THE EVOLUTION OF A TIDEWATER SETTLEMENT SYSTEM

All Hallow's Parish, Maryland, 1650–1783

Carville V. Earle
University of Maryland Baltimore County

THE UNIVERSITY OF CHICAGO
DEPARTMENT OF GEOGRAPHY
RESEARCH PAPER NO. 170

1975

Published 1975 by The Department of Geography
The University of Chicago, Chicago, Illinois

Library of Congress Cataloging in Publication Data

Earle, Carville V.
The Evolution of a Tidewater Settlement System.
(Research Paper—University of Chicago, Dept. of Geography; no. 170)
Bibliography: p. 231
1. All Hallows Parish, Anne Arundel County, Maryland—Economic Conditions. I. Title. II. Series: Chicago. University. Dept. of Geography. Research paper; no. 170.
H31. C514 no. 170 [HC107.M3] 910s [330.9′752′55]
ISBN 0-89065-077-2
75-11554

Research Papers are available from:
The University of Chicago
Department of Geography
5828 S. University Avenue
Chicago, Illinois 60637
Price: $6.00 list; $5.00 series subscription

ACKNOWLEDGMENTS

When the Chesapeake economy went into depression more than two centuries ago, the small planters got by on the credit extended from their more wealthy neighbors. Similarly, the creation of this book occasionally encountered intellectual troughs, and I, like my small planters, incurred numerous debts. Most of what I have learned about the Chesapeake can be traced back to the intellectual challenges and assistance of Lois Green Carr and Russell Menard, and to the atmosphere of scholarliness that they helped forge at the Hall of Records in Annapolis. The bulk of my research was conducted at this magnificent archive, where I received generous assistance from Dr. Morris Radoff, the State Archivist; Gust Skordas; Phebe Jacobsen; and Frank White. Appreciation also extends to the staffs of the Maryland Historical Society and the Library of Congress. At a critical phase in the study Roger Stough unselfishly devoted many hours sharpening my thoughts on systems and helping with the computer program. My gratitude goes out to Vera Curlett and Doris Earle for editing and typing and to Deborah Murry and Francis Silberholz for their renderings of my crude and cluttered manuscript maps.

Several persons read early drafts of the monograph. Both Peter Goheen and Allan Kulikoff offered thorough and indispensable comments. Those who know Peter and Allan will appreciate why I could not incorporate all their tantalizing suggestions. From William Pattison, I borrowed and re-interpreted his notion of settlement systems. The originality of this approach entitled Pattison to some license, but never during our many hours of discussion was he dogmatic or intransigent. I now believe that he was as interested in the process of re-interpretation as he was in the violence that I might inflict on a creative thought. But before I re-interpreted settlement systems and before I found the colonial Chesapeake, I paid heed to Marvin Mikesell's advice that cultural geographers should blend their research specializations with a broad interest and curiosity in all men on the earth at all times. Pursuing this principle, he provided me with intelligent and reasoned guidance on a subject that narrower men would have regarded as beyond their intellectual pale. I am reminded once again of my parish planters; it was the wealthiest among them who could afford to assume the greatest risks.

With these words, "the book" is finished, and the most patient creditors of all, Mary Lou, Rick, Jim, and Randy, must be satisfied.

Woodlawn, Maryland
February, 1975

Carville V. Earle

TABLE OF CONTENTS

LIST OF TABLES

LIST OF ILLUSTRATIONS

Figure		Page

INTRODUCTION

Few Elizabethan Englishmen were more responsible for western planting than the geographer Richard Hakluyt the Elder. His words captured the vigor and hopes of a nation eager to enter the scramble for overseas territory. What distinguished Hakluyt was the breadth of his vision. He foresaw "in time, such league and entercourse . . . between our Stapling seats there . . . that incredible things, and by few as yet dreamed of, may speedily follow tending to the impeachment of our mightie enemies, and to the common good of this noble government."[1] But even Hakluyt would have been astonished by development along the Atlantic Seaboard of North America. By the era of the American Revolution, the two million or more colonists living there nearly equalled England's population in the early Tudor years.[2] Furthermore, these colonists occupied an area more than three times the size of the British Isles.[3] Hakluyt's prediction of "such league and entercourse . . . between our Stapling seats there" also proved correct, and nowhere was this more fully confirmed than in the colonial Chesapeake.

The Chesapeake colonies of Virginia and Maryland quickly developed into

---

[1]Quoted in Wesley Frank Craven, The Southern Colonies in the Seventeenth Century, 1607-1689, ed. by Wendell Holmes Stephenson and E. Merton Coulter, A History of the South, I (n.p.: Louisiana State University Press and the Littlefield Fund for Southern History, The University of Texas, 1949), p. 48.

[2]English population estimates for the Tudor years vary; for the year 1500, the range is from two to three million. Joan Thirsk, ed., The Agrarian History of England and Wales, 1500-1640, IV (Cambridge, England: University Printing House, 1967), 531, 597. E. A. Wrigley, Population and History, World University Library (New York: McGraw-Hill Book Company, 1969), p. 78. Population estimates of the American colonies may be found in U.S., Department of Commerce and Labor, Bureau of the Census, A Century of Population Growth: From the First Census of the United States to the Twelfth 1790-1900, by W. S. Rossiter (Washington, D.C.: Government Printing Office, 1909), pp. 1-15.

[3]The area of the American colonies may be approximated in A Century of Population Growth, pp. 54, 58.

"staple seats" dependent upon "entercourse" with England. The staple crop was tobacco, and its acceptance was complete and enduring. Less than a decade after the founding of Jamestown, tobacco could be found growing in the streets of that village.[1] More than a century later, Benedict Leonard Calvert of Maryland remarked, with resignation, that tobacco is our all and leaves no room for anything else.[2] Nearing the American Revolution, another sagaciously observed that prosperity depended on the gentle rise and fall of tobacco prices.[3] By that date, tobacco culture extended beyond the tidewater region to embrace parts of the Chesapeake back country and North Carolina.[4]

To be sure, dependence on a single staple crop held disadvantages, notably the recurrence of severe economic depressions, but over the long haul the tobacco staple proved beneficent for the economic development of the Chesapeake. In the typical year of the eighteenth century, the Anglo-Chesapeake trade constituted one-third to one-half of the entire trade, by value, between England and the thirteen colonies.[5] Sustained growth in tobacco production propelled the Chesapeake colonies to the top of the heap in export value per capita. They exceeded the colonies of the lower south by 16 per cent; the middle colonies by 64 per cent; and the New England colonies by 112 per cent.[6] The active commerce of the Chesapeake also fostered gains in the personal wealth of plant-

---

[1] Travels and Works of Captain John Smith, President of Virginia and Admiral of New England, ed. by Edward Arber and A. G. Bradley (2 vols.; Edinburgh: n.p., 1910, and reprinted by Burt Franklin, New York, n.d.), II, 535.

[2] Benedict Leonard Calvert to the Lord Proprietary, Oct. 26, 1729, Archives of Maryland, ed. by William Hand Brown and others (72 vols.; Baltimore: Maryland Historical Society, 1883 to present), XXV, 602.

[3] Vertrees J. Wyckoff, Tobacco Regulation in Colonial Maryland, Johns Hopkins University Studies in Historical and Political Science, Extra Volumes, New Series, No. 22 (1936), p. 192.

[4] See especially, Harry Roy Merrens, Colonial North Carolina in the Eighteenth Century: A Study in Historical Geography (Chapel Hill: University of North Carolina Press, 1964), pp. 143-72. James H. Soltow, The Economic Role of Williamsburg, Williamsburg Research Studies (Williamsburg, Virginia: Colonial Williamsburg, Inc., 1965).

[5] U.S., Bureau of the Census, Historical Statistics of the United States, Colonial Times to 1957; a Statistical Abstract Supplement (Washington, D.C.: Government Printing Office, 1960), p. 757.

[6] Computed from James F. Shepherd and Gary M. Walton, Shipping, Maritime Trade, and the Economic Development of Colonial North America (London: Cambridge University Press, 1972), pp. 101-2.

ers. The average Chesapeake planter of 1770 was wealthier than all other persons along the Atlantic Seaboard with the single exception of Charleston, South Carolina and its environs.[1]

In time, the human geography of the Chesapeake took on a distinctive cast unfamiliar to Englishmen. Three landscape characteristics struck travellers most dramatically: the pervasiveness of tobacco, reflected in tobacco houses, old fields, retreating woodlands, and gangs of Negro slaves tending the "weed"; the scattered distribution of rural plantations; and the absence of sizable urban places. In their minds, the patterns of settlement were somehow associated with the peculiarities of tobacco production and marketing--but just how they were associated was not clear. Clarifying these relationships of an enduring staple economy upon people, land, settlement, and circulation is the aim of this book.[2]

Originally, I did not conceive this project as a study of economy and settlement systems in the plantation South. My initial interest stemmed from reading Trewartha's "Types of Rural Settlement in Colonial America," which left me annoyed by the omission of my native Maryland.[3] Maryland's richness lay in her transitional status between southern plantations and middle colony farms. The colony invited comparative inquiry into the origin, growth, and conditions surrounding the development of these two distinctive settlement types. As my research progressed, I realized that comparative study was too ambitious and that one carefully researched local history of the plantation South would be valuable. The result is an examination of All Hallows Parish, Maryland--an area characterized by tobacco culture, dispersed plantations, decentralized trade, and slavery.

---

[1]Alice Hanson Jones, "Wealth Estimates for the Southern Colonies about 1770," Paper presented at the Annual Meeting of the Organization of American Historians (Chicago, 1973), pp. 1-2, 33-35.

[2]Early American history offers numerous opportunities for the reconstruction of past geographies as amply demonstrated by Andrew Clark and his students. A cogent review of this and other work is found in H. Roy Merrens, "Historical Geography and Early American History," William and Mary Quarterly, 3rd Series, XXII (October, 1965), 529-48. In the Chesapeake, Aubrey C. Land's innovative analysis of estate inventories and accounts contains much of value to the historical geographer; the imprint of Land's work upon my own shortly becomes obvious. Aubrey C. Land, "Economic Base and Social Structure: The Northern Chesapeake in the Eighteenth Century," Journal of Economic History, XXV (December, 1965), 639-54.

[3]Glenn T. Trewartha, "Types of Rural Settlement in Colonial America," Geographical Review, XXXVI (October, 1946), 568-96.

Before turning to the parish, a few technical comments are in order. Throughout the monograph I have used the calendar in fashion with one minor adjustment. The Old Style calendar, in use before 1752, is alteréd so that the year extends from January to December instead of beginning on March 25. To convert Old Style dates to New Style, add ten days. Money presents a second problem. At one time or another, tobacco, paper currency, foreign coin, and bills of exchange all served as money. To enhance comparability, these monies are converted to English sterling values; however, the sterling conversions are not adjusted for commodity price inflation or deflation during the course of the colonial period. All quotations retain original spellings and contractions, and superscripts are brought to the line.

On the map scales, distance is measured in rods, which are equivalent to the perches used by colonial surveyors. A rod or a perch equals five and one-half yards or sixteen and one-half feet, while five hundred rods equal 1.56 miles. Finally, I have liberally cited the observations of tidewater travellers, diarists, and others in order to enrich understanding of the parish settlement system. Although several commentators did not visit All Hallows Parish, all believed that the tobacco-producing Chesapeake was a regional unit and, consequently, that their remarks were generally applicable to all parts of the tobacco coast.

CHAPTER I

SETTLEMENT SYSTEMS, AREA, AGENDA

Settlement Systems

Chesapeake settlements had no system, or so it seemed to the seventeenth century English mind. They saw neither historical precedent nor logic in scattered plantations, the absence of towns, and the decentralization of religious, educational, craft, and commercial activities. After all, had not Englishmen lived in villages and towns "for time out of mind?" So also did English colonials in New England, the Dutch in New Amsterdam, and the Spanish in the circum-Caribbean. For the English, the chaos they saw in the Chesapeake was no casual problem. They most dreaded a decay of English culture to the level of the primitive and the animal, and the Chesapeake pattern of settlement gave every indication of a drift toward "barbarism."[1] The pattern of settlement, then, was not simply a matter of better or worse; the choice was a moral issue that separated civilized men from animals. Dispassionate analysis of tidewater settlement systems proved impossible for English travellers who smugly described a provincial backwater which had no towns but only hamlets with pretensions, and for colonial officials and administrators who lamented the commercial and social costs of scattered settlement.

But there was a method to Chesapeake madness, and English blustering did little to change the settlement system. We shall point out frequently in the pages that follow that the dispersed and decentralized system of settlement performed effectively. Trade flourished; wealth accumulated; goods, people and ideas circulated rapidly. Indeed, Marylanders generally knew of English fashions well ahead of provincial Englishmen, or so claimed William Eddis.[2] On a

---

[1] Calendar of State Papers, Colonial Series, America and West Indies, ed. by W. N. Sainsbury and others (44 vols.; London: His Majesty's Stationary Office, 1860 to present), VII, 260-61. Hereafter cited as CSPCS.

[2] William Eddis, Letters from America, ed. by Aubrey C. Land (Cambridge: The Belknap Press of Harvard University Press, 1969), p. 57.

good Maryland horse and a sandy tidewater road, a colonial rider could far outpace his English counterpart. By placing these piecemeal observations into a more unified and explicit framework of settlement systems, we may more fully appreciate how they functioned in the Chesapeake.

An appropriate beginning is to define a settlement system as a portion of the earth's surface that contains places or sites of human activity, which we can call settlements; routes that link these places via traffic; and boundaries that set territorial limits for activities, traffic, and for the system itself.[1] The arrangement of these system elements, of course, varies greatly from place to place. Some systems, as those of the colonial Chesapeake, exhibit dispersed rural housing, scattered merchants, and tiny urban settlements, while other systems present a concentration of settlement into rural villages and urban centers. Quite naturally, geographers are intrigued by these distinctive assemblages, and they have tried to interpret their functions, their origins, and their development over time. But the explanation of settlement types and settlement systems, as Demangeon cautioned us, is usually complex, and the multiple causes are embedded in the society and economy of the area under study.[2] Indeed, we can extend Demangeon's insight one step further. A settlement system is an appendage of its society and economy; settlements, routes, and boundaries exist to serve these other human systems.

Geographers usually study settlement systems in one of two ways: functionally or historically. The functional approach is deliberately static. The

---

[1]The notion of settlement systems has long been implicit in academic geography, and as evidence I submit the functional region, central in the work of Platt and Philbrick, and the study of central places. Cultural and regional geographers have contributed their studies of settlement morphology and boundary analysis. Thus, there is some basis for the claim that settlement system provides an integrating construct for geography. This position is persuasively presented in William D. Pattison, "Geography and the Discovery of Education," Social Science in the Schools: A Search for Rationale, ed. by Irving Morrissett and W. William Stevens, Jr. (New York: Holt, Rinehart and Winston, Inc., 1971), pp. 35-44. Despite close communication between Pattison and me, we found our interpretations of settlement systems diverging. While I approached settlement system from the man-land tradition, checkered by genre de vie and an historical mode of interpretation, he did so from the spatial point of view, emphasizing the abstraction of system elements and functionalist interpretation. My focus became the complex nexus of settlement systems with society, economy, and environment and the external conditions which generated change within the system; Pattison's became the spatial geometry of physical facilities and traffic and the statistical regularities among the system's elements.

[2]Albert Demangeon, "The Origins and Causes of Settlement Types," Readings in Cultural Geography, ed. by Philip L. Wagner and Marvin W. Mikesell (Chicago: University of Chicago Press, 1962), pp. 506-16.

system is examined at a slice in time when conditions are relatively unchanging and presumably the settlement system is in equilibrium. Attention is directed toward the statistical relations among the system elements, with regard to their number, size, and arrangement, and to regularities between systems. Most studies of central place illustrate this approach. The historical approach, which is employed in this study, examines changes in the settlement system. In particular, the focus is upon the timing, rates, and sequence of change among activity sites, routes, traffic, and boundaries. Equally important are the causes which underlay these changes. It is my belief that these causative factors usually arise outside of the settlement system, namely in economic, political, or social systems. Certainly in the Chesapeake, the essential causes of change are economic, demographic, and legislative. A distinct disadvantage of the historical approach to settlement systems is that the documentary record is usually incomplete and precludes full analysis of activity sites, routes, and boundaries. Nevertheless, the Maryland records shed much light upon the plantation, non-agricultural occupations, and economic exchange. And I believe that historical analysis of one Chesapeake parish demonstrates the sensitivity and adaptability of several generations of planters and their settlement system to a fluctuating staple economy.

The Study Area

This monograph examines the evolution of a settlement system in tidewater Maryland between 1650 and 1783. The area of inquiry is All Hallows Parish, an eighty square-mile area centrally located in Anne Arundel County on the Western Shore of the Chesapeake Bay (Figure 1). Although located close to the northern edge of the tobacco region, the parish possessed the typical tidewater qualities of rural dispersal, plantations, tobacco culture, Negro slaves, decentralized trade, and the absence of large towns. All were integral parts of a peculiar settlement system which rapidly adapted to population growth, resource deterioration, governmental legislation, and foremost to the erratic fluctuations of the tobacco economy.

All Hallows Parish is selected for several reasons. The parish belongs to the regional core of the colonial Chesapeake's tobacco coast. The area and population of the parish are a manageable size. Abundant source material, sufficient for statistical compilation, survives for the seventeenth and eighteenth centuries.

All Hallows was clearly within the region of tobacco's dominance, despite

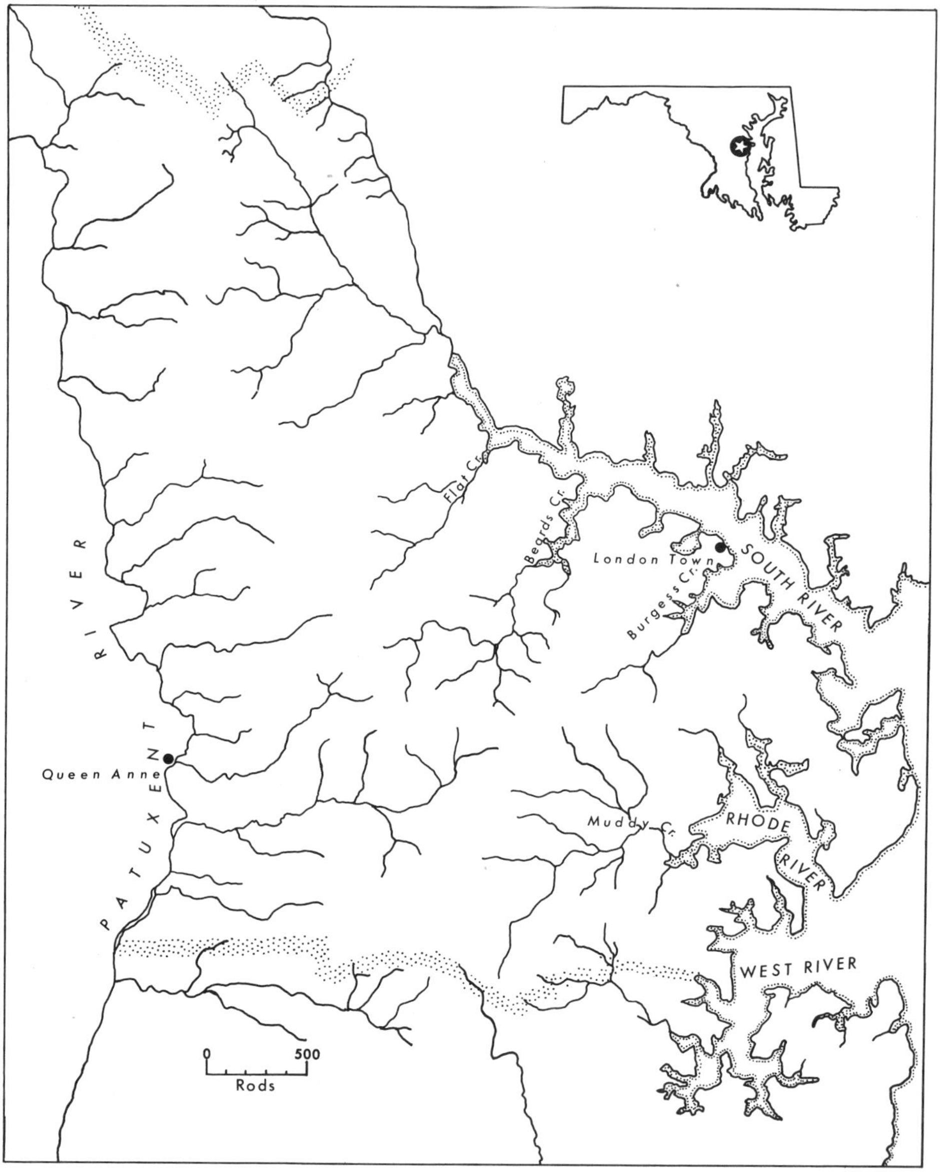

Fig. 1.--Reference Map of All Hallows Parish

peripheral location. The landscape imprint of tobacco was obvious to travellers who passed through the parish at the end of the colonial period. Parish tobacco was reputed among the best in Maryland. Tobacco exports were considerable, and a good proportion of the ships in the annual tobacco fleets called at parish estuaries. The concomitant of tobacco culture, the Negro slave, accounted for 50 per cent of the population by 1776. Probably few areas bordering the tidewater Chesapeake were more committed to or affected by the "stinking weed," tobacco. And in few areas did the process of settlement system change stand out as boldly.

The parish is a manageable size for study. Containing eighty square miles within its boundaries, All Hallows is suitably large to display spatial variations. In fact, All Hallows exceeds the areas of several counties in neighboring Virginia.[1] Also of a manageable size is the parish population which achieved a colonial peak of 3,360 persons by 1776. This modest population is generally adequate for data collection and statistical generalization; however, year-by-year time series of the settlement system are a bit of a problem. This is so because the series derive from probate records of deceased parishioners, who constitute a small and unrepresentative sample in any one year. In order to maintain sensitivity to short-run changes in the system, it is necessary to group the data into discrete periods of three years or more and into continuous running averages.

The surviving documents vary in quality and quantity. Several perceptive travel journals and diaries survive, reminding us that All Hallows lay astride the chief inter-colonial route through Maryland. Three statistical sources document the end of the colonial period; these include a name list census for 1776 and federal property assessments for 1782 and 1783. Earlier periods are covered by the provincial probate records, which provide systematic evidence on tobacco prices and yields as well as plantation activities. These records, known as Inventories and Accounts, list personal property, credits, and liabilities of decedents. Maryland's probate records are unusually full and extend from the 1660's to the Revolution.[2]

---

[1]In 1726, the parish area exceeded the size of Elizabeth City and Warwick counties in Virginia. Louis des Cognets, Jr., English Duplicates of Lost Virginia Records (Princeton, New Jersey: n.p., 1958), pp. 32-41.

[2]For a guide to Maryland's colonial probate records, see Elizabeth Hartsook and Gust Skordas, Land Office and Prerogative Court Records of Colonial Maryland, Publications of the Hall of Records Commission No. 4 (Baltimore: Genealogical Publishing Company, 1968).

Other provincial materials include wills, miscellaneous testamentary business, and the public records of the Governor, Legislature, Provincial Court, and Land Office. At the county level, there are several gaps in the records. Most serious is the absence of the original seventeenth century land deeds and court judgments, which were consumed by a court house fire in 1704. Fortunately, the re-recording of many land deeds after the conflagration permits a reconstruction of seventeenth century land transactions. The destruction of the county judgments, however, is an inestimable loss, because the court made no efforts to re-record these detailed records of roads, ferries, and ordinaries, as well as civil and criminal proceedings. The surviving judgments begin in 1703 and run up to the American Revolution, except for one interruption between 1723 and 1734. Finally, parish records include a register of vital statistics for Anglican parishioners between 1689 and the Revolution, but full reporting seems to prevail only between 1700 and about 1715.

Special Problems Regarding Probate Records

Probate records are very important in this study and their use and interpretation require a few words of caution. The probate records, which include inventories, accounts, and wills, provide us with a sample of the total population of the parish.[1] The most complete of these records, and the most representative, are the personal property lists or inventories of deceased parishioners. When an adult property-owner died, the provincial prerogative court, charged with probate matters, appointed two appraisers to itemize and value the decedent's estate, and to return the written inventory for review by the court. The court usually demanded a detailed rendering of all personal property, so that estate creditors and heirs would not be cheated. When the appraisers failed to meet this standard, the estate was re-appraised. Thus, these lists give insight into the minutiae of plantation life; appraisers listed servants

---

[1] An especially difficult problem is the determination of the residence of the inventoried decedents. The problem arises because the probate records, centrally collected for the colony, rarely distinguish the decedent's parish of residence and even county residence is often omitted in the seventeenth century records. In such cases, residence is inferred from the residence of the estate appraisers, who almost invariably owned land. If both appraisers owned land and lived in the parish, then I include that inventory in the parish sample. If only one of the appraisers resided in the parish, then the inventory and account are scrutinized for further evidence of the decedent's residence. These additional checks include the residence of estate debtors, creditors, and administrators or executors.

and slaves, livestock, implements, boats, craft tools, furniture, books, household goods, and merchandise. Despite the court's attentiveness, numerous eligible decedents were never inventoried. As many as 35 to 40 per cent of the eligible population may have been missed.[1]

Fortunately these omissions are not so serious as they appear for a more important issue has to do with the representativeness of the inventory sample. Representativeness, or the degree to which the sample mirrors the full population, may be checked by comparing known facts about the population with those derived from the inventory sample. The first check compares the per cent of households not owning land in 1675 and 1707.[2] Using various methods, I estimate the non-landowning households in 1675 and 1707 as 20.8 per cent and 33.7 per cent, respectively. By comparison, the inventory sample for non-landowners for 1660 to 1679 and for 1690 to 1699 shows 23.3 per cent and 33.3 per cent, respectively. The closeness of these results confirms that the inventories present a representative portrait of the parish population, at least during the seventeenth century. The next century is a different matter. The inventories are hopelessly unrepresentative after 1769, or so I conclude from a comparison of the per cent of slaveholding households in the 1776 census and in the inventories from 1770 to 1776, which are 54.8 per cent and 96 per cent, respectively. The inventories are, however, fairly representative before 1770. For example, the decade 1760 to 1769 shows 59 per cent of the inventories with bond labor, and this figure compares favorably with the 1776 census proportion.[3] Consequently, in this study the analysis of inventories is confined to those made between 1660 and 1769. They are not a perfectly representative sample of the parish popula-

---

[1]The estimate comes from a study of the burials of white adult males recorded between 1701 and 1710 in the All Hallows Parish register. Inventories survive for twenty-four of the thirty-seven buried persons. The unappraised thirteen include at least two landowners, two overseers, and, in all likelihood, tenants and inmates make up the rest. Annapolis, Hall of Records MSS, All Hallows Parish Register (1689-1721, No. 12200; 1700-1724, No. 12201; 1711-1857, No. 12202). Annapolis, Hall of Records MSS, Inventories & Accounts, Libers 29-32a, various pages. Our estimate of about 35 per cent under-recording of inventories compares very closely to the 36 per cent estimated by Alice Hanson Jones for the middle colonies in 1774. After considerable study, Jones concludes that the wealth of non-probates varies widely, but their median value probably falls below that of probates. Alice Hanson Jones, "Wealth Estimates for the American Middle Colonies, 1774," Economic Development and Cultural Change, XVIII (July, 1970), 86-97, 117.

[2]See Chapter VII for estimates of non-landowners.

[3]Calculated from Table 8 in Chapter III.

tion, but they afford close approximation, with slight biases toward older and more prosperous residents.

Agenda

There exists a logical order to the chapters in this monograph. Their arrangement reflects the sequential changes in the tidewater settlement system. Chapter II examines two decisive parameters or external forces that impinge on the settlement system. They are the state of the erratic trans-Atlantic tobacco economy and the variable quality of the parish resource base, including drainage features, vegetation, and soils. The changing population of All Hallows Parish is discussed in Chapter III. Some emphasis is placed upon establishing fairly accurate population estimates which are prerequisite for the determination of occupational thresholds, tenancy, and man-land ratios. In addition, population growth is examined as an external change which exerted increased pressures upon the land, soils, and timber of All Hallows Parish.

The next two chapters consider the settlement system proper. Chapter IV concentrates on the changing structure and location of urban and potentially urban occupations. They exhibit three distinct spatial phases, with decentralized location prevailing before 1710 and after 1750 and a period of vigorous spatial concentration sandwiched in between. Chapter V describes the predominant type of parish settlement, the plantation, and offers an interpretation of its transformation toward a diversified and more self-sufficient rural settlement. This evolution, which occurs with predictable regularity, is best explained as adaptation to the boom and bust economy and its secular trend. As plantations evolved, so did the interdependence among them. Chapter VI examines the changing circulation of the parish through a consideration of routes, modes of travel, and exchange. The thesis offered here is that the trend toward plantation self-sufficiency, especially in depressions, was manifested in diminished exchanges, particularly for imported European goods. Local exchanges, though subject to retrenchment, were facilitated by a crude but effective transport network of horse roads, ferries, and interpenetrating estuaries. While exchange ebbed and flowed with the tobacco economy, an important spatial change--the appearance of urban-based merchants between 1710 and 1750--produced a central, if transitory, focus for exchange and travel. Lastly, Chapter VII discusses the land as a stabilizing element in a settlement system otherwise in flux. Stability is evident in the endurance of the initial land surveys and the cadastral map, in the continuity in landholding size, and in the slow growth of land ownership. As the parish population grew, many parishioners chose tenancy, but many others joined the voluminous flow of outmigrants seeking opportunities elsewhere. But by the mid-1760's, population growth exerted new pressures on land and boundary stability. For the first time in its history, the man-land ratio of All Hallows proved unfavorable.

CHAPTER II

PARAMETERS OF THE SETTLEMENT SYSTEM

Introduction

Economy and environment were vital considerations for the tobacco planters of the colonial Chesapeake. A bad crop, a year of low prices, or an exhausted plantation meant lower income for the planters. Of course, most planters tried to prevent economic losses through a number of strategies that included altering their plantation activities, trimming back their expenditures, and trying to restore the fertility of their soil. Thus, economy and environment caused a series of changes within the settlement system; and while they were not the only causes, they were sufficiently important to be singled out for discussion at the outset. Specifically, this chapter explores two of the essential parameters of the tidewater settlement system: the changing state of the tobacco economy, as measured by tobacco prices, and the quality and maintenance of agrarian resources such as soil, terrain, water, vegetation, and climate.

Tobacco Prices

"In Virginia and Maryland," lamented Benedict Calvert, "Tobacco, as our Staple, is our all, and indeed leaves no room for anything Else."[1] This singular commitment to tobacco made for a susceptible and unsteady, if profitable, economy. The barometer of the erratic trade in tobacco--its price--pulsated wildly in proportion with European wars and financial crises, with the faddish preferences of European consumers, and with production gluts. Locked into this fluctuating staple economy, the Chesapeake planters gauged their prosperity or poverty, as Charles Carroll succinctly observed, by the rise and fall of tobacco prices.[2]

---

[1]Benedict Leonard Calvert to the Lord Proprietary, Oct. 26, 1729, _Archives of Maryland_, XXV, 602.

[2]Wyckoff, _Tobacco Regulation in Colonial Maryland_, pp. 191-92.

Carroll's observations on the tobacco economy carry considerable weight, for he was not an ordinary man. Yet even astute men are occasionally wrong or ambiguous, and their declarations require restatement as hypotheses. Carroll's hypothesis, that prosperity varies with tobacco prices, becomes more concrete when prosperity is measured by changes in the composition and scale of settlements and these measures are related to tobacco prices over time. Settlement change will be dealt with in a later chapter, and for the moment we direct attention to the reconstruction of a tobacco price series.

An initial attempt at a tobacco price series, 1659 to 1775, appears in Figure 2.[1] Because on-going research in the Chesapeake is continually refining these prices, a clear statement of methodology seems called for. The sources for tobacco prices are estate inventories and accounts. The series between 1659 and 1710 includes prices from the whole colony of Maryland, and thereafter, from Anne Arundel and Prince George's counties. Prices in the probate records appear in local currency, which is converted to sterling by an exchange rate series from the same sources (Appendix A). Price inflation must also be considered. However, this proves exceedingly difficult to measure in the colonial Chesapeake. Commodity price indices offer one way of converting tobacco prices from current value to real value. The continuing research of Russell Menard and Allan Kulikoff has recently produced such an index for Chesapeake commodities, but unfortunately, it became available too late for inclusion in this study. Another gauge of the real value of tobacco--a price index for English wholesale commodities--is available for the period 1697 to 1800.[2] As English commodities constituted such a large share of Chesapeake purchases, it seems reasonable to assume that Maryland commodity prices varied positively with English prices, and that current value Maryland tobacco prices can be converted to real or constant value with the English index. Comparison of the two tobacco price series in Figure 2 confirms their essential similarity, except for the period 1734 to 1739, when the real value of tobacco rose substantially because of falling commodity prices. The closeness of the two price series implies that price inflation is not a serious problem; and accordingly, I consistently use sterling tobacco prices in current value, i.e., unadjusted for commodity price changes.

---

[1]Russell R. Menard, "Farm Prices of Maryland Tobacco, 1659-1710," Maryland Historical Magazine, LXVII (Spring, 1973), 80-85 and Appendix.

[2]A full discussion of these calculations is found in John J. McCusker, "The Current Value of English Exports, 1697-1800," William and Mary Quarterly, 3rd Series, XXVIII (October, 1971), 606-28.

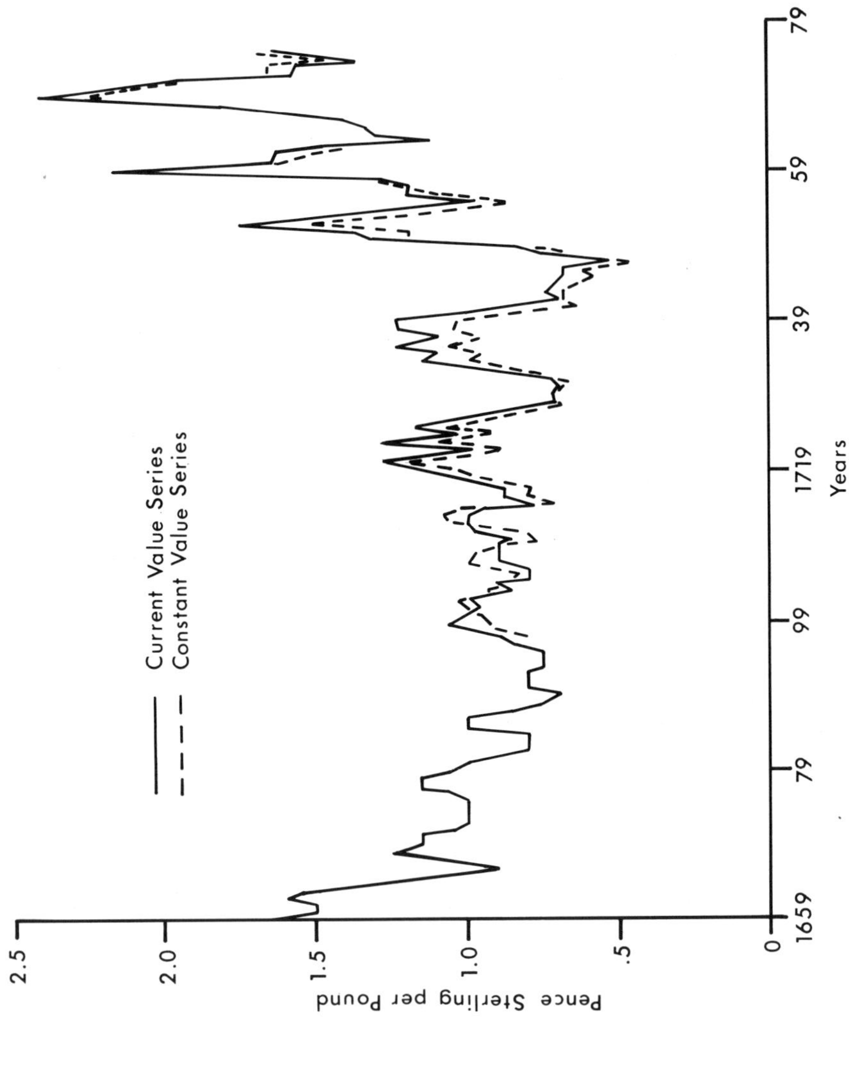

Fig. 2.--Tobacco Prices, 1659-1775

The price series divides into two parts, with a hinge in 1747. Before 1747, tobacco prices tend to fall, but this trend is interrupted by a series of peaks and troughs. Maryland tobacco prices reached their historic low in 1747, and in that same year, the Assembly enacted comprehensive legislation aimed at improving the price of tobacco. Indeed, prices climbed steadily so that by 1769 a pound of tobacco brought four times more than in 1747.[1] Noteworthy, however, is that after 1747 prices fluctuated more rapidly than they had before.

The considerable changes in tobacco prices may be simplified by grouping them into a sequence of boom years of high prices and bust years of low prices.[2] A boom and bust, together, constitute one economic cycle. Booms are defined as a set of sequential years when: (a) the mean tobacco price for the set exceeds one pence per pound; or (b) tobacco, having risen for two years in succession, remains above the level of the second year's price. Busts are the obverse. The sets of booms and busts appear in Tables 1 and 2. Before 1750, the full economic cycle averages over twenty-two years, and busts exceed booms by one and one-fifth years. After 1750, the full cycle condenses to slightly more than eight years, and booms exceed busts by one year. But the shortening of the cycle after 1750 actually is part of a long-run trend. After the initial cycle of 39 years (1659-1697), the succeeding cycles shorten to 21, 15, 16, 7, 10, and 8 years.

Armed with this series of tobacco prices, we will shortly test Carroll's hypothesis in the context of settlement systems. What are the long-term effects of declining prices to 1747, and rising prices thereafter? What are the effects of cyclical fluctuations, and the post-1750 shift from longer to shorter cycles? Some surprises are in store.

The Physical Environment

The second parameter of the settlement system is the physical environment, consisting of water, soils, terrain, vegetation, and climate. Most of these--water, terrain, and climate, for example--changed little and, consequently, may be regarded as constants. By contrast, the tobacco economy exerted enormous pressures on the resources of soil and timber. The traditional

---

[1]Wyckoff, Tobacco Regulation, pp. 164-84.

[2]The idea of a boom and bust economy is elaborated in John M. Hemphill, II, "Virginia and the English Commercial System, 1689-1733" (unpublished Ph.D. dissertation, Princeton University, 1964).

TABLE 1

BOOMS AND BUSTS: 1659-1774

Years	Length	Mean Price in pence	Years	Length	Mean Price in pence
1659-80	22	1.19	1681-97	17	.82
1698-1704	7	.98	1705-18	14	.88
1719-26	8	1.00	1727-33	7	.73
1734-39	6	.98	1740-49	10	.64
1750-53	4	1.24	1754-56	3	.99
1757-61	5	1.53	1762-66	5	1.31
1767-71	5	1.93	1772-74	3	1.56

TABLE 2

MEAN LENGTHS OF BOOMS AND BUSTS: 1659-1774

	pre-1750	post-1750	1659-1774
Booms	10.8	4.7	8.1
Busts	12.0	3.7	8.5
Booms and Busts	11.5	4.2	8.3

historiography of the Chesapeake environment has placed almost exclusive emphasis on soil exhaustion as an endemic problem. I will contend that the traditional interpretation is, at best, a half-truth that betrays a serious misunderstanding of tobacco culture. That exhaustion of soil occurred after a few years of cropping is true enough, but the planters avoided chronic depletion through a clever scheme of field rotation, not unlike that of shifting cultivators in the present day. Here was a transient landscape of frequently shifted fields, abundant old fields, and ragged vegetation in various stages of succession. It is ironic that travellers and scholars alike have used this transience to indict planters and slaves for their laziness and slovenliness. Perhaps the exaggerated emphasis given to soil exhaustion has been responsible for our ignorance of a more serious environmental change. The Chesapeake woodlands early came under full-scale attack by the planters and by the 1730's depleted timber supplies caused serious dislocations in the plantation economy and settlement system.

Estuaries and Necks

The Chesapeake tidewater interwove with the sandy coastal plain, creating a paisley-like pattern of crenated estuaries and necks. At the edge of this intricate shoreline, among the coves, creeks, and rivers, early Marylanders scattered their plantations. They stayed close to the shoreline for good reason. Here they gained vital access to seagoing vessels that brought in the necessities and luxuries from Europe and hauled away the staple crop. During the seventeenth century few planters strayed from the tidewater shoreline--a fact illustrated in Herrman's exquisite 1673 map of Maryland. On the map, plantations spaced between one-fourth and one and one-half miles apart followed the coastal configuration.[1] Perhaps Lord Baltimore saw a draft of this map, for just two years before its publication he pointedly instructed his Surveyor General to limit water frontage to fifteen poles, or 247.5 feet, for every fifty acres patented.[2] As proprietor of all land in Maryland, Baltimore stood to lose a fortune if the planters continued gobbling up these accessible sites.

All Hallows Parish resembled the larger region in coastal configuration and in the planters' evaluation of tidewater sites. Four major estuaries divided the parish into a series of necks. Three of these deep rivers emptied into the Chesapeake Bay. South River, forming the northern boundary of the parish, admitted vessels of three hundred tons to a distance of ten miles, or so claimed Andrew Burnaby.[3] More precisely, he probably meant to the head of the estuary, about eight and one-half miles from the bay. That seventeenth century vessels plied the entire length of the estuary is suggested by a land patent of 1668 called "The Landing," located near the head of the river.[4] The breadth of the river, about three-quarters of a mile at London Town, five miles from the bay, made it a gathering place for tobacco vessels.[5] Proceeding south from this majestic river, mariners rounded a neck of land fronted by a sandy spit for about a mile or so, and then entered Rhode River. Fairly broad at its mouth

---

[1] Augustin Herrman, Virginia and Maryland . . . , Surveyed and Exactly Drawne by Augustin Herrman (London: W. Faithorne, Sculpt., 1673).

[2] Archives of Maryland, V, 95.

[3] Reverend Andrew Burnaby, Travels through the Middle Settlements in North America, 1759 and 1760 (3rd ed.; London: T. Payne, 1798), p. 56.

[4] Annapolis, Hall of Records MSS, Patents 12, f. 135.

[5] Burnaby, Travels, p. 51.

and its middle section, the river tapered off quickly inland. Few ships seem to have called at Rhode River, though there was a landing place where the river joined its main tributary, Muddy Creek.[1] A small peninsula separated Rhode River from West River, which served as the southern boundary of the parish. The Patuxent River, delineating the western boundary of the parish, eventually flowed into the Chesapeake after a long journey on the back side of Anne Arundel and Calvert counties. Vessels of up to three hundred tons burden travelled fifty miles upstream, thus giving access to the planters in western All Hallows at Queen Anne's and Taylor's Landing.[2]

Along these navigable waterways, the early settlers laid out their plantations. But by 1664, after some twenty years of settlement, most of the estuarine sites had been surveyed. The land surveys then proceeded inland, on the backs of the initial surveys, where they occupied the "Ridge" dividing Patuxent and Chesapeake drainage. At about the same time, surveyors laid out large holdings along the navigable stretches of Patuxent. Two wealthy provincial officials, Thomas Taylor and Jerome White, received the lion's share of this land (Figure 3).[3] Further up the Patuxent, beyond the head of navigation, surveying and settling advanced more slowly, and it was not until the 1680's that this land was occupied. But regardless of where men settled in the parish, whether on the estuaries or the ridges, none lived more than five miles from a trans-Atlantic landing, and most were within easy reach of two or three estuaries.

Chesapeake mariners also placed a high premium on these rivers. Their vessels, staying too long in salty waters especially in June and July, came under attack from the "worm" or Teredo navalis, a marine organism which bored and honeycombed vessel bottoms. One remedy for the "worm," certainly known by the eighteenth century, was its destruction by coasting into waters of lower salinity, such as the "freshes" near the heads of estuaries, where salinity was reduced by the infusion of fresh water from coastal plain streams and creeks.[4] Interestingly, the tobacco inspection houses established in 1747 were

---

[1] Resurvey of Beaverdam Neck, June 28, 1705, Patents, IL#B, f. 474.

[2] Burnaby, Travels, p. 56.

[3] Patents, 16, ff. 34-36. Ibid., 12, f. 401.

[4] Robert Beverley, The History and Present State of Virginia, ed. by Louis B. Wright (Chapel Hill: University of North Carolina Press for the Institute of Early American History and Culture at Williamsburg, Virginia, 1947), pp. 121-22. See also Arthur Pierce Middleton, Tobacco Coast: A Maritime History of Chesapeake Bay in the Colonial Era (Newport News, Virginia: The Mariner's Museum, 1953), pp. 35-36.

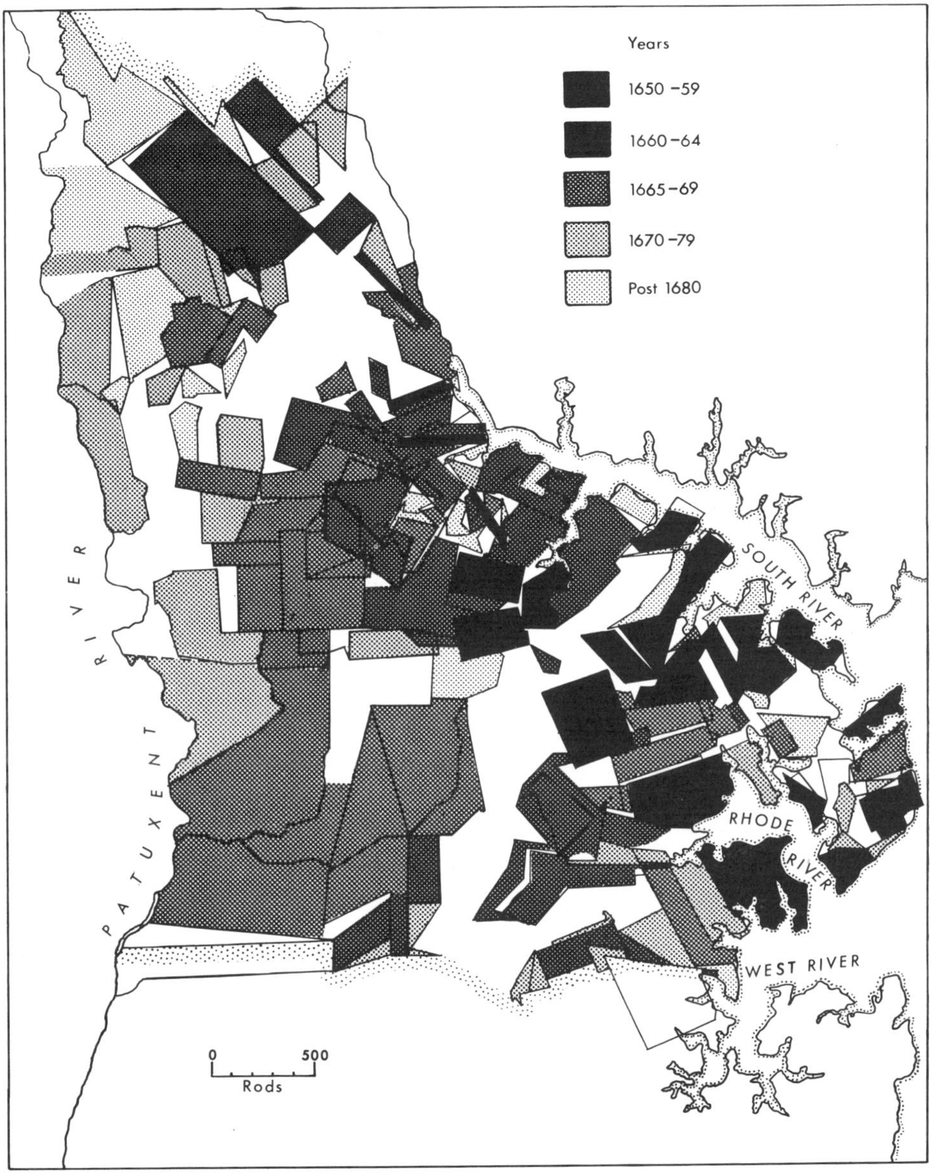

Fig. 3.--Chronology of Surveys in All Hallows Parish, 1650-1700. (White spaces within the parish boundary reflect surveying errors; surveys so separated are usually contiguous. See text, pp. 186-87.)

located in the freshes of South and Patuxent rivers.[1] There, ship captains loaded tobacco and killed the worm at the same time.

Navigation of the Chesapeake estuaries presented few obstacles for experienced mariners. Native pilots, though employed to bring vessels up the bay, were discharged when the rivers were met.[2] The chief obstructions to navigation--branches and trees felled for fishing;[3] ballast unloaded from ships;[4] and waste rock and soil from iron mining operations--proved minor irritants, prompting action by the Assembly.[5] One navigational irritant, sedimentation, never prompted action, probably because sedimentation, and its main cause, surface soil erosion, were slight. Supporting this view is a crude survey of soil taken for Anne Arundel Manor bordering the parish on the south. The 1767 survey classified eroded land as 218.5 acres of 10,894.5 total acres.[6] Soil deposition, though generally insignificant, produced localized impediments to shipping, notably at the heads of the rivers. Such deposition may explain why the inhabitants at the head of South River petitioned in 1712 for a road from their river over to Kilkenny Town near the head of Patuxent navigation.[7] Yet it was at the river mouths where navigational skills were put to the supreme test. Tidal action and shoreline erosion created shoal water graveyards for careless mariners. The sandy headlands changed year to year, and the one at South Riv-

---

[1] Archives of Maryland, XLIV, 608. Ibid., LVI, 47 and 132. Annapolis, Hall of Records MSS, Nov. Court, 1763, Anne Arundel County Judgments, IMB #1, f. 870. Hereafter, Anne Arundel County records are denoted by AACo.

[2] Middleton, Tobacco Coast, pp. 82-83.

[3] In 1733, "An Act to impower the Inhabitants of Anne-Arundel and Prince George Counties, to make the main Branch of the River Patuxent navigable, above Queen-Anne Town, in Prince George County . . ." was passed, followed by a supplemental act in 1736. These acts specifically prohibited obstruction of the branch by hedges, weirs, or fences, or by the felling of trees, "either for the conveniency of fishing or any other reason. . . ." Archives of Maryland, XXXIX, 121-22 and 483-85.

[4] Middleton, Tobacco Coast, pp. 87-88.

[5] "An Act to prevent injuring Navigation to Baltimore Town and the Inspecting House at Elk-Ridge Landing," Nov., 1753, Archives of Maryland, L, 374-75.

[6] Great Britain, Public Record Office MSS, Audit Office 12/79 Maryland Loyalist Claims, 1786-1787, ff. 134-35.

[7] AACo Judgments, TB #3, f. 140.

er receded by thirty to forty yards between 1726 and 1758.[1] All in all, Marylanders protected their river highways to Europe; and given the preeminence of trans-Atlantic trade, their efforts appear quite rational.

Extolling the bay and riverine network was a favorite pastime, and the Reverend Hugh Jones indulged in it. "Noe country can compare with it," said Jones, because "the number of navigable rivers, creeks, and inletts, render it soe convenient for exporting and importing goods into any part thereof by water carriage. . . ."[2] This statement, as so many others about the bay, was hyperbolic. The labyrinth of rivers that facilitated the tobacco trade also set up distinct barriers to local movement and interaction. "You cannot travel any considerable distance in this country," noted William Eddis, "without crossing rivers. . . . Over these, regular ferries are established . . . yet such a number of considerable waters unavoidably occasion great delay."[3] River valleys and estuaries, because they interrupted or slowed land traffic, made logical boundaries for local administrative units. All Hallows, for example, was bounded on four sides by the waters of South River, the Bay, West River, and the Patuxent. Consequently, the spines of the parish meandered along the drainage divides between South and Rhode rivers and the Patuxent and Chesapeake, known as the "Ridge." Along these well-drained interfluves ran the main roads of the parish, and secondary arteries split off from them downslope to the waterside. There, the roads dead-ended, unless a ferry or fording point permitted crossing. Smart travellers followed those roads that skirted the numerous creeks and wound around the heads of the rivers.

The tidewater barrier also affected property lines (Figure 3). In All Hallows, these boundaries never crossed over a major estuary, and rarely ex-

---

[1]Deponents in a land ejectment case produced several estimates of recession, ranging from 15 to 20 yards up to 200 yards, with the median about 30 to 40. Annapolis, Hall of Records MSS, Ejectment Papers, Box #19, Francis Linthicum v Ann Sanders, Depositions of Robert Brown, Ann French, Robert Sanders, James Saunders, and others, March 20, 1758. More recently, between 1860 and 1947, shore erosion on South, Rhode, and West rivers was estimated at .05, .07, and .06 acres per annum respectively; these figures were lower than the county average of .1. Losses were greatest near the river mouths, while deposition was maximum toward the heads. Maryland, Board of Natural Resources, Department of Geology, Mines and Water Resources, Turbit H. Slaughter, "The Shore Erosion Measurements," Shore Erosion in Tidewater Maryland, Bulletin 6 (Baltimore, 1949), pp. 25-26, 28.

[2]Michael G. Kammen, ed., "Maryland in 1699: A Letter from the Reverend Hugh Jones," Journal of Southern History, XXIX (August, 1963), 368.

[3]Eddis, Letters from America, pp. 13-14.

tended over a small creek or bay. Patentees of land confined themselves to the neck or a portion of it.

In sum, estuaries gave excellent access to Europe during the entire colonial period. But within the parish, tidewater areas were more frequently lines of division than lanes of access. Areal unity was found in the necks and along the drainage divides rather than within the drainage basin.

Soils, Tobacco Culture, and Exhaustion

Next to tidewater access, the quality of soil was the preeminent resource for successful tobacco planting. And the soils of south central Anne Arundel County enjoyed a reputation for producing abundant yields of high quality tobacco.[1] In 1837, the area was described by Ducatel:

> What in Anne Arundel County is locally styled the West River district, offers a considerable body of excellent tobacco and corn lands . . . and in their present condition form some of the most valuable plantations in the state. The soil varies from a sandy to a clayey loam, in some places very ferruginous. . . . A soil of the same description extends to the head of South River.[2]

Such technical language was alien to colonial planters, who gauged soil quality by the color and price of the tobacco it produced. And the soils of southern Anne Arundel and Prince George's counties produced some of the finest oronoco tobacco in Maryland, or so declared a French traveller in 1765. Stopping at an inspection house in Prince George's County, he:

> saw some of the bright coloured tobaco which sels so Dear in foreign markets. it is of a light yelow coulour and is much Esteemed as the virginia Sweet Sented: it grows but in particular Soils. The Inhabitants call it bright tobacco.[3]

South River tobacco was touted as precisely the same quality as that of the Pa-

---

[1] U.S., Department of Agriculture, Soil Conservation Service in Cooperation with the Maryland Agricultural Experiment Station, Soil Survey, Prince Georges County, Maryland (Washington, D. C.: Government Printing Office, 1967), pp. 25-26. U.S., Department of Agriculture, Soil Conservation Service, Soil Survey Maps of Anne Arundel County Maryland, Vols. I and II (College Park, Maryland: n.p., 1968). Loaned through the courtesy of Wilson Knowland, SCS agent in Annapolis, Maryland. Maryland Geological Survey, Maryland Agricultural Experiment Station, Soil Map Anne Arundel County, Maryland (n.p., n.p., 1928).

[2] J. T. Ducatel, "Outlines of the Physical Geography of Maryland, embracing its prominent Geological features," Transactions of the Maryland Academy of Sciences and Literature, I (1837), 33-34.

[3] "Journal of a French Traveller in the Colonies, 1765, II," American Historical Review, XXVII (October, 1921), 71.

tuxent, "which has always been found to fit the European markets as well, if not better, than tobacco of the growth of any other part of Maryland."[1]

Tobacco culture exhausted tidewater soils; but turned back to nature, these soils regained their fertility and were cultivated again. The critical point is that exhaustion was temporary, not permanent. The "wearing out" of the soil, manifested in declining yields and profits, occurred routinely after three to four years of continuous tobacco cropping, after which planters abandoned the field to nature and cleared a new parcel of land.[2] The abandonment was temporary while the "old field" rested and recovered its fertility, a period of about twenty years. Through this cyclical shifting of fields, planters maintained tobacco yields. A greater danger to the agricultural system, chronically low yields, became a possibility only when land became so scarce that the old fields had to be cropped without sufficient rest.

The extent of chronic exhaustion in All Hallows may be gauged by the long-term decreases in tobacco yields. Tobacco yields per laborer are calculated from the inventories and accounts which list the size of the tobacco crop and the number of bond laborers. Tobacco yields per laborer in All Hallows Parish between 1660 and 1769 appear in Table 4. However, several cautions must be offered before these data are interpreted. Laborers on the crop are defined as all servant and slave men; all slave women; and servant and slave boys, 12-15 years of age. The aged, infirm, or decrepit are excluded. I follow Tatham in rating men as one share, women as .75, and boys as .5.[3] The free white decedent is counted as a laborer in those estates with less than three servants and slaves. The major drawback to these calculations is that free white labor cannot be included. Another problem is the effects of scale economies, increasing labor output, on estates with numerous laborers. To combat this ambiguity, I include separate calculations of yields on estates with no bond labor. A slight adjustment in labor yields is necessary after 1747, when the tobacco inspection

---

[1] Maryland Gazette, July 19, 1792.

[2] Avery Odelle Craven, Soil Exhaustion as a Factor in the Agricultural History of Virginia and Maryland, 1606-1860, University of Illinois Studies in the Social Sciences, Vol. XIII, No. 1 (Urbana, Illinois: University of Illinois, 1926, and reprinted by Peter Smith, Gloucester, Massachusetts, 1965), pp. 12-13.

[3] G. Melvin Herndon, William Tatham and the Culture of Tobacco Including a facsimile reprint of An Historical and Practical Essay on the Culture and Commerce of Tobacco (Coral Gables, Florida: University of Miami Press, 1969), pp. 101-2.

act required the destruction of "trash tobacco" and "seconds." Contemporaries estimated trash tobacco at one-tenth to one-fourth of a laborer's crop;[1] and with seconds, these estimates rose to as high as one-third of the tobacco crop.[2] These estimates, however, are probably on the low side. Another source, the estate inventories between 1740 and 1747, shows that, on the average, seconds constituted 26.8 per cent of the crop and trash 20.3 per cent (Table 3).[3] Thus, the inspection act discarded about half of a laborer's crop, and to allow for this, post-1747 yields should be raised by 87.7 per cent.

TABLE 3

MEAN PERCENTAGE OF TOBACCO CROPS IN VARIOUS GRADES, 1740-1747

	Top and Good Tobacco	Trash, Grounds, Seconds, Scrub	Trash, Grounds, Scrub	Seconds
Mean Percentage	53.3	46.7	20.3	26.8
Number of Observations	27	27	24	24

In All Hallows Parish, the amount of tobacco produced by a laborer varied from about 1,600 to 2,200 pounds between 1660 and 1769. Higher yields prevailed before 1709 and after 1740, and no clear-cut downward trend indicating chronic exhaustion appears. The long-term fall in labor output, based on all estates, was about seventy to one hundred and ten pounds, or 3.6 to 5.7 per cent. A slightly larger drop of about 18 per cent occurred among those estates with decedents as the only laborers. The effects of exhaustion on labor yield were slight, especially when compared to the 45 to 50 per cent yield reductions occasioned by the inspection act.

Another observation argues against soil depletion of a chronic kind. The Anne Arundel Manor survey of 1767 denoted only 21 per cent of the land as

---

[1] Maryland Gazette, April 7, 1747. Ibid., May 19, 1747.

[2] Ibid., April 28, 1747.

[3] This argument is strengthened by comparing yields per laborer before and after the inspection act. The mean yield for 1750-1759 was 51 per cent of that for 1740-1747 (see Table 4).

TABLE 4

TOBACCO YIELDS PER LABORER, 1660-1769

Years	Observations	Mean Yield in pounds	Post-1747 allowance (x 87.7%)
1660-99	34	1914.0	
1700-09	16	2239.2	
1710-19	23	1687.7	
1720-29	18	1612.8	
1730-39	23	1706.7	
1740-47	28	1863.4	
1700-47	108	1804.6	
1750-59	19	913.6	1714.8
1760-69	27	1032.2	1937.4
1750-69	46	983.2	1845.5
Decedents as the only Laborers			
1660-99	13	2153.1	
1700-39	28	1796.6	

"worn," a term which probably meant exhausted (Table 5).[1]

The stability of tobacco yields for more than a century suggests that planters, their servants, and their slaves were not ignorant abusers of the soil. They averted chronic soil exhaustion by practicing an intensive shifting agriculture, steeped in Indian planting techniques, in an area with a favorable land-man ratio.

Tobacco culture was land intensive, i.e., it involved large inputs of labor relative to land. To produce 1,800 to 1,900 pounds of tobacco per year, a laborer tended about 10,000 plants covering two to three acres.[2] The parish tax-

[1] Audit Office 12/79, ff. 134-35.

[2] The estimate of 1,800 to 1,900 pounds per laborer is based on Table 4. Literary estimates range from 1,000 to 3,500 pounds, and are found in Journal of Jasper Danckaerts, 1679-80, ed. by Bartlett Burleigh James and J. Franklin Jameson, Original Narratives of Early American History (New York: Charles Scribner's Sons, 1913, and reprinted by Barnes & Noble, Inc., New York, 1959), p. 133; Sir Dalby Thomas, "An Historical Account of the Rise and Growth of the West-India Colonies, London, 1690," Harleian Miscellany, IX (London: Robert Dutton, 1810), 427; and Lewis C. Gray, assisted by Esther Katherine Thompson, History of Agriculture in the Southern United States to 1860, Carnegie Institution of Washington Publication No. 430 (2 vols.; U.S.A.: Carnegie Institu-

TABLE 5

SOIL AND TIMBER IN ANNE ARUNDEL MANOR, 1767

	Soil Worn		Soil not Worn	
	Timber lacking	Timber present	Timber lacking	Timber present
Acres	1349.0	929.5	3984.1	4635.9
Per cent of Manor	12.4	8.5	36.6	42.5

ables of 1696, 460 in all, could have cultivated just 1,380 acres of tobacco, or about 2.7 per cent of the total area.[1] Eighty years later in 1776, the area under cultivation, theoretically, rose to 3,468 acres or 6.8 per cent.[2]

Tobacco acreage, though tiny in any one year, wore out quickly as the crop exacted heavy demands on plant nutrients. To counter exhaustion, planters chose one of three strategies: animal manure, crop rotation, or field rotation. The majority preferred the third procedure.

Tobacco fertilized with livestock manure brought complaints that cow-penned tobacco tasted strong and, therefore, received a lower price.[3] A few tenants may have kept cattle on tobacco fields, but most planters restricted the practice to corn fields.[4] Nor did parish planters rely on lime, marl, or plas-

---

tion of Washington, n.d., reprinted by Peter Smith, Gloucester, Massachusetts, 1958), I, 218-19. Yields per acre are rarely given; Gray indicates 1,000 pounds per acre, which seems high in light of present-day fertilized yields. The figure of 10,000 plants on 2 to 3 acres is found in CSPCS, 1696-97, p. 591.

[1]Archives of Maryland, XXIII, 19-20. By 1696, taxables included all persons over sixteen years of age except white women.

[2]Taxables for 1776 are listed on a parish census, which is reproduced in Gaius Marcus Brumbaugh, Maryland Records: Colonial, Revolutionary, County and Church, from Original Sources (2 vols.; Baltimore: Genealogical Publishing Company, 1967), I, 407-16.

[3]Lewis C. Gray, History of Agriculture, I, 217. There is substance to these complaints; cattle manure tends to keep tobacco green and growing too long. And when cured, it lacks color and quality. Other manures are satisfactory. Maryland, University of Maryland Extension Service, W. B. Posey, Tobacco Culture in Maryland, Bulletin No. 65, Revised (May, 1945), p. 17.

[4]See the road petition of Sarah Gresham, Nov. Court, 1743, AACo Judgments, IB#4, f. 297.

ter of paris to restore soil fertility. And only the exceptional planters adopted crop rotations using leguminous plants, grasses, or turnips.[1]

Instead of manuring or rotating crops, planters evolved a form of shifting agriculture which maintained yields. They produced tobacco for three or four years, and followed it with corn for a year or two more. They then shifted to a new parcel, while abandoning the "old field" to colonization by native vegetation.[2] "It will in seven years time, grow up again from seed to substantial Fire-wood; and in Eighteen or Twenty Years 'twill come to be very good Board-Timber."[3] The system of shifting fields maintained yields, so long as the planters permitted their old fields a rest of twenty years or more. Chronic exhaustion threatened the system when the acreage to labor ratio fell below twenty to one. This may be expressed mathematically as:

$$R = \frac{A}{LK_1} K_2,$$

where R equals length of time before recultivation is necessary, A equals area, L equals labor force, K_1 is a constant of three acres cultivated per laborer, and K_2 is a constant of three years which any tobacco land might be cultivated in succession. Applying this formula to the parish in 1776, containing 1,156 taxables and 50,857 acres, old field recultivation would have been necessary after forty-four years, a period exceeding the twenty-year recuperative period. Thus, the favorable man-land ratio staved off chronic soil exhaustion during the colonial years, but that ratio dropped dangerously low by the American Revolution.

Other factors retarded erosion's contribution to soil exhaustion. Soil stripping and gullying made little headway in this coastal plain parish. Nowhere did elevations exceed 200 feet and gentle slopes predominated on the interfluves and the old marine terraces. Slopes rarely exceeded 10 per cent except along

---

[1]Parish inventories indicate that agrarian reform was slow in coming. For an exception, see Letters, John Galloway to Samuel Galloway, Oct. 6, 1774, Oct. 20-21, 1774, Nov. 14, 1774, Annapolis, Hall of Records MSS, Galloway-Maxcy-Markoe Collection, Gift Collection D634. Also, American Husbandry, ed. by Harry J. Carman (New York: Columbia University Press, 1939, reprinted by Kennikat Press, Inc., Port Washington, New York, 1964), p. 189.

[2]American Husbandry, pp. 164-65; Avery O. Craven, Soil Exhaustion, p. 32. The best contemporary description of the system of shifting cultivation is Johann D. Schoepf, Travels in the Confederation, 1783-1784 (2 vols.; Baltimore: Lord Baltimore Press, 1911), II, 32.

[3]Schoepf, Travels in the Confederation, II, 32. Beverley, The History and Present State of Virginia, pp. 125-26.

stream courses where they occasionally rose to 30 per cent.[1] In addition, the permeable coastal plain sands readily absorbed precipitation, and rates of over two inches per hour have been recorded by soil scientists.[2] Crop lands also intercepted runoff. Using Indian planting techniques, the planters set out the row crops of corn and tobacco in "hills," or mounds of earth, excavated from holes one foot deep and square, and hoed up to the knee. They "hilled" first in the spring, preparatory to planting, and again after the removal of the trash ground leaves.[3] The practice created a surface of miniature excavation pits and mounds that impeded the flow of water and its erosive power. Also littering the field and obstructing runoff were decaying tree stumps.[4] At a microscale, the drainage pattern on a planter's field was probably chaotic, and hardly an easy target for erosion.

Vegetation and the Depletion of Timber

The early Maryland colonists, cognizant of England's shrinking forest, fully appreciated the bountiful forests, barrens, and wetlands of the Chesapeake, and they put them all to use. Barrens or grasslands they presumed droughty and inhospitable for cultivation, but excellent for livestock grazing.[5] Lush wetlands, known variously as marshes, swamps, and pocosins, they used for pasturing cattle. Frequently, the lure of the salt grass proved too much for the cattle, and they strayed out in the muck and were mired or swallowed.[6] But

---

[1] Soil Survey Maps of Anne Arundel County, Vol. I. Information on slopes may be found on air photographs which accompany this volume.

[2] These rates apply to the Collington and Sassafras soils which occupy most of the parish. Ibid., II, 1-2.

[3] Herndon, William Tatham and the Culture of Tobacco, p. 113. Gray, History of Agriculture, I, 215-16; and Sir Dalby Thomas, "An Historical Account of the Rise and Growth of the West-India Colonies," p. 424.

[4] At the time of the American Revolution, tree stumps on cleared land often prohibited plowing. American Husbandry, p. 160.

[5] William B. Marye, "The Great Maryland Barrens," Maryland Historical Magazine, L (March, June, and September, 1955), 11-23, 120-42, 243-53. Maryland Gazette, July 14, 1747; ibid., November 8, 1749; ibid., December 6, 1749.

[6] "A Relation of Maryland, 1635," Narratives of Early Maryland, 1633-1684, ed. by Clayton Colman Hall, Original Narratives of Early American History (New York: Charles Scribner's Sons, 1910, reprinted by Barnes & Noble, Inc., 1959), p. 81. And Beverley, The History and Present State of Virginia, p. 125. For mired cattle, see Account of Ralph Williams, April 1, 1675, Inventories and Accounts, 2, f. 238.

more valuable than either of these environments were the luxuriant forest lands. Woodlands in the planter's lexicon meant "fresh lands" for cultivation, and they gauged the quality of the soils from the tree species they supported.[1] The seemingly inexhaustible woodlands served other purposes as well. Their acorns, roots, and assorted plant life provided mast for the hogs and cattle who ranged openly in the seventeenth century.[2] Also, wood was an essential resource in the tobacco economy. Timber was required for hogsheads, cider casks, boats, carts, coffins, and furniture. The rarity of stones in the coastal plain and the slow development of brick-making or brick importation increased the demands on wood for houses, barns, outbuildings, and fences.[3]

In All Hallows, the aboriginal forest was overwhelmingly dedicuous hardwood. Of corner trees identified in land surveys between 1650 and 1700, 64.7 per cent were oaks of various species. White oaks, comprising 18.6 per cent of all corner trees, were good for pipe staves, while red oaks, 19.2 per cent, were used for wainscot. Other oak species included black, spanish, water, live, and ten oaks. Hickories, which probably served for firewood, comprised 12.7 per cent. Less frequent were poplars (7.3 per cent), which made good plank; and chestnuts (3 per cent). Apparently, poplars were concentrated in the eastern portion of the parish near Rhode and West rivers, because three landholdings in this vicinity used "poplar" in their name. Only two conifers were recorded in the list of 506 trees (Figure 4).[4]

Amidst the deciduous forest, scattered pockets of wetlands bordered the estuaries and their tributaries. Small tidal marshes, of no great extent, were numerous along South and Rhode rivers. Swamps appeared inland along the courses of fresh water streams, such as North Runn, Flat Creek, and Muddy Creek. Meadows predominated on the flat floodplain of the Patuxent.

Scattered grasslands occupied the northwestern part of the parish. On the Ridge, five separate tracts of land carried the generic name of "range." And between the head of South River and the Patuxent River, a large stretch of barrens extended along "the back of all the Inhabitants." The citizenry there saw

---

[1] Beverley, The History and Present State of Virginia, pp. 123-25.

[2] "Narrative of a Voyage to Maryland, 1705-06," American Historical Review, XII (January, 1912), 329.

[3] "Maryland in 1699," pp. 367-68.

[4] Patents, various libers between 1650 and 1700. For tree uses, see "Maryland in 1699," pp. 368-69; and "A Relation of Maryland, 1635," p. 79.

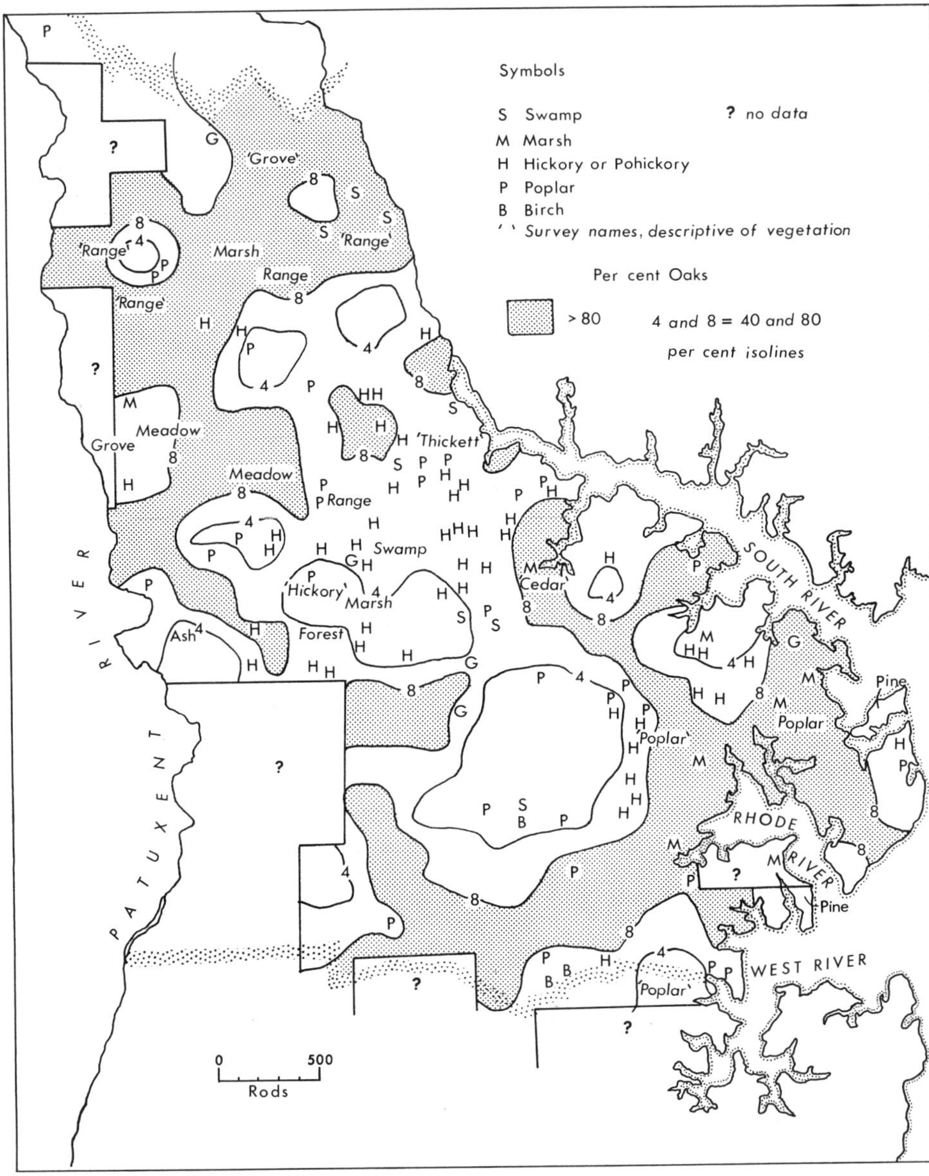

Fig. 4.--Aboriginal Vegetation

these barrens of "Potoxon" as an excellent corridor for a roadway, which would avoid cultivated grounds and road gates while traversing "a more Levell nearer and Convenient way. . . ."[1] Perhaps these grasslands originated with Indian burnings, as is implied by one landholding in the area named "Indian Range."

The bountiful vegetation, particularly the woodlands, came under early attack by the settlers of Maryland and of All Hallows. Tobacco culture placed excessive demands on the woodlands, and their depletion seriously affected the settlement system. In 1699, Hugh Jones detected the assault on the woodlands:

> All the low land is verry wooddy, like one continued fforrest, no part cleared but what is cleared by the English. And tho we are pretty closely seated, yett we cannot see our next neighbours for trees. Indeed in a few years we may expect it otherwise, for the tobacco trade destroyes abundance of timber, both for makeing of hogsheads and building of tobacco houses; besides cleareing of ground yearly for planting.[2]

This forecast proved correct. In the 1770's, the anonymous author of American Husbandry commented that "in the management of their woods, they have shewn the same inattention to futurity with their neighbours, so that in the old settled parts of the provinces, they begin to fear a want of that useful commodity."[3] In All Hallows timber was becoming scarce by the 1720's. A London mortgagor in 1724 asserted that John Belt or his tenants had cut down the woods and let the improvements decay on 200 acres on the Ridge; the property, mortgaged in 1710 at £200 Sterling, was now worth only £30.[4] In 1737, Lewis Duvall petitioned for an act to dock the entail on his land near the head of South River:

> Whereas the said two hundred Acres of land is now near all Cut Downe and the Buildings thereon Old & Decay'd and not more than about thirty or forty Acres of Wood Land Ground belonging to the said Tract & but a small Part of the timber thereon fit for Clap boards whereby the said Lewis Duvall has been Obliged for the support of himself & family . . . to remove therefrom & Settle upon other Fresh Lands. . . .[5]

---

[1] March Court, 1712, AACo Judgments, TB#3, f. 140.

[2] "Maryland in 1699," p. 367.

[3] American Husbandry, p. 189. Fuel was very expensive in Annapolis in 1769, according to William Eddis, Letters from America, p. 21. And in 1750, oaks and chestnuts were valued at £1-10-0 current money each, which was equal in value to 138 pounds of tobacco, or 15 per cent of the annual production of one laborer. Ejectment Papers, Ann Jones v William Disney, February 25, 1750.

[4] AACo Deeds, SY#1, ff. 80-81.

[5] Archives of Maryland, XL, 10; and AACo Deeds, RD#3, ff. 2-4. Also see Archives of Maryland, XLII, 247-48.

About the same time, timber cutting restrictions began appearing in wills;[1] also, woodlands were distinguished according to use as fire or cord wood, board timber, and rail timber.[2]

The thick forest, which visually separated near neighbors in 1699, had given way to a new panorama. In 1767, 49 per cent of Anne Arundel Manor was lacking or scarce of timber (Table 5). When Rochefoucault entered All Hallows at the end of the eighteenth century, he remarked that "the woods upon the road are but few, and these few which remain are cutting down to make room for the sowing of tobacco."[3]

The demands of tobacco culture on the forest were large; timber depletion became evident in the 1690's, and was widespread after the boom years of the 1730's. By the Revolution, the landscape was more open and timber was scarce and expensive.

Weather and Climate

The clearing of the woodlands, some believed, would ameliorate the climate of the Chesapeake region.[4] Yet despite this view, the weather and climate of the Chesapeake did not change appreciably during the colonial period. The planters continued to tend their corn and tobacco under the predictable seasonal regime of a humid continental climate, punctuated by uncertain extremes of drought, humidity, freeze, hail, wind, and rain.

Tobacco culture harmonized nicely with the four seasons in the Chesapeake year. The lengthy frost-free period of 210 days from April 6 to November 2, stretching from the mild Spring through the excessive heat and humidity of late Summer to the coolness of Autumn, permitted the transplanting of tobacco in May and June and harvesting in July and August.[5] Maryland planters suf-

---

[1]Annapolis, Hall of Records MSS, Will of Stephen Warman, May 5, 1740, Wills, 22, ff. 531-33; and Will of Richard Richardson, May 17, 1743, ibid., 23, ff. 261-64.

[2]Aug. Court, 1736, AACo Judgments, IB#2, f. 7; ibid., f. 67; Nov. Court, 1747, ibid., IB#6, f. 608; July 15, 1741, AACo Deeds, RB#1, ff. 69-70.

[3]Duke de la Rochefoucault-Liancourt, Travels through the United States of North America . . . in the Years 1795, 1796, and 1797, trans. by H. Newman (2 vols.; London: R. Phillips, 1799), II, 305.

[4]"Maryland in 1699," p. 369.

[5]Maryland, Maryland Geological Survey, Harold E. Vokes, Geography and Geology of Maryland, revised by Jonathan Edwards, Jr., Bulletin 19 (Baltimore: Maryland Geological Survey, 1957, revised and reprinted, 1968), p. 25.

fered a slight climatic disadvantage, however, as their crops were planted and harvested two to three weeks later than Virginia's; hence it arrived later at the market, and commanded a lower price.[1] Otherwise, the climate and tobacco's requirements synchronized almost perfectly. Precipitation peaked in the Spring and Summer during the growing season. The tobacco harvest came anywhere from late July to September, the later the better. Working in the oppressive heat and humidity of July and August could exact a heavy toll, as it did in the summer of 1747. The Maryland Gazette proclaimed, matter-of-factly, that "We hear from several Parts of the Country, of People Dying by the heat in the Harvest."[2] The parish register of All Hallows tells a solemn story of death in August and September, rivalled only by the coldest month of January (Table 6).[3] Only the affluent or the indolent escaped the heat. The wealthy beat the heat by building homes at higher and breezier sites or by fleeing to the back country heights.[4]

Splashes of color signaled the arrival of Autumn as deciduous leaves prepared to fall. Tobacco was in the barns to cure for six weeks:

> where it is hanged plant by plant . . . til it become powder dry; at which time of the year [October-November] that country is subject to great fogs and mists, which make it become waxy, and if it rises again, than it is fully cured. . . .[5]

This gentle, frontal precipitation continued into winter, alternating with cold dry air out of the northwest. Winters were mild enough for cattle and horses to go unhoused, but too severe for sheep.[6] However, spells of freezing temperatures froze over the rivers, clogged the bay with ice, and decided the justices

---

[1] CSPCS, 1696-97, XV, 582. Higher prices in London for early tobacco are discussed in Letters, Higginson & Bird to Mr. Patrick Sympson, June 30, 1718, Washington, D. C., Library of Congress MSS, Galloway-Maxcy-Markoe Collection, Higginson & Bird Letterbook, 1718-1719, No. 1467; and Higginson & Bird to Madam Walker, Mr. Charles Fleming, and Mr. William Kenney, Dec. 15, 1718, ibid., No. 1836.

[2] Maryland Gazette, July 21, 1747.

[3] All Hallows Parish Registers, 1669-1721, No. 12200; 1700-1724, No. 12201; 1711-1857, No. 12202.

[4] Archives of Maryland, XIV, 326.

[5] Sir Dalby Thomas, "An Historical Account of the Rise and Growth of the West-India Colonies," p. 424.

[6] William Eddis, Letters from America, p. 74.

TABLE 6

NUMBER AND PERCENTAGE OF BURIALS BY MONTHS IN ALL HALLOWS, 1700-1712 AND 1700-1776

Jan.	Feb.	March	April	May	June	July	Aug.	Sept.	Oct.	Nov.	Dec.
1700-1712											
26	13	19	18	12	6	7	27	26	15	14	13
13.3%	6.6%	9.7%	9.2%	6.1%	3.1%	3.6%	13.8%	13.3%	7.7%	7.1%	6.6%
1700-1776											
50	27	36	35	29	14	15	40	39	41	32	37
12.7%	6.8%	9.1%	8.9%	7.3%	3.5%	3.8%	10.1%	9.9%	10.4%	8.1%	9.4%

to adjourn the county courts.[1]

Regardless of the season, spells of drought occasionally plagued the Chesapeake planter. Most dry spells came in the spring and summer months, when a lack of rainfall was compounded by high rates of evapo-transpiration. Spring rain was especially critical for the planter because he hesitated to transplant his tobacco without a "season," meaning a steady rain, to strengthen his plants. But perhaps the most disastrous droughts occurred in cold winters, such as that of 1767-1768. The real impact came in April of 1768 when the vegetation, which was normally sparse in early spring, had made "but little appearance."[2]

With some feeling for the economy and the environment of the Chespeake, we may now turn to the people, both whites, servant and free, and blacks, overwhelmingly slaves.

---

[1] Maryland Gazette, Dec. 23, 1746. Ibid., Jan. 11, 1749.

[2] Ibid., April 7, 1768.

CHAPTER III

THE CHANGING POPULATION OF ALL HALLOWS PARISH

Introduction

The first settlers arrived in Anne Arundel County in the mid-seventeenth century. Growing rapidly by immigration, the parish added English freemen and indentured servants in large numbers; a smattering of Scots and Irish; and numerous Negro slaves. White immigration and slave importation dwindled around the turn of the eighteenth century, and the parish population grew more gradually than it had before. An accumulating excess of births over deaths, or natural increase, constituted the chief source of population growth. Economic conditions continued to affect the timing of that growth, albeit with less directness than during the frontier years. During boom years, immigration picked up speed and native child births increased. As the economy turned down, births tended to fall, outmigration became more common, and the population held steady or declined. But the relationship between the economic cycle and population growth was not always simple and direct, and indeed the few population statistics that have survived make any general statement a tentative one.

Population Growth

The population statistics for colonial Maryland appear primitive in comparison to modern censuses. A few comprehensive surveys are available; but aside from these, the student of Maryland demography must estimate population by resourcefully juggling such indicators as taxables, houses, and militiamen. Our estimates of population rely extensively on taxable figures, because they survive more fully than other indicators.[1] In colonial parlance, a taxable meant a person capable of working in the fields and, therefore, one assessable

---

[1]These and other population data used in this chapter are conveniently listed in Arthur E. Karinen, "Numerical and Distributional Aspects of Maryland Population, 1631-1840" (unpublished Ph. D. dissertation, University of Maryland, 1958), Appendix A, pp. 175-207.

for the poll or head tax. The taxable's legal definition, though varying at first, was fixed once and for all by a 1681 statute declaring as taxables all persons sixteen years and over, with the exception of white women.[1] Thus, total population exceeded taxables by some multiple, which can be determined when both figures survive in the same year. Some discrimination should be used when estimating an unknown population with the taxable multiple because it varies with the age, sex, and racial structure of the population. Karinen, after much study of these multiples, concluded that a multiple of 2.4 applied best before 1676; 2.6 between 1676 and 1705; and 3.0 thereafter.[2]

Estimates of this sort form the basis for Figure 5 which graphically depicts the growth of taxables, households, and population in All Hallows Parish. The cautious reader, before plunging into the graph, will want to know its sources and the assumptions that underlie it.

The first set of curves, A and A', describe the change in parish taxables. Curve A' is based on actual parish taxables for 1696 and between 1761 and 1776, and estimated taxables for the years 1697-1760. The latter estimates are accomplished by assuming that All Hallows's taxables grew at the same rate as they did in St. James' Parish, which bordered All Hallows on the south and where taxable figures survive more fully.[3] The index of St. James' taxable growth (1696-1761) when applied to All Hallows produces Curve A'; note, however, that the index estimates too many taxables in 1761. The gap results either from All Hallows loss of western territory and population to Queen Caroline Parish in 1728 or from a slightly higher growth rate for St. James.[4] Assuming the latter, the growth index can be adjusted downward for the entire period. This adjustment uniformly deflates the number of All Hallows taxables, and the estimates come into line with the actual number of parish taxables in 1761 (Figure 5, Curve A). Henceforth, in discussing taxable growth, I shall always refer to the adjusted Curve A.

Parish taxable figures do not survive before 1696. But an estimate is pos-

---

[1] Archives of Maryland, II, 399, 538-39, 547. Ibid., VII, 233.

[2] Arthur E. Karinen, "Maryland Population: 1631-1730: Numerical and Distributional Aspects," Maryland Historical Magazine, LIV (December, 1959), 365-67.

[3] St. James' Parish taxables are listed in Karinen, "Numerical and Distributional Aspects," pp. 179-205. The two parishes were similar in population size, composition, ethnicity, religion, and economy.

[4] Archives of Maryland, XXXVI, 285-86.

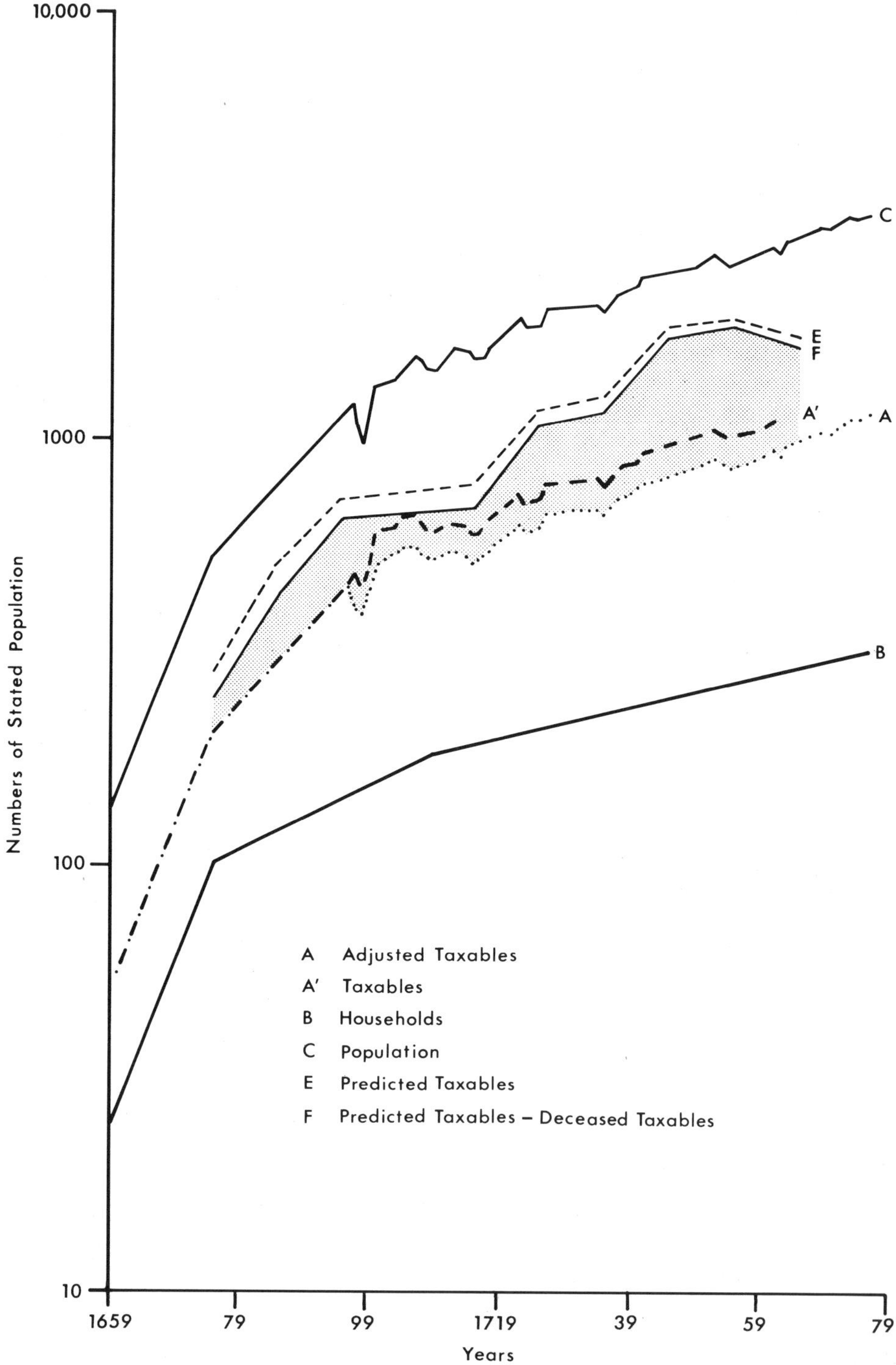

Fig. 5.--Growth of Taxables, Households, and Population, 1659-1776

sible for the year 1675, when Anne Arundel County numbered 816 taxables.[1] How many of these taxables resided in All Hallows Parish? The estimating procedure proceeds on the assumption that the parish's share of taxables resembled its share of related demographic indicators, namely land surveyed up to 1675; houses shown on Herrman's map of 1673; and taxables in 1696.[2] The parish's proportions of these indicators appear in Table 7, along with the taxable estimates that they produce. The low taxable estimate of 206 seems correct on the following grounds. First, the estimate derives from Herrman's map, compiled just a few years before 1675. Second, the estimate of 206 taxables, when converted to a household estimate of 101, provides the closest fit to the number of resident landowners (80) in 1675.[3]

TABLE 7

ESTIMATES OF PARISH TAXABLES
AND HOUSEHOLDS, 1675

Parish-County Ratios	Apportioned Estimates of Taxables	Estimates of Households
Acres surveyed to 1675, 43.6%	357	176
Herrman's map, houses, 25.2%	206	101
1696 Parish taxables, 29.4%	240	119

Even more important than taxables, from the geographer's point of view, are the number of households in the parish. Household figures, however, are non-existent before the census of 1776, and earlier years are estimates, which appear as Curve B in Figure 5. The curve is based on spot estimates for 1675 and 1707 and on the census of 1776. To obtain these estimates, divide the average number of taxables in inventoried households into the total number of parish taxables. (For purposes of definition, an inventoried household is an estate con-

---

[1] Ibid., XV, 51.

[2] The sources are: for land surveys, various libers of Patents; for parish and county taxables in 1696, Archives of Maryland, XXIII, 17-21; for houses, Herrman, Virginia and Maryland.

[3] For more detail, see Chapter VII.

taining at least one bed and some pots, pans, or dishes. The inventoried taxables include all slaves and male servants over sixteen years of age and the male decedent.) Inventoried households between 1671 and 1680 averaged 2.03 taxables and for 1701-1710, 3.18.[1] Dividing these figures into the parish taxables for 1675 and 1707 yields 101 and 184 households, respectively.

An earlier estimate of households is also possible. On the assumption that the parish landowners in 1659 were heads of households, and that no tenants resided in the parish, then the area contained twenty-five households. These assumptions seem appropriate for a frontier region, settled just nine years. This household estimate permits a taxable estimate of 51 persons, which is achieved by multiplying the 25 households by the 2.03 taxables residing in inventoried households (the mean for 1671-1680). Then, given household figures or estimates for 1659, 1675, 1707, and 1776, the intervening years may be determined graphically.

Total population of the parish appears in Curve C. The only exact figure is for 1776. Other years are estimated by the taxable multiples suggested by Karinen.

The complexity of these estimates stands in contrast to the simplicity of the pattern of population growth. The parish population grew rapidly during the first half-century of settlement. Taxables increased by an annual rate of nearly 9 per cent between 1659 and 1675; by 3.3 per cent from 1675 to 1705; and by 4.3 per cent for the period 1659 to 1705.[2] These spectacular advances were not, however, linear. As will be shown in the next section, population growth responded mainly to changes in immigration, which fluctuated sharply from year to year.[3]

Population growth eased off to about one per cent during the eighteenth century (1705-1776), but again episodic spurts of growth alternated with plateaus of little or no growth. The first of these spurts between 1696 and 1705

---

[1]The inventories for 1671-1680 are from Testamentary Proceedings, Libers 1-5, and Inventories and Accounts, Libers 1-7A. For 1701-1710 inventories, see Inventories and Accounts, Libers 20-33.

[2]Growth rates calculated on the formula

$$r = \frac{\log P - \log P_O}{\text{years}}$$

[3]Immigration to Virginia in the seventeenth century is the subject of a pathbreaking book by Wesley Frank Craven, White, Red, and Black: The Seventeenth-Century Virginian (Charlottesville: The University Press of Virginia, 1971).

coincided with a short-lived economic boom and parish taxables shot up from 460 to 560. Over the next ten years, taxable numbers declined occasionally and population did not grow appreciably during this period of low tobacco prices. A sharp increase ensued during the late teens and early twenties, when taxables rose to about 660. But population levelled off once again, not to resume upward until 1735 to 1741 when nearly 800 taxables resided in All Hallows Parish. This close association of population and economic cycles prevailed until 1741, but not afterward. Population augmented gradually, irrespective of economic conditions, and even a severe depression such as occurred in the 1740's did not slacken the rate of growth. Sporadic declines of population in 1753, 1762, and 1770 were brief exceptions to the trend.

By 1776, All Hallows contained 3, 360 persons residing in 312 households. By comparison to 1659, there were twenty-three times as many taxables and twelve times as many households. Population grew spectacularly until 1675 and with moderate speed into the first third of the eighteenth century. Yet, during this entire period, population fluctuated in conjunction with conditions in the tobacco economy. The severity of these fluctuations disappeared after the mid-1730's, as the parish population expanded slowly, steadily, inexorably.

Immigration

Until 1710, the parish population expanded through the immigration of whites and of Negro slaves. Before 1690, Negro importations were trivial, and the parish newcomers were overwhelmingly white, English freemen and servants. The precise number of English entering into the parish probably can never be known, but we are permitted a crude approximation, owing to the proprietor's policy of granting "head rights" to fifty acres of land for every white person transported into the colony between 1651 and 1683.[1] With some qualification, the acreage surveyed in the parish constitutes a rough measure of white immigration, with each fifty acres of survey equal to one white immigrant.[2]

---

[1] Marshall Harris, Origin of the Land Tenure System in the United States (Ames, Iowa: Iowa State College Press, 1953), pp. 215-19.

[2] The qualifications are that land warrants for head rights sometimes circulated, almost as a form of currency, thus prolonging the time between immigration and survey; and that the immigrants may have settled in one area, while their head right was used to survey land in another area. Such was the case when ship captains received head rights for a boat load of servants without indentures; the captains could have sold both the servants and the rights independently.

Because surveys were made several months or more after the arrival dates of immigrants, the timing of immigration should be lagged slightly when interpreting Figure 6.

The tempo of immigration to parish and colony closely corresponded. Parish immigration peaked in the early 1650's, between 1658 and 1663, and again in 1669, when it achieved a maximum of about eighty persons per year. New arrivals diminished during the 1670's, but small bursts occurred in 1672, 1675, and 1678. Maryland immigration accelerated in roughly the same years, specifically, 1650-1651, 1658-1659, 1661, 1663-1664, 1669-1671, 1673, and 1677.[1] And like the colony-wide immigrants, those who came to the parish were predominantly English servants transported to the colony when the tobacco economy was in good health.[2]

The immigration of white indentured servants continued into the 1680's, in seeming defiance of adverse conditions. Tobacco prices sagged, and in 1683 the Proprietor abolished his custom of granting land for the transport of immigrants. Yet a growing European tobacco market encouraged an expansion in output, compensating for the drop in prices. Parish planters raised tobacco production by importing English servants to toil on the tobacco plantations for their indentures of four to seven years, and by pushing the servants to produce greater outputs of tobacco per laborer--a trend evident in Table 4 and the data on which that table is based. More servants worked on the average parish plantation during the 1680's than in any other decade of the colonial era. From this peak of 3.6 servants per estate with bond labor, their numbers plummeted to .68 in the 1690's, and then rose slightly to 1.23 in the first decade of the eighteenth century (Table 8). But by then, servant labor was on the way out, except

---

[1]Russell Menard, "The Growth of Population in Early Colonial Maryland, 1631-1712," unpublished MSS (Annapolis, 1972), pp. 6-7 and tables.

[2]In the debate on the regulating causes of Chesapeake immigration, Menard argues for economic conditions in the Chesapeake and Craven hypothesizes English economic conditions. Russell R. Menard, "Immigration to the Chesapeake Colonies in the Seventeenth Century: A Review Essay," Maryland Historical Magazine, LXVIII (Fall, 1973), 323-29. Craven, White, Red, and Black, pp. 16-17. My assessment is that Menard has the better argument; however, the correlation between Chesapeake tobacco prices and immigration is not, in all cases, especially strong. Perhaps we should tie Craven's observation that immigration was heaviest from 1650 to 1675 to the notion that a general prosperity prevailed in these years. A good portion of this prosperity, I submit, resulted from the expanding Dutch trade to the tobacco colonies--a trade that was finally smashed by the English mercantilists about 1675. H. Roy Merrens and I will address the immigration issue in a forthcoming study of the southern colonies.

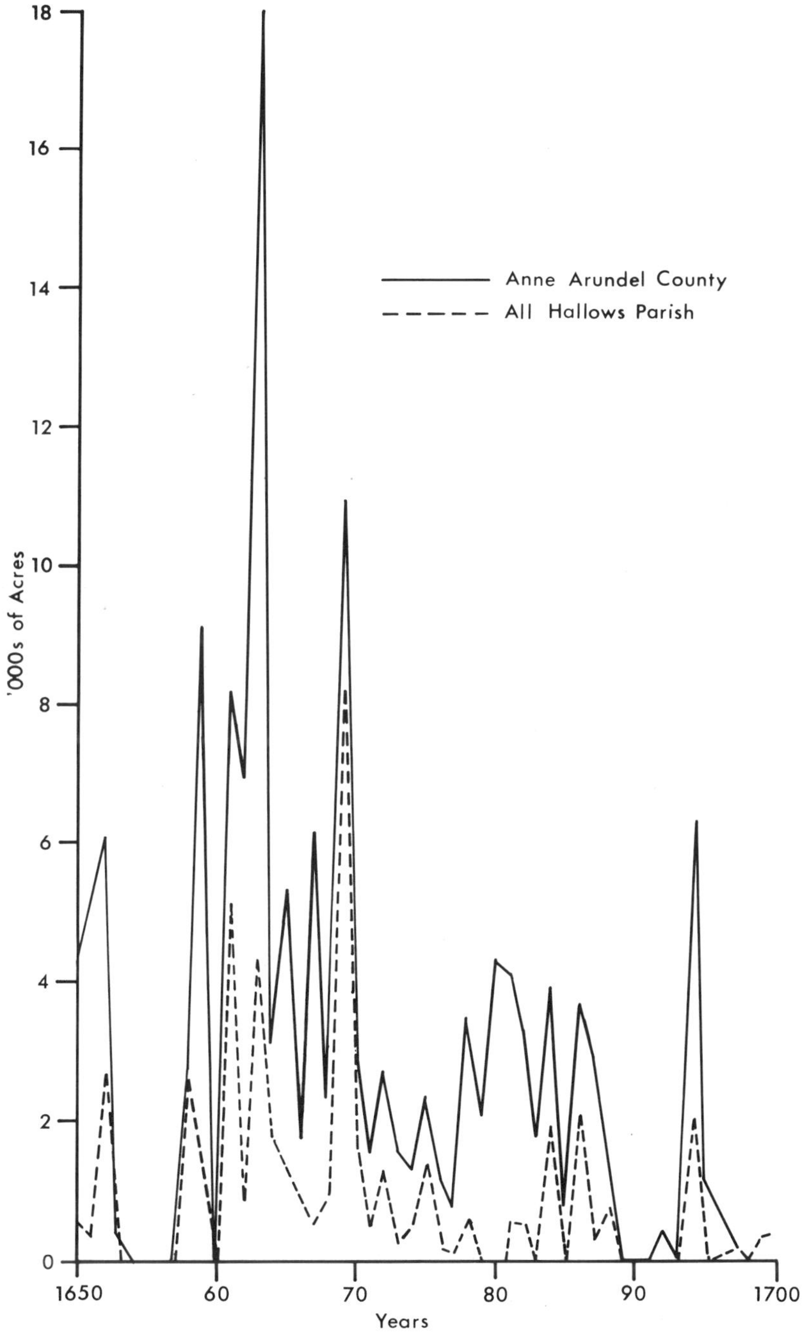

Fig. 6. --Acres Surveyed by Common Warrant in All Hallows and Anne Arundel County, 1650-1700.

TABLE 8

SERVANTS AND SLAVES IN ESTATE INVENTORIES, 1660-1769

Years	No. of Estates	No. of Estates with Bond Labor	All Estates		Estates with Bond Labor		
			Mean No. of Bond Laborers	Mean No. of Slaves	Mean No. of Bond Laborers	Mean No. of Slaves	Mean No. of Servants
1660-79	37	17	1.76	.53	3.82	1.12	2.71
1680-89	55	29	2.66	.74	5.03	1.41	3.62
1690-1700	39	19	3.18	2.85	6.53	5.84	.68
1701-10	44	26	3.39	2.75	5.73	4.65	1.23
1711-20	54	26	4.09	3.80	8.50	7.89	.62
1721-30	46	29	4.61	4.09	7.31	6.48	.83
1731-40	54	34	6.67	6.32	10.59	10.03	.56
1741-50	63	47	6.49	6.32	8.70	8.47	.23
1751-60	52	43	8.33	7.92	10.07	9.58	.49
1761-69	61	36	7.30	7.23	12.36	12.25	.11

for a slight resurgence in the 1720's; slave labor had displaced the servant.

Slave importation to All Hallows Parish was brief, but voluminous.[1] In the final decade of the seventeenth century, the parish inventories recorded a remarkable addition of Negro slaves. Before 1690, the average planter owning bond labor had 1.41 Negroes or less on the plantation; in the 1690's, that figure jumped to nearly six Negroes. This lightning increase in black population, unparalleled during the colonial period, can be explained only by massive importation, as parish planters radically shifted their labor investment from white servants to Negro slaves. Negroes, comprising about 10 per cent of the parish population in 1675, made up 35 per cent by 1700.[2] Thereafter, slave importation waned as a force in the growth of the black population in All Hallows. As with the white population, the natural increase of blacks became the chief source of growth.

Natural Increase

The critical shift from immigration and slave importation to natural increase can be documented in several ways. For the white population, we use replacement rates; for blacks, the balance of sex and age structures of that population.

White replacement rates indicate the average number of sons who replace their deceased fathers. The rate provides an approximate measure of the excess of births over deaths. The tabulation is simply achieved by counting the sons in the will of their father.[3] The data are grouped according to the dates when the fathers wrote their wills. These dates are surrogates for the precise death dates, which are rarely given. The replacement rates, appearing in Table 9, may be back-dated to give the probable birth dates of the surviving children. Birth dates are back-dated sixteen years from the will dates following

---

[1]The terms "Negro" and "slave" are here used interchangeably. They are not perfectly synonymous, but the small number of exceptions--the free Negroes and mulatto slaves--are insignificant for the aims of this study. For example, the 1755 census of Anne Arundel County shows 99.4 per cent of the Negroes as slaves, and 98 per cent of the slaves as Negroes. "An Account of the Number of Souls in the Province of Maryland, in the Year 1755," Gentlemen's Magazine, XXXIV (June, 1764), 261.

[2]The evidence for this assertion is found in the next section of this chapter.

[3]On replacement rates, and their relation to birth rates, see T. H. Hollingsworth, Historical Demography, The Sources of History: Studies in the Use of Historical Evidence (Ithaca, New York: Cornell University Press, 1969), pp. 375-88.

TABLE 9

FREE WHITE REPLACEMENT RATES, 1645-1769

Years of Recordation	Years of Probable Birth	No. of Wills	Replacement Rates
1661-70	1645-54	7	.57
1671-80	1655-64	15	1.00
1681-90	1665-74	27	1.67
1691-1700	1675-84	17	1.82
1701-10	1685-94	18	1.33
1711-20	1695-1704	18	1.11
1721-30	1705-14	22	2.23
1731-40	1715-24	24	2.46
1741-50	1725-34	31	2.90
1751-60	1735-44	18	2.17
1761-69	1745-54	21	2.14

Hollingsworth's argument that the sons in the will averaged sixteen years of age, or the midpoint of a thirty-two-year generation.[1] These probable birth dates also appear in Table 9.

White replacement rates during the seventeenth century were generally low. The rate hovered near unity or fell below it in the early years of settlement. The pre-1664 parish resembled other frontier communities with an overwhelmingly male population, many of whom died before forming families. Replacement rates rose to moderate levels of 1.67 to 1.82 during the generally prosperous years from 1665 to 1684. The trend reversed abruptly in the economically depressed 1680's and 1690's.

A decisive turning point in parish demography came with the large cohort of 1705-1714, when 2.23 sons replaced their fathers. This sharp increase in parish children reflected the new families formed by the sizable native cohorts born in the 1670's and 1680's and by freed servants imported during the brief boom of 1698 to 1704. The replacement rate pushed even higher, reaching a maximum of 2.90 between 1725 and 1734. This largest of parish cohorts came of age during the severe depression of the mid- and late 1740's; indeed, their labor probably contributed to the tobacco glut that sent prices spiralling.

Slaves did not leave wills; and therefore, it is impossible to develop replacement rates comparable to the white population. Yet the shift from importa-

[1]For the use of a 32-year generation for pre-industrial populations, see <u>ibid.</u>, p. 377.

tion to natural increase can be documented by the changing age-sex structure of the slave population. Slave sex ratios and adult-child ratios become very imbalanced, favoring adult males, during periods of importation. The ratios approach unity or less than unity (the ratios become more balanced) under natural increase.

Slave-buying planters preferred to purchase adult males. These Negroes made ideal field hands, and their output exceeded Negro women by one-quarter and boys by one-half.[1] Males predominated the parish inventories from the 1670's to the 1760's, but the imbalance rose acutely in just two decades, the 1690's and the 1720's. After each of these decades of importation, sex ratios trended downward. By 1776, after forty-six years of natural increase, the Negro population of All Hallows approached a balance of males and females (Table 10).[2]

TABLE 10

SLAVE AND SERVANT SEX RATIOS, 1660-1769

Years	No. of Slaves Counted	No. of Servants Counted	Slave Sex Ratio	Servant Sex Ratio
1660-79	6	39	1.00	2.25
1680-89	26	93	1.36	2.00
1690-99	92	13	1.79	1.17
1700-09	88	19	1.52	2.80
1710-19	118	11	1.41	1.75
1720-29	179	24	1.59	2.00
1730-39	315	15	1.52	4.00
1740-49	368	11	1.47	4.50
1750-59	365	21	1.31	1.33
1760-69	335	13	1.35	2.25
1776 Census*	879	?	1.11	?

*Adult sex ratio only.

Further evidence of black natural increase comes from the changing ratio of slave adults to slave children. When planters exercised their preferences in the slave import market, the ratio became very imbalanced in favor of adults,

[1] Herndon, William Tatham and the Culture of Tobacco, pp. 101-3.

[2] Slave and servant sex ratios are calculated from those inventories that specify the sex and/or the names of bond laborers. Sex can be inferred from the forenames, in most cases.

as for example, during the seventeenth century and in the 1720's (Table 11).[1] The ratio became more balanced from 1700 to 1720 and from 1730 to 1776 as slave reproduction augmented the black population. These dependent slave children, in roughly equal sex proportions, were the least desirable slaves from the planter's point of view. He preferred adult males, adult females, and children, in that order.

TABLE 11

SLAVE AND SERVANT ADULT-CHILD RATIOS, 1660-1769

Years	No. of Slaves Counted	No. of Servants Counted	Slave Adult-child Ratio	Servant Adult-child Ratio
1660-79	19	46	2.80	10.50
1680-89	32	98	3.00	5.13
1690-99	101	19	2.89	.90
1700-09	102	21	2.09	1.33
1710-19	133	15	1.38	2.00
1720-29	187	24	2.34	3.00
1730-39	341	16	1.81	7.00
1740-49	320	11	1.29	10.00
1750-59	365	19	1.25	1.71
1760-69	318	12	1.04	1.00
1776 Census	1763	?	.99	?

The parish population, both whites and blacks, grew by natural increase during most of the eighteenth century. Yet despite high replacement rates, the parish population did not grow rapidly, owing to the decline of immigration and slave importation and to attritions caused by outmigration and death.

Outmigration and Death

Hundreds of freemen, servants, and slaves immigrated to All Hallows Parish during the seventeenth century. The flow reversed in the eighteenth century, as native parishioners, seeking opportunities elsewhere, left the parish. Outmigration achieved extraordinary dimensions by the 1740's and 1750's when

[1] Adult-child ratios are also calculated from estate inventories. Children are defined as persons less than sixteen years of age or persons referred to as "boy" or "girl." "Wenches," "lads," "women," and "men" are recorded as adults. Confirmation for the age division between adults and children is found in several inventories containing both ages and age terminology for bond labor. Adult terminology comes into usage when the servant or slave child reached sixteen years of age.

over half of the parish taxables departed for new lands.

Estimating how many persons left the parish is very difficult since neither tax lists nor censuses survive until the end of the study period. The complicated procedure used here to arrive at estimates of outmigration is, in itself, commentary on the crudeness of these estimates. The procedure requires several steps. First, the number of actual taxables (Figure 5, Curve A) is compared to the predicted taxables, or those who should have been in the parish according to the wills and inventories (Figure 5, Curve E). The space between Curves A and E is divisible into those taxables who died and those who migrated out of the parish. The number dying is determined by death rates calculated from wills and inventories. Then, subtracting the deceased taxables from the predicted taxables leaves the outmigrants, appearing graphically as the space between Curves A and F (Figure 5). All outmigration estimates are based on the data presented in Table 12.

A concrete example of the procedure may prove helpful at this point. The example calculation of outmigration is for the 1740's, a time when many parishioners left the parish. After describing each step in the calculation, the appropriate figures for the 1740's are inserted in parentheses. The outmigration estimate begins with the actual parish taxables from Figure 5, Curve A (810 taxables for 1745). Next, the calculation of predicted taxables contains several steps. The mean number of taxables per household (7.43), determined from wills and inventories, is the sum of free white (3.90) and bond taxables (3.53) per household. The number of free white taxables (3.90) includes the mean replacement rate plus one--the free taxable who died. Bond taxables per household (3.53) are counted from the inventories (Table 8). These two are summed to give predicted taxables per household (7.43), which is then multiplied by the number of parish households at mid-decade (for 1745, 249 households, Figure 5, Curve B) producing total predicted taxables (1850.07). This figure always exceeds actual taxables (810), and the excess divides into death and outmigration. Deaths are estimated by constructing a death rate for predicted free white taxables, which is assumed to apply for bond taxables also. The first step in calculating the death rate is estimating the proportion of predicted taxables (1850.07) who are free white. This proportion (52.49 per cent, Table 12, Column C) is derived from the figures in Table 12, Columns A_0, A_1, and A_2. The number of predicted free white taxables (971, Table 12, Col. D) may be determined with this proportion. Next is the calculation of a death rate, which requires a population at risk (the 971 predicted free white taxables) and the number of deaths in

TABLE 12

STEPS IN THE ESTIMATION OF OUTMIGRATION, 1660-1769

Years	Predicted Taxables per Household (Col. A)		
	Free Whites (Col. A_0)	Bonded (Col. A_1)	Total (Col. A_2)
1661-70	1.57	2.00	3.57
1671-80	2.00	.83	2.83
1681-90	2.67	1.61	4.28
1691-1700	2.82	2.16	4.98
1701-10	2.33	1.83	4.16
1711-20	2.11	2.02	4.13
1721-30	3.23	2.36	5.59
1731-40	3.46	3.89	7.35
1741-50	3.90	3.53	7.43
1751-60	3.17	4.00	7.17
1761-69	3.14	2.91	6.05

Year	Predicted Taxables (Col. B)	% of Predicted Taxables per household who were free white (Col. C)	Predicted free white Taxables (Col. D)	Free White Taxable Death Rate per 1,000 (Col. E)	No. of Deaths of all predicted Taxables (Col. F)	Outmigrants/ Predicted Taxables (Col. G)	Persistence Rate (Col. H)
1665	?	?	?	?	?		?
1675	285.83	70.67	202	138.61	39.55	40/285	83.8%
1685	517.88	62.38	323	157.99	81.82	136/518	68.8%
1695	722.10	56.63	409	95.35	68.85	213/722	67.4%
1705	744.64	56.01	417	105.52	78.57	106/745	84.1%
1715	797.09	51.09	407	135.14	107.72	171/797	75.1%
1725	1173.90	57.78	678	64.90	76.19	488/1174	55.6%
1735	1274.52	47.08	600	86.66	110.45	484/1275	58.4%
1745	1850.07	52.49	971	60.76	112.41	928/1850	46.6%
1755	1921.56	44.21	850	41.18	79.13	972/1922	47.2%
1765	1760.55	51.90	914	59.08	104.01	657/1761	60.4%

this population, and here we use the number of white adult males who died and left inventories (59 such inventories survive for 1740-1749). From these, a decadal death rate per 1,000 free white taxables is calculated (Table 12, Col. E, 60.76). Applying this rate to the total population at risk--the predicted taxables--gives the total number of deaths (112.41). Finally, subtracting this figure and the actual taxables from the predicted taxables leaves the number of outmigrants (Table 12, Col. B, 928). The persistence rate (47.2 per cent), which appears in Column H of Table 12, is simply the proportion of predicted taxables remaining in the parish after subtracting those who died.[1] These estimates of outmigration describe an increasingly mobile population.

Parishioners left All Hallows at varying rates between 1660 and the American Revolution. The largest exodus came during the severely depressed 1740's and continued into the next decade. During these two decades alone, over 1,800 taxables probably left All Hallows, and the persistence rate fell below 50 per cent. Before 1740, outmigration tended to increase, but with marked fluctuations. During the boom of the 1670's, outmigration dwindled; 83.8 per cent of the taxables remained in the parish, no doubt, because land and opportunity were still plentiful. But in the next two decades, 1680 to 1700, persistence rates fell to 67 per cent. Contributing to this substantial outmigration were a combination of events including generally depressed tobacco prices, slave importation, and the survival of children to adulthood. Competition for parish land, nearly all of which had been surveyed by 1700, became intense owing to the influx of slave labor in the 1690's and, more importantly, to the coming of age of the sizable birth cohorts of 1665 to 1684. The frontier era had come to an end by the turn of the century.

To use a metaphor, the first twenty years of the eighteenth century were a calm before the storm. Despite low tobacco prices from 1704 to 1718, opportunities improved for parish planters and fewer of them left the parish. Persistence rates rose to 75 per cent or more. Competition proved less intense because the replacement rate for free whites fell toward unity and the death rate remained high at over 100 per 1,000 taxables. But these halcyon days were not

---

[1]These outmigration estimates may be strengthened by more direct evidence of movement out of the parish. From the name lists in the 1776 census and the assessments of 1782 and 1783 can be calculated parish persistence rates, unadjusted for deaths. Of those heads of households present in 1776, 59.7 per cent appear in the assessments six years later. The rate for landowners is 72.7 per cent and for non-landowners, 49.2 per cent. Landowners constituted about one-half of the households at this time.

to last; the parish entered its most crucial demographic phase in the third decade of the new century. Land scarcity and a population burgeoning by natural increase encouraged outmigration. Death rates fell off abruptly, probably because immigration and the high death rates experienced during the "seasoning" period had diminished. If fewer parishioners died, more were born, as evidenced by the rise of replacement rates to a peak of 2.37 in the 1740's. Facing dwindling economic opportunities in the parish, 44 per cent of the parish taxables departed in the 1720's. Outmigration pushed even higher during the 1740's depression, but this economic turndown simply exacerbated problems set in motion earlier by a fixed resource base and a demographic transition of rising birth rates and declining death rates. Where did these migrating parishioners go and how well did they fare are questions deserving of study. As tantalizing as these questions may be, we must lay them aside and confine our attention to the affects of outmigration on the composition of the parish population and on the settlement system.

Population Composition

By 1776, the population of All Hallows Parish resembled other tobacco producing areas in the tidewater region. The population was half white and half Negro, half free and half slave. But because of white outmigration and the rapid increase in slave reproduction, the black population tested the long-held numerical superiority of the English and Anglican whites.

Negroes barely outnumbered whites in the census of 1776, but the demographic indicators pointed toward further imbalance.[1] Negroes comprised 52.5 per cent of the total parish population of 3,360. Among children alone, Negroes made up a slightly larger share of 54.9 per cent. Perhaps higher fertility rates prevailed among Negro women, who averaged 2.12 children each compared to 1.55 for white women. Also contributing to the black majority was the heavy outmigration of whites, many of whom owned no slaves. Landless, slaveless whites migrated out with greater frequency during the 1770's than did landed, slaveholding planters.[2] The average household during the 1760's contained 3.14 white taxables (Table 12, Column A_0); by 1776, it contained 1.29 taxables. By contrast, a very slight decrease occurred among bond taxables per house-

---

[1]For the census, see Brumbaugh, Maryland Records, I, 407-16.

[2]Supra, p. 53. Even a casual inspection of the 1776 census and the federal assessments of 1782 and 1783 show that landless men were also slaveless men.

hold, most of whom were Negroes, falling from 2.91 in the 1760's (Table 12, Column A_1)[1] to 2.82 by 1776. The abrupt drop in white taxables seems to indicate that many poorer whites left the parish and that slaveowning planters remained. The continuation of differential outmigration and Negro fertility guaranteed the numerical dominance of the Negro in the parish during the Revolutionary era.

Despite the large number of Negroes in 1776, many parish households, 45.2 per cent, contained none. The typical planter had a small labor force. The median household contained just two laborers (taxables), and the modal household, only one laborer. At the other extreme, one planter claimed 61 taxable persons, and the 31 largest households (the top 10 per cent) domiciled 467 taxables or 40.4 per cent of the total. Most of these taxables were, of course, slaves. The median slaveowner quartered 7 slaves, but one planter owned 93 slaves.

The contrasts between white and black population and slaveowning and nonslaveowning planters varied sharply from south and east to northwest by the end of the colonial period. According to the federal assessment of 1783,[2] South River Hundred on the northwest side of the parish departed radically from the rest of the parish and from the stereotypic image of the "tobacco coast." This area, extending from the head of South River west to the Patuxent, contained fewer Negro slaves (39.6 per cent), less slaves per household (3.79), and a lower ratio of Negro adult males to white adult males when compared to other parts of the parish. In addition, the sex ratio was acutely imbalanced with only 50 males for every 100 females (Table 13). The demographic peculiarity of this portion of the parish hints at different causal processes such as lesser eco-

---

[1]Technically, the figure of 2.91 represents the number of bond taxables per household during the 1760's, and is not exactly comparable to the number of Negro taxables per household in 1776. However, the number of servants in the parish during the 1760's was so small as to make the difference negligible. During that decade, the mean number of servants per household was .11. Subtracting this figure from the 2.91 bonded taxables per household in the 1760's produces 2.80 Negro taxables per household, which figure is even closer to the 2.82 Negro taxables per household in 1776.

[2]Baltimore, Maryland Historical Society MSS, Scharf Collection, Federal Assessment of 1783. This assessment taxed real and personal property, and hence the definition of taxable person differed from the head or poll taxes of the colonial years. In 1783, some of the taxable persons may have lived in the households of other taxables; and therefore, they are not strictly comparable to the household entries which appear in the 1776 census.

TABLE 13

POPULATION SUMMARY BY HUNDREDS
OF THE 1783 ASSESSMENT

	Lower Rhode	Upper Rhode	South River	Totals
% of Population Slave	48.4	51.6	39.6	47.1
White Sex ratio	1.28	1.35	.49	.92
Slave Adults/ Slave Children*	1.33	1.10	.79	1.04
Male Slaves, 14-45 years/ White Males, 16-50 years	1.49	1.26	.86	1.16
Mean no. of Slaves per person taxed	4.06	5.42	3.79	4.48

*Adults were those 14 years of age and over.

nomic opportunity and considerable outmigration. In contrast, the remaining hundreds of Upper and Lower Rhode River reflect what we have come to expect along the tobacco coast. Negro slaves made up nearly half or more of the population, and adult male slaves exceeded adult male whites by one-tenth to one-third (Table 13).

The white population, though slipping numerically behind their slaves, maintained a kind of unity found in their common religion and ethnic origins. The planters were predominantly Anglican in religion and English in national origin or descent. Quakers and Scots, however, added a touch of religious and ethnic variety.

Quakerism made sizable inroads among the Puritans who settled Anne Arundel County in the 1650's. By 1672, Quakers had established meetings at West River, immediately south of the parish, and at Herring Creek in southern Anne Arundel County. During the 1680's South River Quakers conducted a "Disorderly and Separate" meeting.[1] Although the number of residents becoming

[1]J. Reaney Kelly, Quakers in the Founding of Anne Arundel County, Maryland (Baltimore: J. H. Furst Company for The Maryland Historical Society, 1963), p. 49. On the South River meeting, see Kenneth L. Carroll, "The Anat-

convinced Quakers will probably never be known, by 1675 at least sixteen of the eighty parish landowners were or had been Quaker. About half of these Quaker landowners resided in the southern part of the parish between Rhode and West rivers.[1]

Quaker numbers diminished in the eighteenth century, particularly after the establishment in 1692 of Anglicanism as the official religion of Maryland. Religious back-sliding was evident in an Anglican religious survey of 1724. Quakers comprised about 27 per cent of the households in St. James' Parish, south of All Hallows, and none in St. Anne's Parish immediately to the north of All Hallows. A negligent minister failed to return the figures for All Hallows, but by interpolation, the parish contained about 12 per cent Quaker households.[2] The proportion may have been even smaller, as indicated from estate administrators. Beginning in the 1720's, the prerogative court specified those estates administered by Quakers. Of 195 parish estates with probated accounts taken between 1720 and 1769, just 11 or 5.6 per cent had Quaker administrators. In sum, Quaker households constituted perhaps 20 per cent of the parish in the 1670's and perhaps 5 to 12 per cent in the next century. The trend was toward fewer Quakers once the area was erected as an Anglican parish.

The establishment of Anglicanism as the official Maryland religion in 1692 insured an Anglican majority in All Hallows Parish. Shortly after the creation of the parish in that same year, a register of vital events recorded the minister's strenuous schedule. Between 1701 and 1710, he conducted 193 marriages, 156 burials, and 310 baptisms for a population of about 1,150.[3] Such were the ministerial demands in a parish where 80 to 85 per cent of the residents professed Anglicanism.

These Anglicans and Quakers of All Hallows were Englishmen, as were most whites in the Chesapeake. Englishmen, according to one authority, contributed over 90 per cent of the white immigrants to the Maryland colony before

---

omy of a Separation: The Lynam Controversy," Quaker History, LV (Autumn, 1966), 67-78.

[1]The names of landowners in 1675 are from Rent Rolls, Liber 1, and various libers of Deeds. Quaker membership is found in the carefully documented work by Kelly, Quakers in the Founding of Anne Arundel County.

[2]Papers Relating to the Church in Maryland, A.D. 1694-1775, ed. by William Stevens Perry (n.p., privately printed, 1878), pp. 193-95, 204.

[3]All Hallows Parish Register, 1669-1721, No. 12200, and 1700-1724, No. 12201.

1680.[1] A similar proportion came into All Hallows. English predominance endured in the next century, despite the immigration of a few Scots and Scots-Irish. For example, over 90 per cent of the surnames listed in the parish census of 1776 are of English origin. Of the 32 non-English names listed in the census, 29 were common to other parts of the British Isles, one may have been German (Romalls), and two were French (Duvall).[2] Twenty-four Scottish and Scots-Irish surnames were listed in the census. Twelve of these carried the name of Stewart, followed by Anderson (7), Mitchell (1), Strachan (1), Buchanan (1), Dick (1), and Ferguson (1). Irish representatives included Ryan (1), Sullivan (1), and Mulliken (3). In summary, nine out of ten white families in the parish at the beginning of the American Revolution were of English origin. The other was a non-English Briton.

Population Density and Distribution

White Britons and black Africans transformed All Hallows Parish from a sparsely settled frontier area to one of the more densely settled sub-regions of the tobacco coast by 1776. These changes in population density, which will be referred to repeatedly in our later discussion of settlement, appear in Table 14. The density figures in this table are derived from population estimates given above, and from estimates of the occupied area, as measured by the acreage surveyed. The latter deserves brief comment. During the seventeenth century, the land area of the parish expanded along with population growth. By 1675, 56.12 square miles were surveyed, and thirty years later the parish surveys encompassed 78 square miles. Few additions occurred after 1705, so that in 1783 the federal assessment recorded 79.46 square miles for the parish. Accordingly, the density calculations for the years 1675 to 1705 use the amount of acreage surveyed by the appropriate date. For 1715 and 1725, the acreage of 1705 is used, and afterward the 1783 area is used.

---

[1]This proportion appears in Howard F. Barker, "National Stocks in the Population of the United States as Indicated by Surnames in the Census of 1790," Annual Report of the American Historical Association, XXXI (1931), 256.

[2]Ibid., pp. 126-359. The pitfalls in inferring national origin from surnames are many. Genealogical inquiry is less inferential, but the average person left little evidence of his or her family's homeland. The method used here is to check the surnames and national origins given in Barker against parish names. Surnames which had currency in England and one or more other areas are recorded as non-English; thus, if there are errors in assignment of national origin, they probably increase the number of non-English

TABLE 14

POPULATION DENSITIES IN ALL HALLOWS, 1675-1783

Year	Densities per Square Mile		
	Taxables	Households	Population
1675	3.67	1.80	8.81
1685	4.73	1.91	12.31
1695	6.23	2.05	16.20
1705	7.19	2.30	18.69
1715	6.65	2.48	19.95
1725	7.83	2.70	23.50
1735	8.73	2.93	26.19
1745	10.19	3.13	30.58
1755	10.95	3.37	32.85
1765	12.59	3.66	37.76
1776	14.55	3.93	42.55
1783	?	3.78	43.56

Parish population densities varied in space as well as in time. The 1783 density of forty-three and one-half persons per square mile rose to over forty-eight persons per square mile in the south and southwestern part of the parish known as Upper Rhode River Hundred. Densities fell to about thirty-eight in South River Hundred, which once again stands out for its deviation from the rest of the parish. Along the main stretches of South and Rhode rivers, densities nearly duplicated the parish mean.

These spatial variations in density probably had their origins early in the eighteenth century. A comparison of 1783 densities with landholdings surveyed by 1707 shows a close correlation between small and medium-sized surveys early in the century and areas of high density later on. More specifically, the valley of Flat Creek to its confluence with South River, containing numerous small, overlapping surveys, and the neck of land between South and Rhode rivers, holding small and medium-sized parcels (Figure 7), were both areas of higher densities in 1783. By contrast, along the Patuxent Valley over to the head of South River vastly larger surveys of 500 acres and more prevailed, and in these areas, densities were lowest as of 1783.

For earlier periods, densities are less pertinent than the directions taken by settlement. So long as planters acquired land on easy terms, they surveyed and patented as much land as they could, and this process helped spread settlement thinly across the parish. The initial planters located along the Chesa-

Fig. 7.--Initial Surveys, 1650-1707

peake estuaries, and later immigrants moved beyond them to the north and west, and a few others pushed up the Patuxent Valley from Calvert County (Figure 3). The small, jumbled surveys along Flat Creek were taken up in a second wave of surveys between 1660 and 1665, when immigration to All Hallows was at its highest (Figure 6).

As the parish filled with people, a distinctly rural way of life prevailed, yet the dependence on tobacco as a commercial staple tied the planters into an Atlantic economy that was organized in English port cities and eventually in Chesapeake towns. It is to these urban settlements and their emergence in All Hallows that we now turn.

CHAPTER IV

URBAN SETTLEMENT

Introduction

The settlement system of All Hallows Parish passed through three spatial phases. Before 1710, a handful of specialized occupations were scattered among the dispersed rural plantations. During the second phase between 1710 and 1750, these specialists, and particularly the merchants, clustered into a small town on South River. During this period of intense urban concentration, London Town sheltered perhaps half of the parish's secondary and tertiary occupations. The rapid rise of this town, small though it remained, signalled a new prosperity in the tobacco trade. Meanwhile, the rural population continued to live on dispersed plantations, but these settlements had undergone a fundamental restructuring since the seventeenth century. Planters somehow had to cope with a cyclical economy of boom and bust; they buffered these fluctuations by diversifying their agricultural operations, by improving their crop processing capabilities, and by making and repairing their own goods and equipment. In short, they turned inward toward plantation self-sufficiency. These restructured plantations seriously undermined urbanization in the parish during the third locational phase after 1750. Economic depressions increasingly spelled a dwindling market for town merchants; their plantation customers retrenched by substituting home-produced goods for the merchants' store goods. Several other problems confronted the parish's urban merchants. The meteoric growth of Baltimore, Alexandria, and Georgetown helped re-orient Maryland highways and traffic away from the parish; and far-reaching tobacco legislation in 1747 produced major shifts in local marketing centers of tobacco. The town merchants of London Town on South River saw that economic opportunities lay elsewhere; their relocation to these more promising places merely hastened the decline of the town, and of the parish's brief encounter with urban life.

The merchant exodus from London Town returned the parish to a settlement pattern of dispersed plantations and decentralized urban functions, reminiscent of the seventeenth century. But the resemblances were superficial.

Within the plantations, changes of enormous proportions had altered activities and conduct; the planters had adapted their plantations to an erratic and unpredictable economy.

Urban and Decentralized Sites

Commercial agriculture employed 80 per cent and upwards of the households in colonial All Hallows; yet the other 20 per cent or so contributed much to the settlement system, and particularly to its changing spatial pattern. These merchants, coopers, carpenters, innholders, tailors, shipwrights, doctors, and ministers--or more broadly, specialists in secondary and tertiary economic activities--constituted a group which toiled in both urban and rural settings. If urban settlements were to arise in the parish, this group of specialists would provide the personnel; and hence, we designate them as potentially urban. This potential for clustering together was activated in the first half of the eighteenth century. The prevailing pattern of decentralized locations gave way; one-third to one-half of the potential urbanites swarmed into London Town, swelling its population to about 200. All over the tobacco coast, small towns advanced in size and vitality. And urban centralization, though meager compared to the big towns of Boston, New York, and Philadelphia, thoroughly revolutionized Chesapeake life by re-locating activities, rearranging travel patterns, and mediating and expediting commercial relations with England and European markets. This potential urban population of All Hallows Parish bears closer examination.

The Structure of Potential Urban Occupations

The white men of All Hallows Parish were distinguished by name and by their economic task or honorific title. This convention affords us a useful guide to the occupational structure of the parish. An especially complete list of occupations is contained in the parish land records. Although a fire in 1704 destroyed the seventeenth century land records, the re-recording of many of these deeds permits a rough reconstruction of the early occupational structure.[1] Yet even in the land records, a few occupational specialists are missed. One underenumerated group is the tenant-at-will, whose verbal lease agreements went unrecorded by the court. Another group is obscured by the use of honor-

---

[1]John M. Hemphill II, "Annapolis: Colonial Metropolis and State Capital," The Old Line State, ed. by Morris L. Radoff, Maryland Hall of Records Commission Publication No. 16 (Baltimore: Twentieth Century Printing Company, Inc., 1971), p. 180.

ific titles, such as "Esquire" or "Gentlemen." But because these prominent men appeared frequently in the public record we can usually identify their principal economic function. The completeness of enumeration also varies with fluctuations in the land market, with fuller reporting corresponding to periods of active land transaction.

Bearing these problems in mind, we can point to one other advantage of the land records as a source of occupational data, particularly for the geographer. He can better pin down the location of occupational specialists because the land records often specify the residence of the parties, or because a clue to their residence is contained in the location of their landholdings. With the precaution that the land records understate occupations, particularly of tenants-at-will, and that their locations are crudely approximated in a number of cases, we can examine the changing occupational structure of All Hallows Parish as it appears in Table 15.

Number and Variety of Occupations

In All Hallows Parish, specialized persons were few in number and limited in variety. Probably at no time during the colonial period did they exceed 20 per cent of all parish households (Table 16). Specialist occupations did vary, however, becoming more numerous between 1710 and 1739 and again in the decade in the 1760's when they comprised 10 to 17 per cent of all households. The remaining households were made up of planters--invariably the predominant occupational group, especially between 1680 and 1709, and, to a lesser extent, between 1740 and 1759. In any case, the proportion of secondary and tertiary specialists was small, and substantially less than in southeastern Pennsylvania, where one-third or more of the heads of households had occupations other than farmer.[1]

The thirty-two different occupations professed by parish residents covered a narrow range of colonial jobs. What is most interesting about the list of parish occupations is the numerous craft and service activities that were absent or performed by quasi-specialists on the plantation. So far as the land records indicate, the parish lacked bakers, butchers, barbers, perukemakers, printers, painters, brewers, potters, and metalsmiths, excepting blacksmiths. Nor were there specialists in brick manufacture, the making of cloth, candles, or guns,

---

[1]James T. Lemon, The Best Poor Man's Country: A Geographical Study of Early Southeastern Pennsylvania (Baltimore: The Johns Hopkins Press, 1972), p. 8.

TABLE 15

SELECTED SECONDARY AND TERTIARY OCCUPATIONS, 1660-1769

	1660-1679	1680-1689	1690-1699	1700-1709	1710-1719	1720-1729	1730-1739	1740-1749	1750-1759	1760-1769
Total	11	11	9	17	31	25	41	28	33	39
Resident	11	10	6	11	31	24	36	24	26	33
Non-resident	0	1	3	6	0	1	5	4	7	6
Resident Only Merchants	4	5	4	2	13	13	14	12	9	9
Woodworkers	2	1	0	3	6	3	10	2	6	4
Leatherworkers	0	0	0	1	1	1	4	3	1	5
Tailors	2	1	0	0	3	0	1	2	3	2
Innholders	1	0	1	1	3	2	2	1	1	1
Doctors	1	0	2	2	1	1	0	0	0	0

Note: "Woodworkers" includes carpenters, coopers, joiners, boatwrights, and sawyers.
"Leatherworkers" includes cordwainers, shoemakers, tanners, saddlers, furriers, and hatters.

Source: Deeds, various Libers.

TABLE 16

PROPORTION OF HOUSEHOLDS WITH OCCUPATIONAL TITLES, 1660-1769

Date	Residents with Titles	% of all Households with Titles
1660-79*	11	10.99
1680-89	10	8.26
1690-99	6	4.14
1700-09	11	6.14
1710-19	31	16.06
1720-29	24	11.43
1730-39	36	15.79
1740-49	24	9.64
1750-59	26	9.70
1760-69	33	11.34

*Non-comparable due to 20-year grouping.

or the provision of transport services. Of the thirty-two occupations represented in the parish, two distinctive groups can be identified. Persistent occupations endure throughout the colonial years. Higher-order occupations appear at later dates when conditions of entry are satisfied.

Persistent Occupations

The skeletal structure of parish occupations emerged during the seventeenth century. Merchants, carpenters, coopers, and tailors, to name a few occupations, appeared early and persisted for the remainder of the colonial years. These persistent occupations provided continuity into the next century when the occupational structure was enriched by higher-order occupations.

Among these persistent occupations, merchants consistently supplied the largest number of specialists. Between 1660 and 1769, they comprised 41 per cent of the 212 persons with occupational titles. During the seventeenth century, merchants numbered four to five per decade; but between 1710 and 1719 they increased abruptly toward an equilibrium of twelve to fourteen merchants per decade. This equilibrium position prevailed until 1749, and then the number of merchants fell to nine per decade.

Equally persistent were wood craftsmen. Skills in cooperage and carpentry were always critical in a growing tobacco economy, and this is reflected in the wood craftsmen's ranking as the second largest occupational group with almost 18 per cent of all occupational persons. More specifically, this group included carpenters, coopers, turners, joiners, sawyers, boatwrights, and shipwrights. An unusual feature of the woodworkers is their sharp peak during the prosperous 1730's, when the parish contained six carpenters, one cooper, two boatwrights, and a shipwright. This boom period evidently touched off a spate of shipbuilding and plantation construction, and, recalling our earlier discussion, of timber depletion.

After the wood craftsmen came tailors and innholders, or ordinary keepers. Tailors accounted for about 6.5 per cent of the total; but their numbers never exceeded four per decade, and one or two was most usual. Innholders comprised about 6 per cent of all specialists, and the typical decade found between one and three innholders, with a peak of three occurring in 1710-1719.

The remaining persistent occupations produced only one or two representatives in a decade. These included ministers, mariners, millwrights, plasterers, and blacksmiths.

Persistence also characterized the medical profession, at least until 1740, when doctors, physicians, and chirurgeons simply disappeared from the parish records. At least two doctors resided in the parish during the 1670's.[1] Between 1700 and 1720, four doctors practiced in the parish, and in 1735 Dr. Richard Hill made his home in London Town.[2]

Perhaps the demand for doctors diminished after 1720 as the death rate tumbled lower. As important may have been the competition provided by medical dabblers. Moderate- and well-to-do planters increasingly administered their own cures and preventions with medicines, drugs, and instruments.[3] These medical paraphernalia were relatively rare in estate inventories between 1710 and 1739, where they appeared only four times (2.5 per cent of the inventories). But in the next twenty years, they appeared in thirteen inventories (11.6 per cent).

---

[1]For the 1670's, see the inventories of Jacob Neale, "Chyrurgeon," and Dr. William Jones. Testamentary Proceedings, 5, f. 40; and Inventories & Accounts, 5, ff. 429-35. Two other doctors, Michael Cusack and Francis Stockett, died in the parish in the 1680's. Ibid., 8, ff. 499-501; and ibid., 9, f. 445.

[2]Raymond P. Stearns, Science in the British Colonies of America (Urbana: University of Illinois Press, 1970), p. 277.

[3]For numerous examples of planter doctoring, see The Secret Diary of William Byrd of Westover, 1709-1712, ed. by Louis B. Wright and Marion Tinling (Richmond: The Dietz Press, 1941).

Higher-order Occupations

As the parish matured and population densities increased, new occupations catered to the wants of the parishioners. These higher-order occupations, so-called because they depended on minimum supportive population densities, consisted of leatherworkers and a motley assortment of others. Leatherworkers--shoemakers, cordwainers, tanners, and saddlers--comprised 7 per cent of all persons with occupational titles; yet, they did not appear until the first decade of the eighteenth century. Then, with population densities exceeding 18 per square mile, a cordwainer made the initial entry into the parish occupational structure. Further additions awaited the 1730's when suddenly the parish sheltered four shoemakers or cordwainers, one of whom doubled as a saddler. Leatherworkers declined over the next twenty years, but their numbers rose again in the 1760's. Perhaps the prosperity of the 1730's stimulated these trades, and in the 1760's the decimation of parish cattle created an abundant supply of the leatherworker's raw material--hides.[1] Two of the five leatherworkers in the 1760's were tanners. Another tanner-cordwainer opened his shop earlier in 1742, but he did not persist into the 1750's.

A few other specialist occupations participated in the parish settlement system. These higher-order occupations included, in order of entry: a fuller, clogmaker (probably employed in a fulling mill), weaver, bricklayer, furrier, hatter, and lawyer (Table 17). In summary, wool-associated specialists made their appearance during the 1730's and 1740's, when population densities reached 25 to 30 persons per square mile. In the next two decades, trades associated with the embellishment of houses and attire were added. Presumably sufficient demand existed for landscape and personal beautification after the mid-eighteenth century, a period aptly described as the golden age of colonial culture.[2]

Scale and Scale Thresholds

We have dwelt thus far on the expanding consumer market as an essential precondition for the entry of parish craftsmen and merchants. Their success, however, depended equally as much on the entrepreneur's resources. Each occupation required peculiar combinations of capital, goods, equipment, and labor, adding up to a minimum investment, or scale threshold.

---

[1]For the decimation of the cattle population during the 1760's infra, p. 124.

[2]Thomas J. Wertenbaker, The Golden Age of Colonial Culture (Ithaca, New York: Great Seal Books, 1949).

TABLE 17

OCCUPATIONS, DATE OF ENTRY, AND POPULATION DENSITIES

Date of Entry	Population Density (at mid-decade)	Occupations
1680-89	12.31	Millwright Blacksmith
1690-95	16.20	
1700-09	18.69	Minister
1710-19	19.95	
1720-29	23.50	Schoolmaster
1730-39	26.19	Fuller Ironmaster Saddler
1740-49	30.58	Clogmaker Tanner Weaver
1750-59	32.85	Joiner Turner Bricklayer
1760-69	37.76	Furrier Hatter Lawyer

A crude measure of minimum investment is contained in the monetary value of estates belonging to occupational specialists. Fortunately, 61 of their estate inventories have survived. By occupation, these inventories are distributed as follows: merchants, 33; woodworkers, 9; doctors, 8; tailors, 4; leatherworkers, 3; innholders, 2; schoolmasters, 1; and ministers, 1.

Merchants.--Merchant estates were much larger than those of other occupations. Between 1660 and 1769, the scale of 33 merchant estates averaged £1464.51. This figure exceeded the average of the remaining 28 specialists--£129.48--by over eleven times. Without question merchants numbered among the wealthiest parish residents and full-time mercantile activity required substantial capital. Almost 70 per cent of the merchants possessed £500 or more at death, although merchant scale varied widely, from £26 to £5792.

Mercantile activity became more expensive during the eighteenth century. Before 1710, merchant estates averaged £1221.47; between 1710 and 1769, the value rose to £1529.94 between 1710 and 1769, and the minimum scale hovered between £400 and £600 (Figure 8). Six hundred pounds was a lofty sum beyond the reach of most parishioners. Just 12.09 per cent of all parish estates after 1710 exceeded £600, and merchants made up over half (55 per cent) of these (Table 18). These wealthy estates appeared more frequently during the 1730's, 1750's and 1760's; but these increments produced few new merchants, because merchant numbers remained static or declined in these years.

The establishment of mercantile scale thresholds before 1710 is clouded by a small sample of seven merchant inventories. These definitely indicate lower thresholds of between £120 and £325 (Figure 8). Regardless of the precise level of the threshold, mercantile activity in the seventeenth century required decidedly less capital--perhaps as much as £100 to £200 less--than in the next century. The lower scale threshold meant also that more parishioners were eligible to enter merchant ranks. Thirty-six per cent of all pre-1710 inventories surpassed the lower threshold of £120, and 14 per cent surpassed the upper threshold of £325. The capital requirements for merchants rose during the colonial period, but at all times, substantial sums were a prerequisite for success. Also prerequisite for merchant success was the appropriate expenditure of these grand sums.

The large scale of merchant activities was necessary for facilities, store goods, and liquid capital. The merchant invested a small amount in facilities. Most possessed a store where they retailed European goods and collected tobacco from their planter customers. A crude building sufficed, and construction costs rarely exceeded £5 to £10 sterling.[1] Decentralized merchants usually erected an inexpensive store, placed amidst their plantation buildings; more ambitious traders, seeking a commodious site in London Town, had to pay expensive land prices and rentals ranging from £1 to £15 per acre.[2]

The typical store contained a bewildering assortment of goods. Rochefoucault captured the peculiarity of this settlement institution in his warning to fellow Frenchmen:

---

[1]On construction costs, see AACo Judgments, RC#2, f. 89; ibid., TB#1, ff. 730-32; Inventories & Accounts, 32, ff. 40, 77; Testamentary Proceedings, 6, f. 33.

[2]One house in London Town rented for £4-11-8 current money in 1755, while another leased at £14-15-0 current money per annum. Accounts, 37, ff. 143-46; and ibid., 54, ff. 29-33. In 1770, one lot in London Town was rented at £18 currency per annum. Annapolis, Hall of Records MSS, Original Wills, Box F, folder 5.

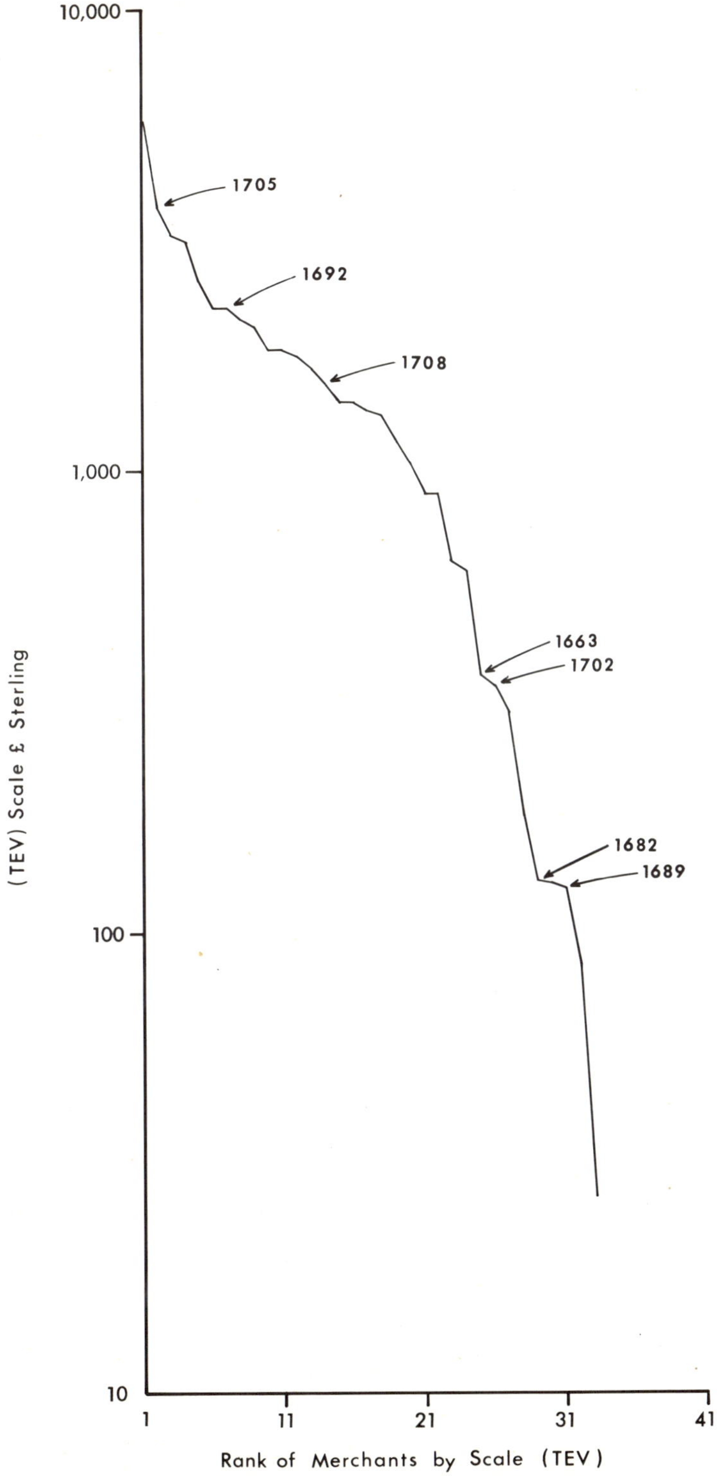

Fig. 8.--Rank-order of Merchant Scales, 1660-1769

TABLE 18

INVENTORIED ESTATES EXCEEDING MERCHANT SCALE THRESHOLD OF £600, 1710-1769

Date	Number	% of all Inventories
1710-19	5	9.62
1720-29	4	7.69
1730-39	7	12.90
1740-49	6	9.38
1750-59	9	18.75
1760-69	9	14.75

> The french translation of the term store is magazin: but it is frequently expressed by the word boutique; and yet neither of these words conveys its meaning completely, according to the peculiar character, object and use of store in America; and especially in places thinly inhabited. The words magazin and boutique may be met with repeatedly in books of travels, but the reader will never be able from them to form an idea of the meaning which belongs to store in America. A store is a shop or place where all kinds of commodities intended for consumption are to be found, and sold by retail; nothing is excluded from it: here are candles and matches, as well as snuff and tape.[1]

Even these comments understate the range of goods found in Samuel Peele's stores at his death about 1733.[2] Of Peele's total estate, £1550 sterling, or 26.8 per cent, was invested in store goods or merchandise. Fine linens comprised 16 per cent of the total value of store goods; "Pershon Silk," 4.5 per cent; coarser cloths, 12.6 per cent; sail line, 6.1 per cent; "habardashary," 8.9 per cent; shoes, 4.5 per cent; hats, 6.5 per cent; buttons and mohair, 1.6 per cent; stockings, 3.0 per cent; spices and grocery, 4.0 per cent; stationery, .8 per cent; saddles, 2.4 per cent; upholstery, 1.9 per cent; "cutlary ware," .9 per cent; pewter and brass ware, 1.2 per cent; tin ware, .6 per cent; iron ware, 7.2 per cent; and earthenware, .8 per cent. Few merchants were as wealthy nor had as many goods as Samuel Peele, but for most the variety of goods was similar.[3] Parish merchants were diversified retailers and wholesal-

---

[1] Rochefoucault-Liancourt, Travels through the United States, I, xxii-xxiii.

[2] Inventories, 18, ff. 150-76, 518-19.

[3] In 1730, Peter Hume of London Town offered for sale Barbados Rum, bareled beef, Madeira wine, lime juice, and muscovado sugar. Between 1745

ers. There was no room for those who sold a few specialized lines of goods.

The retailing of European goods was a chief function of parish merchants; yet, they invested only small amounts in tertiary items, such as new goods and merchandise, scales and weights, cash, and silver plate. Of 32 parish merchants, the average investment in tertiary items barely exceeded 10 per cent of total estate value (scale). One reason for small retailing inventories, at least in value, was that customers demanded a great variety of basic but inexpensive goods, such as buttons, tape, cloth, thread, implements, and so on. The merchant with a small expenditure could provide a cornucopia of consumer goods.

A few merchants supplemented their own stock of goods with those consigned by English merchants, who paid a commission on sales. Maryland merchants went to some pains to conceal these consignments from their customers, or so it appears from the correspondence of Patrick Sympson, chief factor in Maryland for the London company of Higginson and Bird. On his departure from England, the company instructed Sympson to dispatch one John Belt up the Bay:

> in some place where you have not already many debts owing . . . afsd Goods are consigned to you and you should commit them to John Belt. . . . you need not take Notice to any person that the affair is wholly under Mr. Belts care which we desire you will observe & let nothing be said of it but between you & he. . . .[1]

Secrecy served the company's interest and the factor's. His customers perceived him as a local fellow, an independent merchant owning his own goods. At the same time, the factor gained access to the accumulated capital and marketing services of a British merchant house. How successfully merchants obscured their consignment dealings is an open question, but we do know that several parish merchants engaged extensively in consignment and factorage.[2] Five of our thirty-three merchants invested such small amounts, less than £5, in goods and other tertiary items that they scarcely could have conducted a mercantile operation, unless it were underwritten by an English merchant house.

---

and 1748, London Town merchants advertised nails, German steel, sloop anchors, grapnels, and a great variety of cloths, and "sundry other European goods." Maryland Gazette, March 10, 1730; ibid., November 15, 1745; ibid., August 15, 1746; ibid., February 17, 1748.

[1]Higginson and Bird to Mr. Patrick Sympson, December 2, 1718, Higginson & Bird Letterbook, 1718-1719, No. 1727.

[2]Other factor agreements are found in Testamentary Proceedings, 6, ff. 506-7. Annapolis, Hall of Records MSS, Testamentary Papers, Box 17, folder 8. AACo Judgments, 1720-1721, ff. 271-75.

Independent parish merchants also supplemented their own goods and credit with those of the English merchant.[1]

Slave trading engaged some parish merchants, but the African trade in human lives required enormous capital, well beyond the reach of most parishioners. In their lifetime, few accumulated the £500 required for a one-eighth share in a slaving venture to Angola in 1718.[2] But at least three parishioners, all merchants, had the funds and the stomach for the slave trade. In 1718, the London merchants Higginson and Bird urged their Maryland factor Patrick Sympson to talk with Richard Snowden of All Hallows and several others about venturing in the African slave trade, since "we are ambitious of such Gentlemen being concerned with us."[3] The Snowden overture may have failed. Eleven years later, the same Richard Snowden teaming with Peter Hume of London Town and Daniel Dulany, gave notice "that there's a Ship arrived in South River, with about Two Hundred choice Slaves, which are to be sold by" us.[4] Later, in 1748, the Scottish merchant James Dick of London Town advertised the sale of "ten choice Negroes," "a likely Negro Man and a country-born Negro Boy."[5]

A small, infrequent, and less-costly slave trade thrived between the Caribbean and the Chesapeake, and parish merchants undoubtedly imported West Indian slaves, though no direct evidence of such a trade survives.[6] The endurance of mercantile connections between All Hallows and Barbados, the chief slave island, from the 1680's to the 1730's should reassure us on this point.[7]

---

[1]For example, Samuel Peele was occasionally titled "factor," probably for his brother John in London. AACo Deeds, SY#1, f. 297.

[2]Higginson and Bird to Coll. Edward Lloyd, September 27, 1718, Higginson & Bird Letterbook, No. 1557.

[3]Higginson and Bird to Patrick Sympson, December 2, 1718, _ibid._, No. 1727.

[4]_Maryland Gazette_, March 10, 1730.

[5]_Ibid._, May 11, 1748; _ibid._, April 20, 1748.

[6]A concise and thoroughly documented account of the seventeenth century slave trade to Maryland and Virginia is found in Middleton, _Tobacco Coast_, pp. 134-35, and especially footnotes 11 through 16, p. 388.

[7]William Burges of London Town corresponded with Coll. Elliott of Barbados in the 1680's. Inventories & Accounts, 18, ff. 108-10. Also in the 1680's, Thomas Taylor, Maryland merchant, was consigned four Negroes from Jane Bishop in Barbados. This may have been the same Thomas Taylor who lived on the "Ridge." Annapolis, Hall of Records MSS, Provincial Court Land Records, WRC#1, f. 392. For Barbadian connections in the 1730's, see AACo Deeds, 1730-1733, ff. 335-36.

Amazingly, the parish merchant laid out a small sum for goods, store, and land. A hypothetical merchant at the threshold scale of £600 sterling invested about £60 for tertiary items, perhaps £10 for building a store, and £10 to £50 for land, adding up to £120. Many planters had access to £120, and so it must be asked why so few shifted toward mercantile activity . Certainly, planters occasionally dabbled in the mercantile world. A more precise estimate of this can be gained from the parish inventories which show that 18 per cent of the estates between 1660 and 1769 contained new goods or merchandise. Yet these same inventories reveal that the majority of investments were small, indicating a flirtation with retailing and the tobacco trade.

Serious merchant activity required far more than capital for land, buildings and goods. Even more pivotal was the merchant's ability to extend short-term credit which in turn depended on his access to liquid capital. He drew this capital from one of three sources: his own readily negotiable assets; collateral capital, which rested on his less liquid assets; or capital gained by affiliation with London merchants. With this capital, the merchant extended enormous amounts of consumer credit. For example, twenty merchants, exceeding the £600 threshold and dying between 1710 and 1769, extended, on the average, credit (accounts receivable) amounting to 28.77 per cent of total estate value (scale). Returning briefly to our hypothetical merchant with an estate of £600, this meant credit extensions of £172.6 compared to £120 for land, store, and goods. Occasionally, a merchant tied up even larger sums in credit, as did Thomas Lloyd who had 88 per cent of his estate in accounts receivable.[1]

Other Services and Crafts.--A yawning gulf separated the merchants of the parish from craftsmen and purveyors of services. The twenty-eight craft and service occupations represented in the inventories averaged £129.5 in total estate value (scale)--a figure one-tenth that of the average merchant. The twelve craftsmen's inventories averaged £128.6 compared to £130.1 for the sixteen service inventories. Among craft occupations, scale ranged from James

---

[1]Thomas Lloyd's executors were James Dick and Andrew Strachan, who were merchants in London Town. Lloyd seems to have operated a store in St. James' Parish, for his estate was charged with the "Cartage of sundry goods of decds estate from the swamp [near Herring Creek in St. James'] to London Town." Annapolis, Hall of Records MSS, Original Wills, Box L, folder 38. Accounts, 36, ff. 124-33. Three bits of evidence suggest that Lloyd operated as a factor for larger merchants, perhaps Dick and Strachan: the location of executors some distance from Lloyd's place of business, the hauling of his goods to London Town, and the vast amount of credit extended to Lloyd.

Masson, Joiner, £4.25 (1749) to John Belt, Cooper, £525.9 (1700); and for services, John Holland, Innholder, £18.3 (1718) to Thomas Miles, Innholder, £421.2 (1670).

For these occupations, the possession of specialized skills counted more heavily than investments in capital goods and stocks. Expenditures for tools and equipment ranged from nothing to £52 (Table 19). The capital goods needed by a tailor cost less than a cow; by a carpenter, less than a feather bed; by a blacksmith, doctor or minister, less than a Negro boy; and by an innholder, less than a prime Negro male. Yet despite the inducement of low capital costs, the parish and the Chesapeake region failed to foster a large and vigorous group of craft and service specialists. Further research into this weak link in the occupational structure may clarify whether skilled Englishmen simply avoided emigration to the Chesapeake or, if they came, the tobacco economy channeled them to the plantation way of life.

Occupational Specialists and Potential Urbanization

In All Hallows, sizable urban places were precluded by the small number of secondary and tertiary occupational specialists. Hypothetically, if all of these specialists had located in urban places in 1776, the urban population would have been less than 620 persons and the level of urbanization less than 20 per cent. However, the number of specialists, or the potentially urban population, varied considerably during the colonial years. Potential urban population, which is calculated by multiplying the number of specialists during a decade by the mean number of persons per household,[1] ranged from 70 in 1685 to a peak of 360 in 1735 (Table 20).

These hypothetical urban populations provide a standard against which the centralization or decentralization of the settlement system can be gauged. Of course, complete centralization was never achieved in the parish, but during the eighteenth century the clustering of many specialists produced significant urban growth, even though town size was sharply limited by the small number of occupational specialists in the parish.

---

[1] A mean of seven persons per household is used before 1720, and a mean of ten thereafter. The former results from the 1704 census of Anne Arundel County. Archives of Maryland, XXV, 256. The exclusion of slave children from the census is adjusted by doubling the slave population. Also an error in the number of masters of families is corrected from 716 to 765. See Menard, "The Growth of Population," pp. 25-26.

TABLE 19

INVESTMENT IN THE "TOOLS" OF SELECTED OCCUPATIONS

Occupation	Person, Date	"Tools" and Materials	Capital Expenditure in pounds sterling
Tailor	Andrew Roberts, 1682	Shears; "linning," 8 dozen buttons; 2 yards cotton.	1.23
Tanner	Edward Sarson, 1689	Bark mill, frame, and stone, bark, bark knife and tray, etc.; 88 hides "in sundry conditions"; 79½ tanned hides; 2 buckskins; 6 doe skins.	52.33
Carpenter, Shipcarpenter	John Hill, 1705	6 hand saws; 8 augers; 6 mallets; 2 malls; claw hammer; 2 marking irons; 5 planes; cooper's tools; nails; 2 whip saws; 1 cross-cut saw; 2 saws; 1 axe.	5.77
Blacksmith	Enoch Bolton, 1679	200 lbs. iron; 20 bu. coals; more coal, smith's tools including vice, anvil, fordage tools, bellows, screw-plate; and a parcel of steel.	7.22
Innholder	Thomas Miles, 1670	2 bu. malt; 6 beds; linen; mashing tub; 7 dishes; 2 basins; plates; 3 saucers; drinking pots & cups.	32.59
Minister	Joseph Colebatch, 1735	Books; horse & saddle.	10.76
Doctor	John Moss, 1694	Chest of medicines.	13.00
Schoolmaster	John Wilmott, 1765	Nothing.	0

Sources: Inventories and Inventories & Accounts.

Locational Changes of Specialized Occupations

In All Hallows Parish, the location of specialists proceeded through three phases, which were: Phase I (Scattered Specialists, 1650-1709); Phase II (Spatial Concentration, 1710-1750's); Phase III (Decentralization, 1750's-1776).

TABLE 20

POTENTIAL URBAN MAXIMUM
POPULATIONS, 1680-1769

Date	Urban Maxima
1685	70
1695	42
1705	77
1715	217
1725	240
1735	360
1745	240
1755	260
1765	330

Confirmation of these three distinct periods appears in the locational maps of parish specialists between 1660 and 1769 (Figures 9 through 16). The several maps depict all occupational specialists identified in the land records as well as the location of secondary and tertiary activities gleaned from inventories, wills, judgments, and miscellaneous sources. Accurate location of these specialists is impossible in many cases, and the best that can be achieved is the probable tract on which the specialist resided.

Phase I (Scattered Specialists, 1650-1709)

During the first sixty years of settlement in All Hallows, towns were insignificant both in size and as coordinators of an agrarian settlement system. The spatial alternative was a loose scattering of occupational specialists along the estuaries.

The seventeenth century pattern of settlement in the parish resembled other areas of the Chesapeake.

> The people there not affecting to build nere each other But soe as to have their houses nere the Watters for convenience of trade and their Lands on each Syde of and behynde Their houses by which it happens that in most places there are not fifty houses in the space of Thirty myles.[1]

After forty-four years of settlement (1678), the province's largest town and capital at St. Mary's numbered "not above thirty houses, and those at consider-

[1]Archives of Maryland, V, 266.

able distances from each other."[1] Little had changed by 1699, since:

> We have not yett found the way of associating ourselves in towns and corporations. . . . There are indeed severall places allotted for towns, but hitherto they are only titular ones, except Annapolis. . . . There are in itt about fourty dwelling houses.[2]

In a province where capital cities captured only 30-40 houses, the prospect for town growth in other areas was unlikely.

Visitors and observers deemed the absence of towns absurd and proprietary officials lamented the consequences for trade. Laying plans for the settlement of South Carolina, Lord Ashley urged that great care be taken to keep houses orderly and convenient to one another, since he found "by the experience of both Virginia and Maryland that men will expose themselves to the inconvenience and barbarism of scattered dwellings in unknown countries."[3] One R. G. went further and forecast the curse of God upon these scattered settlements.[4] The lack of towns perplexed proprietary officials as early as 1658. They held fervently to the dogma that towns stimulated trade, and ancillary was the belief that much of the profit would accrue to them.[5] Their convictions came to the test after 1683, when the Assembly passed a general town act, appropriately entitled "An Act for the Advancement of Trade."[6] An initial attitude of nonchalance greeted the bill in the lower house of the Assembly, as the Assembly tied the passage of the town act to proprietary concessions on other bills.[7] Vocal opposition to the act surfaced by 1686, and the Maryland Council proclaimed:

> that any words spoken or published to the effect that building of towns is not for the good of the country shall be construed as disaffection to the Government, and punished accordingly.[8]

---

[1] Ibid. [2] "Maryland in 1699," pp. 371-72.

[3] Letter, Lord Ashley to Sir John Yeamans, September 18, 1671, CSPCS, 1669-74, VII, 260-61.

[4] R. G., "Virginia's Cure: or an Advisive Narrative Concerning Virginia," in Tracts and Other Papers Relating Principally to the Origin, Settlement, and Progress of the Colonies in North America, ed. by Peter Force (4 vols.; n.p., no publisher, 1844, reprinted for Peter Smith, Gloucester, Massachusetts by the Murray Printing Company, Forge Village, Massachusetts, 1963), III, 4-5.

[5] "Journal of the Dutch Embassy to Maryland, by Augustine Herrman, 1659," Narratives of Early Maryland, p. 322. CSPCS, X, 226-27.

[6] Archives of Maryland, VII, 609-19. [7] Ibid., pp. 491-93.

[8] CSPCS, 1685-88, XII, 243.

KEY TO MAPS OF OCCUPATIONAL LOCATIONS

SECONDARY OCCUPATIONS

L	Leatherworkers (Cordwainer, Saddler, Shoemaker, Tanner)
●	Mills and Millwrights
T	Taylors
W	Woodworkers (Boatwright, Carpenter, Cooper, Joyner, Sawyer, Shipcarpenter, Shipwright, Turner)

TERTIARY OCCUPATIONS

▲	Churches, Ministers, and Meeting Houses
D	Medical Profession (Doctor, Chyrurgeon, Physician, Surgeon)
□	School Houses and Schoolmasters
✪	Merchants
	Landings
☆	Inspection Houses for Tobacco

Vertically stacked symbols indicate that these occupations are located on the same site.

Key to Figures 9-16

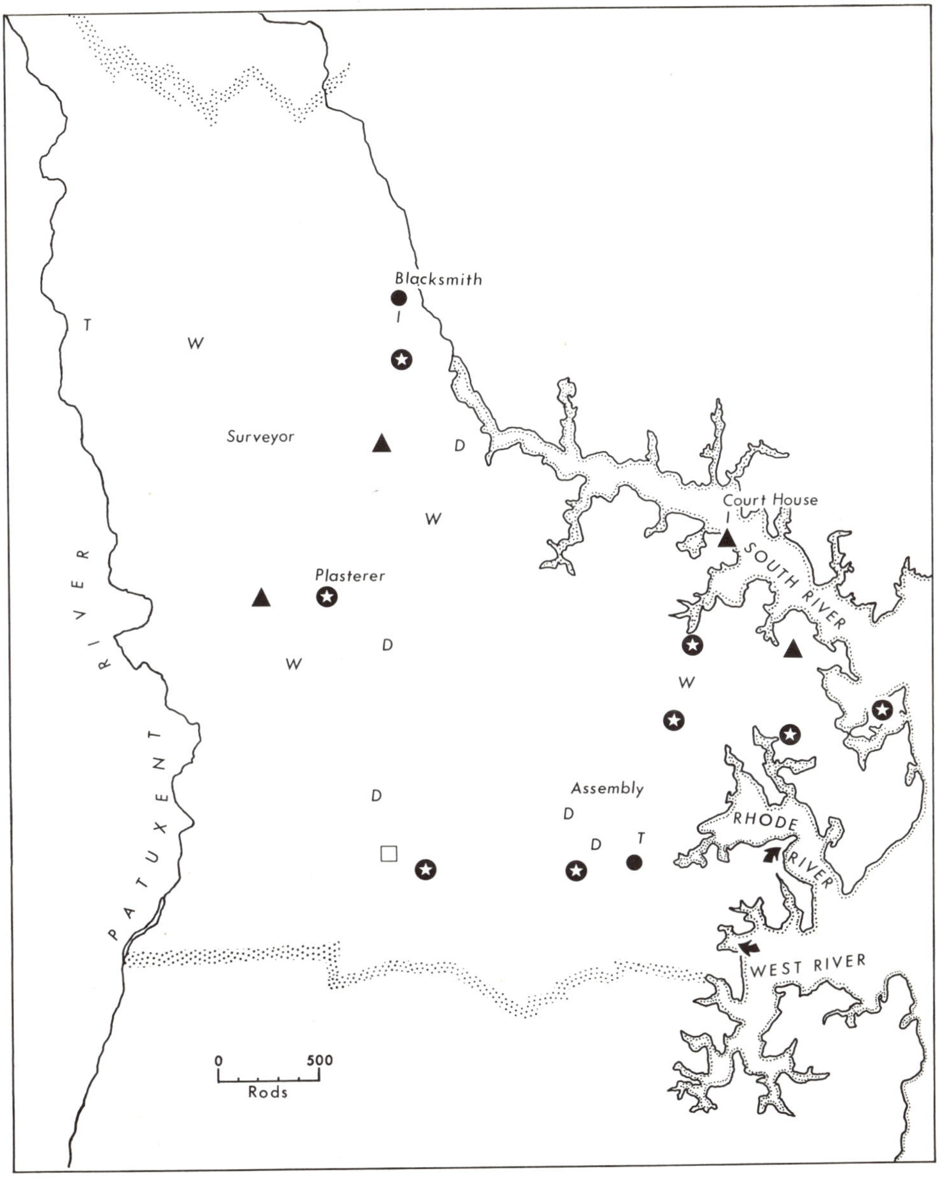

Fig. 9.--Location of Occupational Specialists, 1650-1699

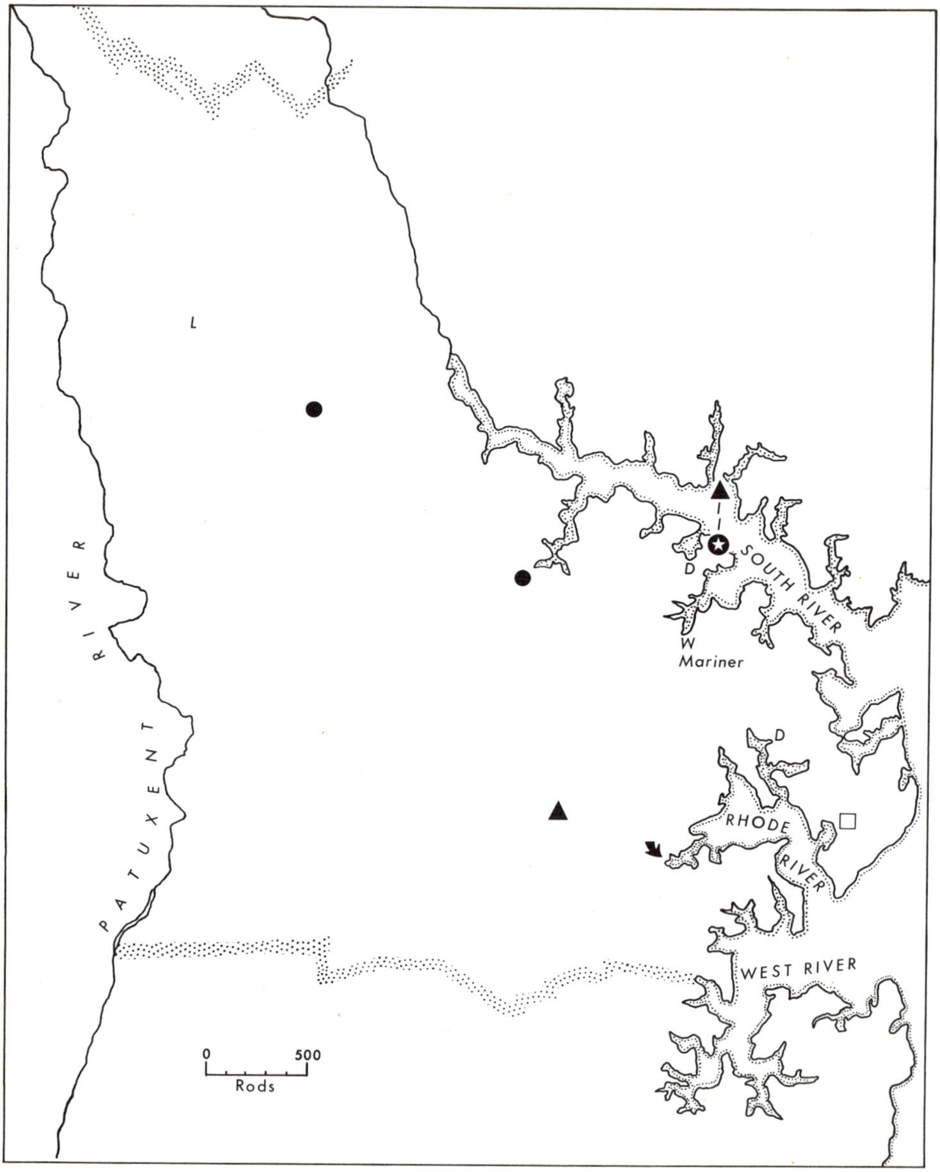

Fig. 10.--Location of Occupational Specialists, 1700-1709

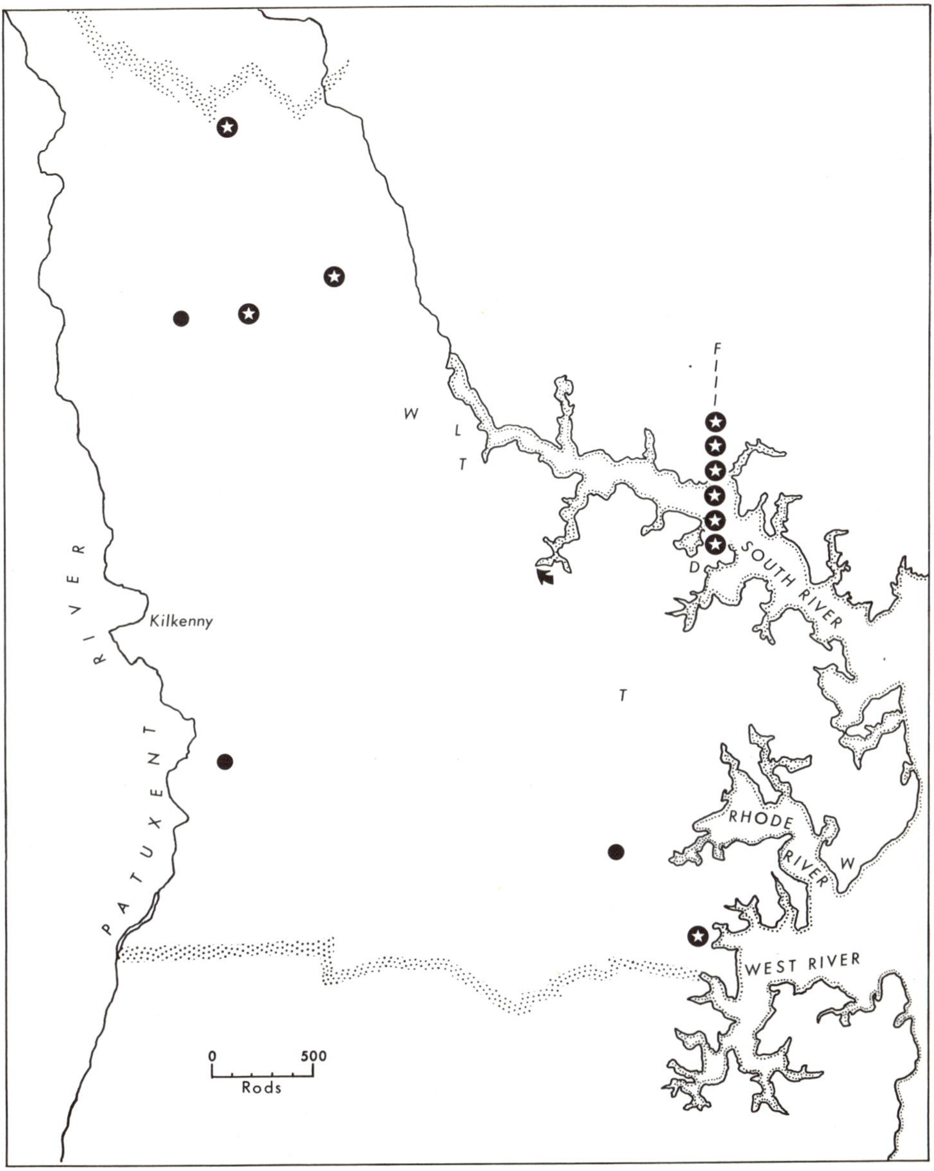

Fig. 11.--Location of Occupational Specialists, 1710-1719

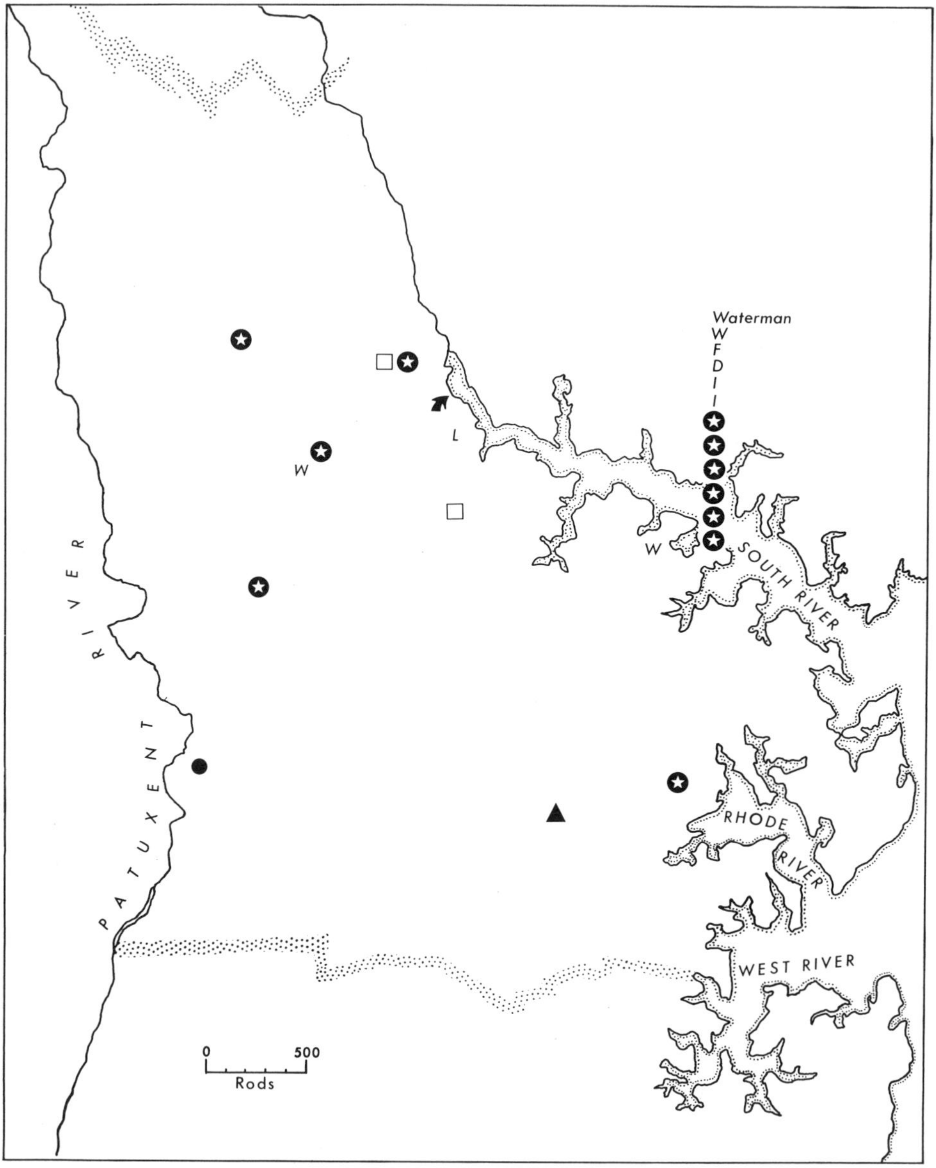

Fig. 12.--Location of Occupational Specialists, 1720-1729

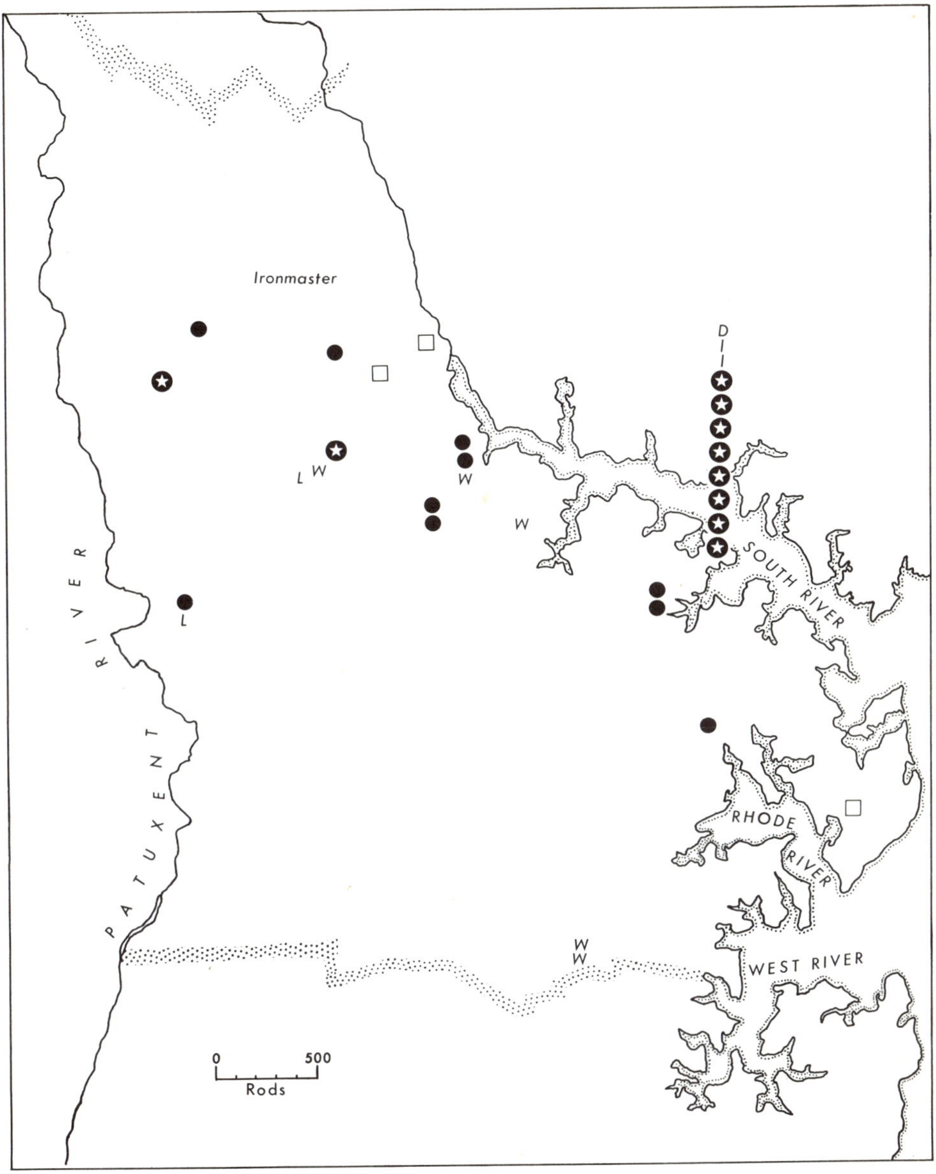

Fig. 13.--Location of Occupational Specialists, 1730-1739

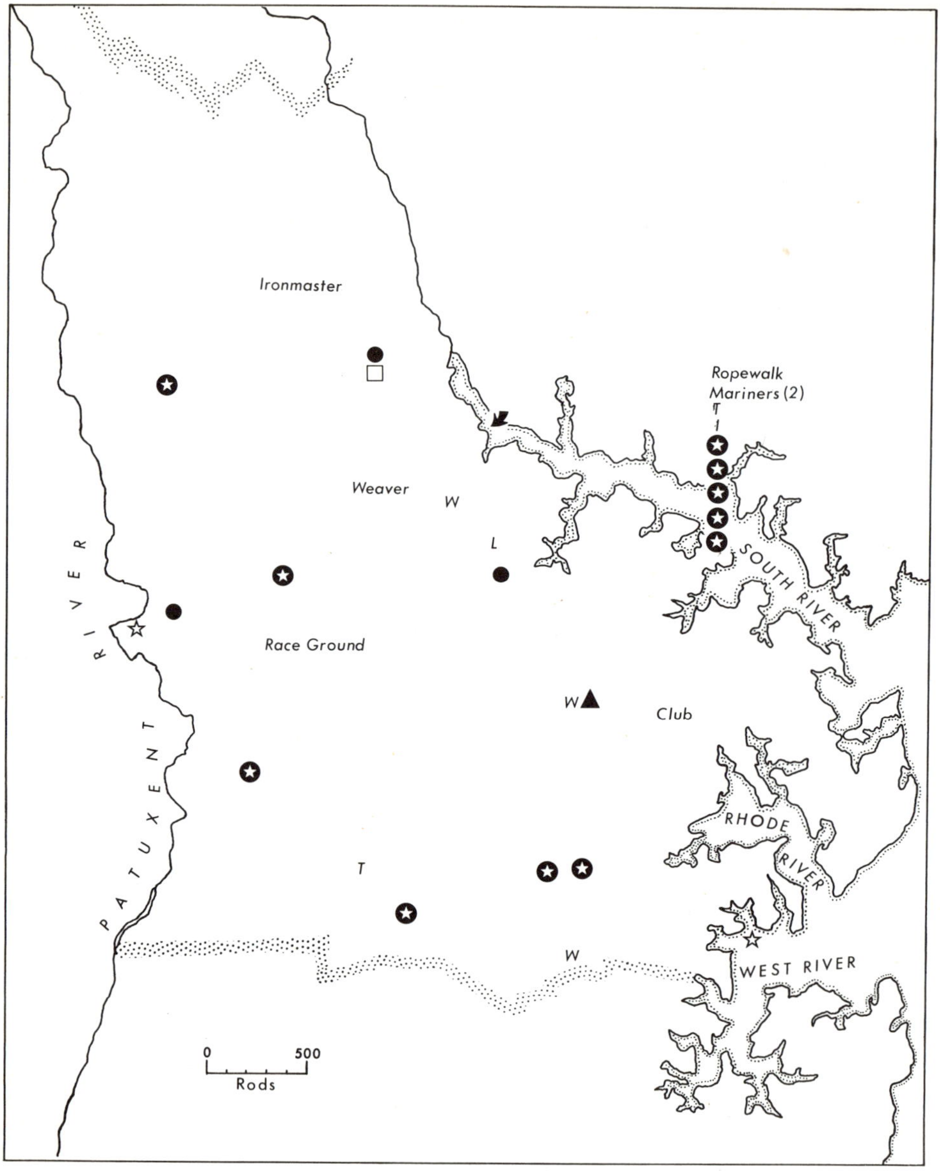

Fig. 14. --Location of Occupational Specialists, 1740-1749

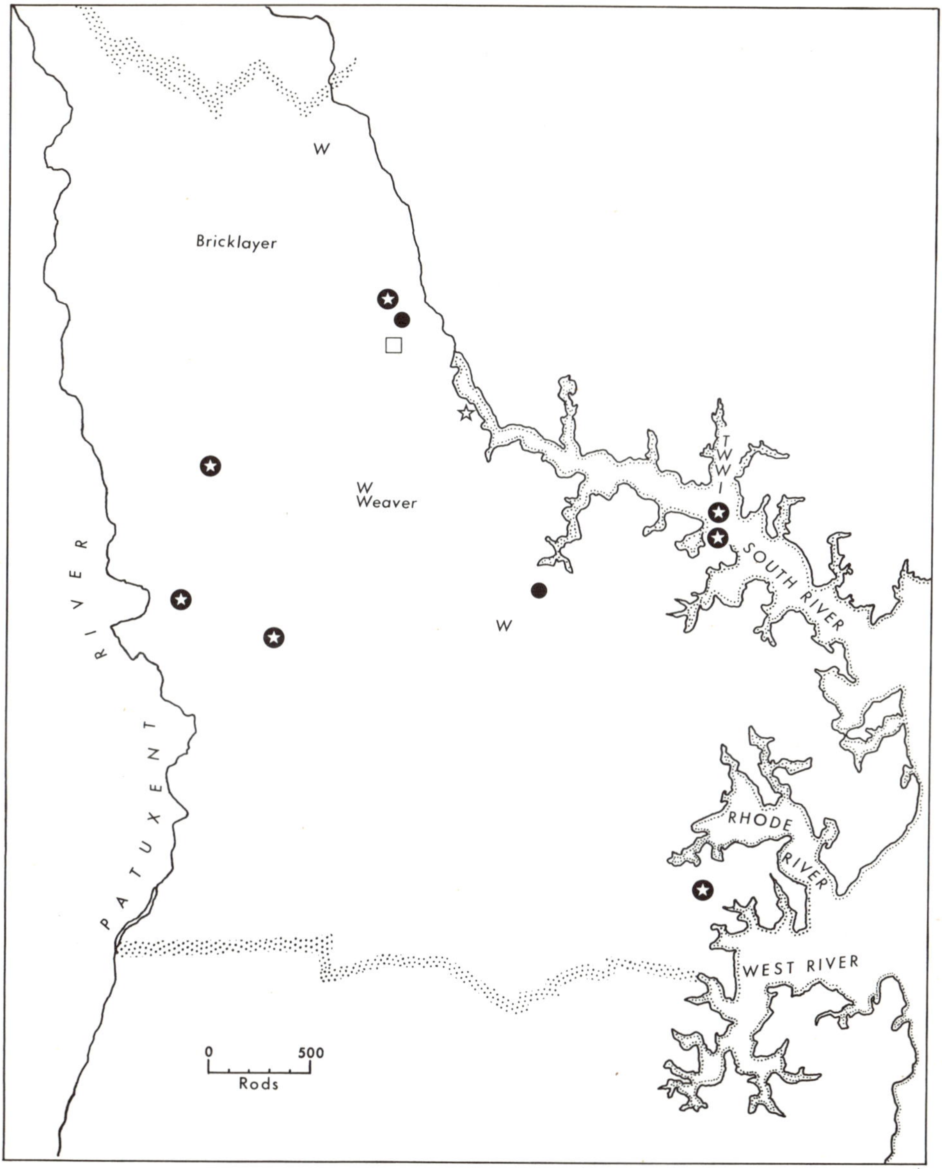

Fig. 15. --Location of Occupational Specialists, 1750-1759

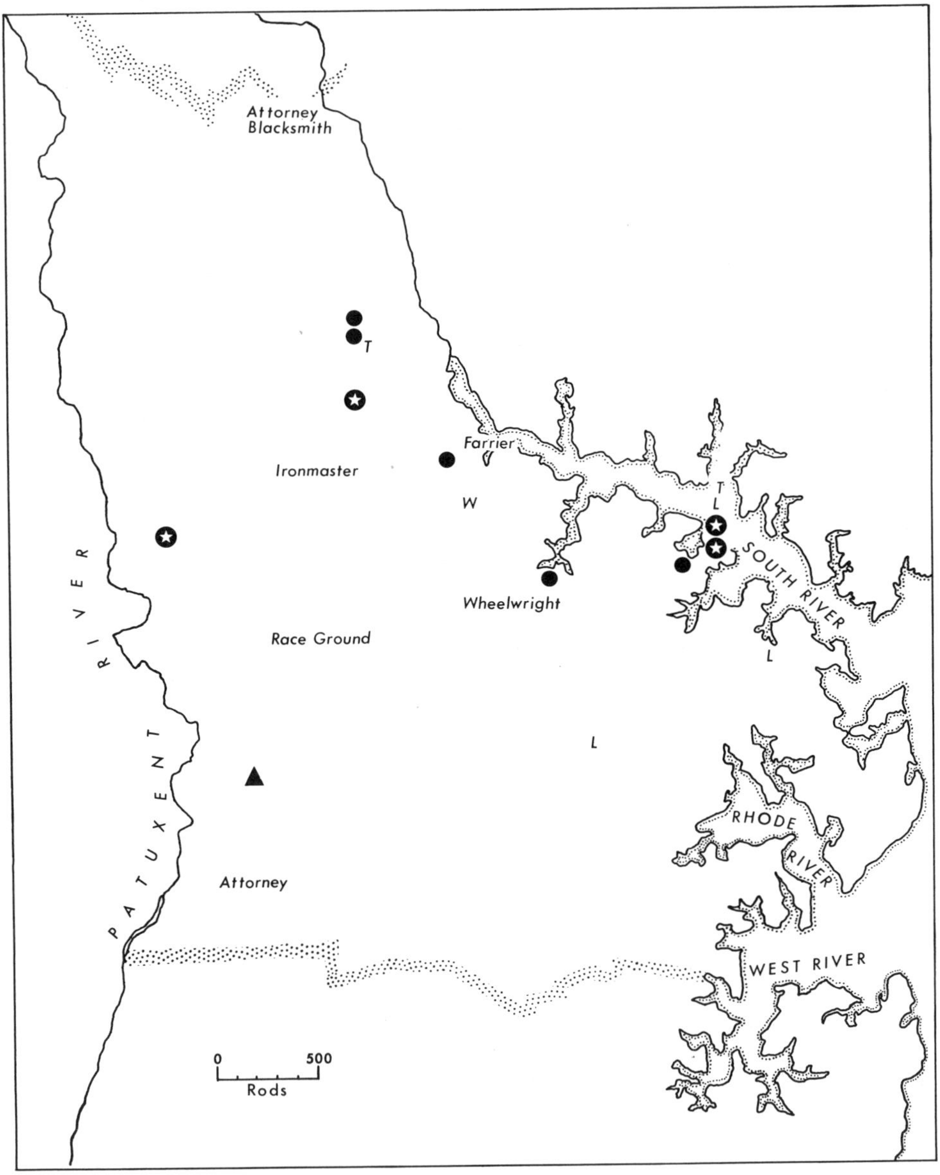

Fig. 16.--Location of Occupational Specialists, 1760-1769

Implementation was also dilatory, and "many frauds are dayly committed."[1] Nonchalance, vocal opposition, and delay were clear messages. Most seventeenth century Marylanders were satisfied with the on-going decentralized settlement system.[2] By century's end, the "titular" and "paper" towns dotting Maryland's shoreline testified to the futility of statutory coercion.

The decentralized location of seventeenth century occupations reflected the estuarine distribution of the parish population (Figure 9). Almost half of the specialists occupied sites near tidewater; this was especially true along Rhode River and the lower portion of South River, which contained over 60 per cent of all specialized sites. In these two areas, though merchants were overrepresented, with six out of eight, clustering around specific sites did not occur. These merchants scattered unevenly among the interlacing necks and estuaries. Second in importance was the area near the head of South River. The area attracted diverse occupations, including a merchant, millwright, blacksmith, boatwright, innholder, and a doctor. The pattern in the rest of the parish was diffuse, although specialist sites tended to string along the drainage divide, known as the Ridge, between Patuxent and Chesapeake drainage. Interestingly, each of the three areas of specialist location contained at least one doctor and one Quaker meeting site, probably for weekly meetings.[3]

Prior to the general town act of 1683, no urban centers existed in All Hallows Parish. In that year, London Town on South River was established; and though the evidence is fragmentary, this legislative creation had little impact, until after 1710, in centralizing the scattered specialists. According to the act of 1683, one hundred acres of land adjoining Shipping Creek, now Almshouse Creek, was to be laid out and subdivided into acre lots and streets. Optimism must have reigned, for a bid to locate the town on West River had been thwarted;[4] and the Proprietor seriously considered the South River area as the site for the provincial capital. On November 6, 1683:

> His Lop [Lordship] being moved by this house, to nominate a place for the Court house & Doth say and Declare that when a conveniency shall be pro-

---

[1] Archives of Maryland, V, 564-65.

[2] English merchants seemed satisfied too. See Commissioners of Customs to Lords of Trade and Plantations, December 12, 1681, CSPCS, 1681-85, XI, 152.

[3] Kelly notes that weekly and monthly meetings of Quakers were held at John Belt's and at Ann Lambert's. These appear on Figure 9. Kelly, Quakers in the Founding of Anne Arundel County, p. 86. The third meeting was held at John Lynam's. Carroll, "The Anatomy of a Separation," pp. 67-78.

[4] Archives of Maryland, VII, 554.

vided in South River in An Arrundell County, sufficient for reception of his Lordsp and Councill and for holding of Assemblyes & provinciall Courts and the severall and respective offices, thereon depending his Lop will make use thereof for such ends soe long as he shall see convenient.[1]

A building was erected to house the court, but hopes were dashed when, in 1694, the royal government abandoned the old capital at St. Mary's City and moved to Annapolis.[2]

Aside from the court house, London Town's urban accoutrements were few. A lot was designated for the parish church, but it was erected eventually more than one mile south of town on the drainage divide.[3] In addition, the town probably served as the mercantile base for William Burges, who originally owned the town land.[4] Finally, there may have been two or three ordinaries or inns, catering to the county residents during "public" or court times. John Larkin probably operated one of the ordinaries before 1699.[5] In 1703, the county court licensed an ordinary in London Town to Hester Groce.[6] And two years later, a license was issued to Mehittable Peirpoint, who may have been John Larkin's daughter.[7] Her license was followed by one to David Macklefresh in 1707.[8]

A man of some wit, Macklefresh styled himself as the Lord Mayor of London Town in 1709.[9] Along with the inn and the town, he operated the public ferry over South River.[10] The individual dominance of London Town by this relative newcomer was symptomatic of its malaise. Planter families of long residence in the parish, such as Linthicum, Welsh, Taylor, and Ridgely, were

---

[1]Ibid., p. 601.

[2]AACo Deeds, IB#2, ff. 545-47. For the shift of the capital to Annapolis during the Royal Period, see Archives of Maryland, XXXVIII, 23-25.

[3]AACo Deeds, CW#1, ff. 473-75.

[4]Wills 4, f. 244; Inventories & Accounts 18, ff. 89-108.

[5]AACo Deeds, WT#1, ff. 10-11; ibid., IB#2, ff. 545-47.

[6]AACo Judgments, G, f. 106.

[7]AACo Judgments, TB#1, f. 168; AACo Deeds, IB#2, ff. 545-47.

[8]AACo Judgments, TB#1, f. 688. [9]AACo Deeds, PK, f. 235.

[10]AACo Judgments, TB#2, f. 231. Macklefresh was also very active in acquiring town land, purchasing at least four lots and two houses between 1693 and 1703; AACo Deeds, WT#2, ff. 56-58, 143-45.

selling off town lots rather than buying.[1] Despite the peripatetic Macklefresh, town growth awaited persons with more capital, at least more than the £37.8 left by the Lord Mayor at his death about 1712.

Phase II (Spatial Concentration, 1710-1750's)

Between 1713 and 1720 a major revision occurred in the settlement system of All Hallows Parish, and this change established a pattern which endured until the 1750's. The locus of change was London Town, where at least 30 per cent of all occupational specialists were concentrated by 1719. For the next thirty years, this proportion varied narrowly between 30 and 40 per cent until the precipitous decline of the town in the 1750's and 1760's. By 1747, London Town rivaled the size of the provincial capitals of the seventeenth century. Several vexing questions arise. What accounted for such rapid growth and equally rapid decline? Why, after the town's sharp take-off, did town growth level off for thirty years?

The centralization of occupations into London Town was rapid and selective.[2] In less than a decade, at least ten households with perhaps 70 people had clustered at the town. Although these households comprised only 5 per cent of the total parish population, they accounted for over 30 per cent of all occupational specialists. The impetus for this urban growth came, almost exclusively, from the merchant community. Between 1714 and 1728, at least nine merchants, one doctor, one innholder, and one shipwright took up residence in London Town. These were not typical men, for most were newcomers having access to capital and credit. Patrick Sympson, who entered in 1714, was the chief Maryland factor for the London firm of Higginson and Bird.[3] William Chapman "of London, merchant," left that place in 1713 with a letter of attorney from Mr. Phillip Smith, London merchant; by 1716, William was in London Town to remain until his death about 1762, leaving an estate of over £1400 ster-

---

[1] Ibid.

[2] One other ill-fated town was created in 1707. Kilkenny was to be laid out on Patuxent River, opposite Queen Anne's Town in Prince George's County. Archives of Maryland, XXVII, 69. The town appeared infrequently in the public record, and the most that may be said is that the town had one house in 1747. Maryland Gazette, November 25, 1747.

[3] Higginson and Bird to Patrick Sympson, December 2, 1718, Higginson & Bird Letterbook, No. 1727.

ling.[1] Also in 1716 came Samuel Peele, the factor or perhaps the partner of his brother John, London merchant.[2] Two local merchants acquired lots in 1718; one of these, William Nicholson, may have been the same person who earlier was the "attorney in fact" for "Mr. Peter Paggen & Co.," London.[3] William Black arrived by 1720, and departed from London Town six years later for London, appointing Peter Hume his Maryland attorney.[4] Hume lived in London Town for a time and acted as Black's agent and was also involved in the importation of 200 slaves in 1729.[5] This nucleus of London-connected merchants attracted other traders such as Richard Moore, a Philadelphia merchant;[6] Dr. Richard Hill, probably from the same place; and local merchants such as Turner Wootton and James Mouat.[7]

Merchants initiated urban growth in London Town, and subsequently, they dominated town life until the 1760's. But the extent of urban growth was severely limited by the small number of parish merchants, which as noted before reached an equilibrium position about 1710 to 1719. Further growth required the attraction of other specialists, but the town's centralizing power was weak. Between 1710 and 1750, the town acquired a few innholders, and an occasional shipwright or tailor (Figures 10 through 15). Other secondary and tertiary activities remained scattered. Thus, the London Town of 1725 probably resembled the town of 1747, when it contained between thirty and forty buildings.[8]

The revisions in the settlement system introduced by London Town were in part superficial. The decentralized pattern of the seventeenth century persisted for half or more of the occupations and institutional sites. Mills, woodworkers, schools, churches, a social club, and a race track remained scattered in the rural countryside.

---

[1] AACo Deeds, WC#1, ff. 33-36; Inventories, 79, ff. 34-38.

[2] AACo Deeds, RD#2, f. 76; and ibid., SY#1, f. 297.

[3] AACo Judgments, G, f. 646.

[4] AACo Deeds, CW#1, f. 227; ibid., SY#1, f. 321.

[5] Maryland Gazette, March 10, 1730.

[6] AACo Deeds, CW#1, f. 499; ibid., ff. 5, 499-505.

[7] AACo Deeds, RCW#2, ff. 223-24; ibid., RD#1, ff. 16-19.

[8] Karinen, "Numerical and Distributional Aspects," p. 195.

Water mills occupied the gentle gradients of runs and creeks. Only two mills were located in the sluggishly drained area near the mouths of South and Rhode rivers. Upstream from London Town, however, nearly every major tributary of South River had a mill. During the 1730's boom, no less than eleven mills or mill dams dotted the parish map. On Flat Creek alone there were four mills including two water mills, one fulling mill for cleaning wool, and one grist mill. Nearby, probably on Beard's Creek, Richard Moore erected both a water mill and a bolting mill valued at £25 and £9, respectively.[1] Evidently, the main considerations in the siting of mills were water power and proximity to areas of agricultural diversity, which produced sheep, corn, and wheat.

The location of woodworkers was also decentralized. They avoided the long-settled southeastern quarter of the parish, and preferred sites along the upper half of South River. A plausible interpretation, but one lacking firm evidence, is that in these older, more densely settled areas near the bay, timber depletion left few resources for wood craftsmen. But even in the seventeenth century, there were few woodworkers in these areas, though some shipbuilding occurred.[2] Sites along the upper reaches of South River possessed several locational advantages for woodworkers. Shipwrights surely preferred the navigable waters in the freshes, thus avoiding the "worm." As for carpenters and coopers, the area was accessible to timber, to mills for sawing, and to the markets of planters and shipwrights.

Sites of religious, educational, and recreational activities were fewer in number, and they followed their own rules of location. Such was the case for the parish church. Upon establishment as the official church, the Anglicans carved Maryland into parishes, each containing a church and a minister. The shape and size of the parishes had great effect on church location. In All Hallows, a lot in London Town was initially reserved for the church; but apparently it was never constructed. The first clue of the church's location came in a deed in 1747, placing the church on "Brewerton," about three and a half miles south of the town, and on the high ground between South and Rhode rivers.[3] The

---

[1]Inventories, 21, ff. 12-15.

[2]Shipbuilding was significant along South River by 1697. During the five preceding years, it is probable that both of the ships or brigantines built or building in Maryland were erected on South River; likewise, were one of the eight sloops, and four of the eleven shallops. Archives of Maryland, XXV, 595.

[3]AACo Deeds, RB#2, ff. 363-64.

church was probably built on this site much earlier, since by 1708 the rector, Joseph Colebatch, had acquired land on a nearby tract called "Larkin's Hills."[1] In the first decade of the eighteenth century, "Brewerton" lay close to the population center of the parish. Nonetheless, this site was not the geometric center of the parish, and as population grew and spread, the church's location became more eccentric and inaccessible. In 1709, residents at the heads of South and Severn rivers petitioned the legislature for a "chapel of ease."[2] Almost one year later, a convenient site at the head of South River was agreed upon by the vestrymen of All Hallows and neighboring St. Anne's.[3] Inaction resulted. Convinced of the uncertainties of the chapel and of this life, Amos Peirpoint bequeathed £5 sterling for the building of the chapel, if and when it commenced.[4] His bequest lay idle for the chapel of ease was never constructed in All Hallows during the colonial era. However, the religious needs in the northwestern area were eventually ministered by the new parish of Queen Caroline, created in 1728, and by a chapel-of-ease built about 1729 in neighboring St. Anne's Parish.[5]

In summary, church location was decided by territorial boundaries and centrality to the parish population at the time of the decision. The parish bounds split drainage basins, and hence, the most central location was along the drainage divide. London Town was more suited to merchants who required a ccess to British ships.

Perhaps three widely scattered schools were conducted in the parish during the entire colonial period. Two of these school houses were privately operated. In 1682, a school house was recorded in the inventory of Henry Stockett, who resided in the south central part of the parish on the Ridge.[6] Another school house, erected about 1709, was located between South and Rhode rivers near the bay; this school was still standing in 1759.[7] The third school house was a special case. In 1723, the General Assembly authorized a county school for Anne Arundel. A central location was imperative for this publicly financed

---

[1]Ibid., PK, ff. 51-57.

[2]Archives of Maryland, XXVII, 427.

[3]Ibid., p. 520.

[4]Wills, 14, f. 680.

[5]Archives of Maryland, XXXVI, 285-86; Maryland Gazette, March 11, 1729.

[6]Inventories & Accounts, 8, ff. 12-14.

[7]Deposition of Robert Brown, Thomas Linthicum agt. Ann Sanders, August 28, 1758, Ejectment Papers.

school, drawing students from the entire county.[1] In 1724, the "Visitors" or regents of the school met at London Town:

> to treat with any person or persons who are inclinable to sell one hundred Acres of Land as near [the] Center of the County, as may be in order to fix a Free School. . . .[2]

They agreed with Richard Snowden to purchase 150 acres of his land on the south side of the head of South River.[3] Later, they contracted with Thomas Gassaway to build a rather sumptuous structure for £138 current money.[4] Gassaway fulfilled the contract, and a schoolmaster was secured. In 1745, he advertised that:

> Reading; Writing, in the most usual Hands; Grammar, Arithmetic, Vulgar, Decimal, Instrumental, Algebraical; Merchants accounts, With the Italian Method of Book Keeping; Geometry; Trigonometry, Plain or spheric; with their Application in Surveying, Navigation, Astronomy, Dialling; Likewise the Use of the Globes, and sundry other Parts of the MATHEMATICS, are concisely and expeditiously taught at Anne Arundel County School, near the Head of South River. . . .[5]

Parish recreational sites were also dispersed. The "Ancient South River Club," comprised of select gentlemen from the parish, had its clubhouse on the drainage divide between South and Rhode rivers, about one mile from the parish church.[6] "Batchelors Race Ground" was located on the "Ridge,"[7] and a fair, with horse racing, held forth in John Conner's old fields in 1745.[8]

This dispersal of specialized sites was a continuing legacy of the seventeenth century. It was this legacy which eased the transition of the settlement system into its third phase of urban denouement.

Phase III (Decentralization, 1750's-1776)

Wayfarers through London Town chronicled the swiftness of its decline. In 1747, there were 30 to 40 dwelling houses;[9] a French visitor in 1765 noted that

---

[1] Archives of Maryland, XXXIV, 740-46.

[2] Annapolis, Hall of Records MS, Proceedings of the Visitors of the Free School of Anne Arundel County, 1724, Gift Collection, G610, March 17, 1724.

[3] Ibid., April 24, 1724.

[4] The details of this contract appear in ibid., August 13, 1724.

[5] Maryland Gazette, May 27, 1745.

[6] AACo Deeds, RB#1, ff. 13-14.

[7] Ibid., BB#2, ff. 346-47.

[8] Maryland Gazette, October 18, 1745.

[9] Karinen, "Numerical and Distributional Aspects," p. 195.

"this is a very Small place not above a Doz'n houses."[1] In the same year, another declared it a "pleasant village."[2] Ten years later, a traveller misnamed the town New London.[3] In the 1790's, Rochefoucault failed to mention the town, though he passed through it.[4]

The decline of London Town was underway by the 1740's; however, there remained a lingering optimism. In 1748, Stephen West, Jr. erected a rope walk:

> and makes all sorts of Cables, cordage and Rigging for Ships, and other Vessels; as also Sail-Twine, Logg-Lines, deep-sea Lines, Housline and Marline; and white Rope for Country Uses. . . .[5]

By 1765, West had removed to Prince George's County, and reestablished his factory there.[6]

Others followed West's lead and by 1760 the specialist occupations in London Town had dwindled by one-half. Merchant numbers fell even more drastically to two by 1760, and for the first time since 1700-1710 they were outnumbered by other specialists. The town's fortune was sealed, and in the 1760's, though the parish occupational structure expanded, there were no additions in London Town. Town merchants either died or left, not to be replaced. Concurrent with the decline of London Town, the parish resumed a decentralized occupational structure, reminiscent of seventeenth century patterns.

Ironically, London Town owed its collapse primarily to legislation aimed at rescuing the tobacco trade. The state of the trade and the economy reached their low points in 1747 when tobacco earned less than half a penny a pound. Earlier statutes aimed at lowering supply through stinting or burning of the crop now appeared woefully inadequate. In a sweeping law passed in 1747, the Assembly superseded these earlier laws and established a comprehensive inspec-

---

[1]"Journal of a French Traveller," p. 71.

[2]Lord Adam Gordon, "Journal of an Officer Who Travelled in America and the West Indies in 1764 and 1765," Travels in the American Colonies, ed. by Newton D. Mereness (New York: Macmillan Company, 1916), p. 409.

[3]J. F. D. Smyth, A Tour in the United States of America (2 vols.; London: J. Robson and J. Sewell for G. Robinson, 1784), II, 211.

[4]Rochefoucault-Liancourt, Travels through the United States, II, 304.

[5]Maryland Gazette, May 11, 1748.

[6]Fred Shelley, ed., "Ebenezer Hazard's Travels through Maryland in 1777," Maryland Historical Magazine, XLVI (March, 1951), 50.

tion system modeled after Virginia.[1] The Assembly intended to improve tobacco's quality and price by eliminating trash and second tobacco from the market. The act provided for the inspection of all tobacco at conveniently located inspection houses, where inspectors issued receipts for good tobacco and burned the bad. Thus, the law compelled parish planters and merchants to carry their tobacco to the inspection houses and this involved a considerable realignment of the settlement system.

The 1747 law specified two inspection houses for All Hallows--one in the freshes of South River and the second in the Patuxent River freshes. The Assembly specified another house on the southeastern boundary of the parish, at Watkins Creek near the mouth of West River; however, jurisdiction over its operation was given to St. James' Parish.[2] Remarkably, the legislators did not delegate an inspection house for London Town on South River. They chose instead a site a few miles upstream at Howard's Point, also called Macklefish Point. But apparently the site proved less than satisfactory, and within the year petitions requesting a new location circulated.[3] Hard on the heels of these petitions came complaints about the negligence of the warehouse proprietor, one Thomas Rutland.[4] A decade later, fire consumed the warehouse,[5] and at that point the Assembly acquiesced and shifted the inspection house to a tract called "The Land of Ease" at the confluence of Flat Creek and South River.[6] Meanwhile, planters on the western side of the parish continued to deliver their tobacco at the inspection house at Taylor's Landing, situated near the unsuccessful town of Kilkenny and across the Patuxent from Queen Anne's Town in Prince George's County.[7]

The net effect of the 1747 inspection act was to shift the foci of local tobacco marketing from London Town to the statutory inspection houses on South,

---

[1]For the background to the 1747 inspection act and previous measures, see Wyckoff, Tobacco Regulation; and Middleton, Tobacco Coast, pp. 120-26.

[2]This was the Sprigg's Point Warehouse. Archives of Maryland, LVIII, 486.

[3]Ibid., XLVI, 19.

[4]In 1752, the tobacco inspectors contended that Thomas Rutland had refused to make repairs, build a shed, or erect four prizes. AACo Judgments, ISB#2, f. 429; ibid., f. 761.

[5]Archives of Maryland, LVI, 47, 49. [6]Ibid., p. 132.

[7]Maryland Gazette, November 25, 1747.

Patuxent, and West rivers. London Town lost its reason for being--the tobacco trade--and collapse was imminent. But these new points of trade proved unworthy successors. They failed to attract clusters of merchants, craftsmen, and service personnel. Their impotence as centralizing forces was largely a matter of economic conditions and a decline in merchant numbers.

In the past, rising tobacco prices heralded a general prosperity for planters, merchants and towns. Yet past conditions did not apply after the inspection act of 1747. Prices indeed rose after the act, but these gains were more than offset by severe reductions in the annual tobacco crop. Chesapeake tobacco exports rose by about 25 per cent during one year when the Maryland act was suspended.[1] One critic of the 1747 act anticipated the impact of quantity reductions upon planters:

> I hope the poorer sort of people among us are to be regarded as well as the better sort; then let us consider how many of them are obliged to rent land; let us otherwise consider too, what the yearly rent is that they pay, which is generally 800 lbs. of Tobacco. Well, let us suppose a man has a wife and severall small children to maintain . . . and supposing him to make 1000 lbs. Top Tobacco, and 500 lbs. of good second Tobacco, which will be a good crop when he [has] to pay his landlord for his rent, he will have left 200 lb. of Top Tobacco, and 500 lb. of Second Tobacco to maintain [his] family; which is but a small quantity: But now let us Suppose, that if we had an Inspection Law, what would he have [left] to maintain his family? Why, he would have but 200 lbs. of Tobacco, because his 500 lb. Second Tobacco must be destroyed; which at the prices Tobacco sells at now, the Top at 12s6d per cent. and the second at 8s. per cent. will produce him 3£5s. whereas, if he had but the 200 lb. Top Tobacco allowing it to sell for 16s8d per cent. he would only have 1£13s4d to support his family; which would be debarring the man of above half his profit. . . .[2]

This perceptive critic understated his case, at least for All Hallows Parish.

---

[1]U.S., Department of Commerce, Bureau of the Census, Historical Statistics of the United States, Colonial Times to 1957; A Statistical Abstract Supplement (Washington, D. C.: Government Printing Office, 1965), p. 766. After the inspection act the number of tobacco hogsheads exported per year from Maryland between 1756 and 1760 was less than the quantity exported in 1731 and 1733. Similarly, when the inspection act expired in 1771, exports increased from the 23,700 hogsheads in 1770 to 29,140 in 1771 and 33,480 in 1772, or respective increases of 22.9 per cent and 41.2 per cent over 1770 exports. Charles Albro Barker, The Background of the Revolution in Maryland, Yale Historical Publications Miscellany, XXXVIII (New Haven: Yale University Press, 1940, and reprinted by Archon Books, 1967), pp. 340-44, 381.

[2]The critic also noted that the average taxable produced 150 pounds of trash tobacco, in addition to the 500 pounds of seconds. "Mr. Q. in the Corner," "Letter to the Editor on 'Mercator's Reflections on an Inspection Act,'" Maryland Gazette, April 28, 1747.

Recalling the estimates in Chapter II, nearly half of the planter's crop was rendered non-merchantable by the inspection act. To compensate for quantity reductions, the price per pound of tobacco had to double. Seen from this perspective, the post-1747 years were less than prosperous. Between 1748 and 1776, the average price of tobacco, deflated by half for quantity reductions, was less than a penny per pound in every year but two (1759 and 1769 were the exceptions). A virtual state of perpetual depression existed which bridled planter purchases and, in turn, deterred merchant revenues and recruitment.

While it would be patently unfair to place exclusive blame on the inspection act of 1747 for Maryland's economic miseries, the act did seriously undermine urbanization. Inspection reduced the annual output of tobacco, and fewer merchants were required for marketing the parish crop. The remaining merchants redistributed customers, hinterlands, and occasionally their store locations. The sequence of events can be traced in All Hallows. The inspection act probably halved parish tobacco production as per labor yields fell from 1804.6 pounds to 913.6. Parish merchants found themselves in a keenly competitive marketing situation. Before the act, each of the twelve merchants marketed, on the average, about 129, 329.7 pounds of tobacco produced by 71.7 taxables. The parish altogether produced an estimated 1, 551, 956 pounds of tobacco; but after the act, parish production fell to 785, 696 pounds of tobacco, or 65, 474.7 pounds for each of the twelve merchants. Strong pressures were set in motion and merchants attempted to maintain their tobacco volume by increasing their customers. These competitive pressures surfaced immediately and in a decade, merchants declined from twelve to nine. The survivors increased their volume, again on the average, to 87, 299.6 pounds of tobacco while serving 95.6 taxables. What had happened was that the surviving merchants had gained 24 new taxables from the departed merchants, and in the aggregate this redistribution involved 216 taxables or 25.1 per cent of all parish taxables. There can be little doubt that the settlement system was in flux as customers and hinterlands were redistributed, merchants were pared, and new foci for the tobacco trade were imposed. Realignment was inevitable.

On balance, the tobacco inspection act of 1747 was a failure for All Hallows Parish. The act may have improved tobacco prices and quality, but such improvements did not compensate the small planter or tenant who lost half his crop to the inspectors. Impoverishment translated into smaller expenditures at the merchant's, the carpenter's, and so on. Even more disastrous were the act's effects on the urban node in the parish settlement system. That system churned and realigned for two decades after the law went into force. Given the far-reaching consequences of this statute, we must wonder about the motivations, intentions, and foresight of the men who constituted the Assembly of 1747. Did they anticipate the effects of the act on merchants and existing urban centers? Did these colonial legislators design to benefit decentralized native merchants by penalizing town-based merchants with strong ties abroad? These issues await a comprehensive political history of the 1740's--a project beyond both the scope of this work and the capabilities of this author. When that study is completed we shall perhaps know the motivations of the assemblymen; until then, we may conclude that their actions seriously undermined London Town and the town's London-affiliated merchants.

CHAPTER V

RURAL SETTLEMENTS: THE PLANTATIONS

Introduction

Agrarian activities dominated the settlement system of All Hallows Parish. For every merchant or craftsman, the parish countered with eight or nine planters. These planters practiced a commercial agrarianism, emphasizing the production of tobacco for European markets. They gambled that European demands would hold firm and bring prosperity to the Chesapeake, but these distant markets shifted mysteriously with fashion, taste, and population. A rupture in these faraway markets left the planters with a worthless luxury crop--worthless in price and worthless in the sense that they could not use it for household consumption. Thus, tobacco planting proved a risky business, much riskier than grain farming in the colonies to the north, where if markets collapsed, the farmers and animals could at least consume the food.

Planters enmeshed in a trans-Atlantic economy quickly learned that this delicate trade suffered severely from European disruptions.[1] Wars closed down continental markets and foreign privateers confiscated Chesapeake tobacco in transit to Britain. European financial crises threatened British merchants who urgently demanded credit remittances from their Chesapeake correspondents. Their enormous indebtedness reflected the planters' heavy reliance on English and European manufactured goods, which flowed unevenly into the Chesapeake. The fineries and necessities from European factories were at times abundant and, at other times, scarce depending on the market strategies of British merchants and the size of the annual tobacco fleet. Powerless to control the European end of the trade, Chesapeake planters and legislators at-

---

[1]The details of this trans-Atlantic economy may be found in Middleton, Tobacco Coast, pp. 93-177; Hemphill, "Virginia and the English Commercial System"; John M. Hemphill II, "Freight Rates in the Maryland Tobacco Trade, 1705-1762," Maryland Historical Magazine, LIV (March, 1959), 36-58; Jacob M. Price, "The Economic Growth of the Chesapeake and the European Market, 1697-1775," Journal of Economic History, XXIV (December, 1964), 496-511.

tacked over-production and marketing inefficiencies at home. Their actions, though a palliative, seem to have had little effect in dampening price fluctuations or improving planter income. The individual planter had little choice but to fall back on his own initiative; and in the aggregate, they devised an adaptive and flexible response to a trans-Atlantic economy of boom and bust. That response became manifest in the increasingly self-sufficient plantation.

Adaptive Change to an Economy of Boom and Bust

During the colonial period, individual action was the most efficient way of coping with an erratic trans-Atlantic economy. Planters buffered the extremes of depression by expanding the variety of plantation activities, thus reducing their reliance on English goods and the tobacco market. When prosperity returned, they participated as usual in the commercial economy, stepping up imports and exchange as revenues warranted. These adjustments in plantation activities and expenditures came about slowly and unevenly, and, in transit, the plantation was transformed from a specialized agricultural site dependent on Europe to a diversified and potentially self-sufficient settlement.

Plantation Variables

Colonial vocabulary permitted at least five usages for the term "plantation." These included a tract of land, a parcel of cleared land, an overseas expedition of colonists, a rural habitation and associated outbuildings, and a rural settlement which produced tobacco.[1] The most frequent usage in All Hallows was as a generic settlement term. The term encompassed virtually all rural settlements and, so far as I can tell, it carried no connotation of scale, buildings, population of the settlement, land area, or variety of activities.

---

[1]Examples of the multiple use of the term are abundant. As a tract of land, see AACo Deeds, WT#2, ff. 59, 310-12; as a parcel of cleared land and an overseas colony, see Governor Seymour to the Council of Trade and Plantations, August 21, 1706, CSPCS 1706-08, XXIII, 194; as a settlement, see "Narrative of a Voyage to Maryland, 1705-1706," American Historical Review, XII (January, 1907), 329; as an agrarian operating unit based on tobacco and slaves, see American Husbandry, pp. 177, 187; also see the comments of Isaac Weld in Edgar T. Thompson, "The Plantation as a Social System," Plantation Systems of the New World, ed. by Vera Rubin, Social Sciences Monographs, VII (Washington, D. C.: Pan American Union, 1959), p. 36, quoting Isaac Weld, Jr., Travels Through the States of North America and Provinces of Upper and Lower Canada during the Years of 1795, 1796, 1797 (4th ed.; London: J. Stockdale, 1807).

Following the contemporary lexicon, we can describe the rural settlements of All Hallows as "plantations." Their evident variety invites consideration which is made all the easier by an exquisite series of parish estate inventories from 1660 to 1769. These records, though falling short of telling us all we want to know about the plantation--they do not detail holding size nor list capital improvements such as buildings and fences--do reveal the diverse activities and the labor force of the plantations for over a century.

Before dissecting these records, we should clarify who is included in the sample. The 494 parish inventories include planters--a vast majority--and a handful of secondary and tertiary specialists, most of whom engaged in agriculture along with their specialization. A small methodological problem cropped up regarding several large planters who owned home plantations and one or more outlying "quarters." Occasionally, these "quarters" lay outside of the parish. Are these units separate plantations or simply parts of one plantation? To resolve the question, I consistently observe the following rule: if all of the holdings lie in the parish, they are collectively considered as one plantation; holdings beyond the parish are excluded. In any case, multiple holdings are the exception and not the rule. Most parish planters owned or rented just one parcel of land.

A great deal may be learned about the plantation and planter behavior by slicing these inventories into a series of variables. Eight plantation variables are important in this study, and they are: plantation activities, including primary, secondary, tertiary and consumption; labor; scale or total estate value; the degree of specialization and potential self-sufficiency.

The first set of variables--primary, secondary, tertiary, and consumption activities--may confound the non-geographer, so before we infer and measure these concepts from the inventories, some brief definitions are in order.

Primary activities are those which extract resources from nature, such as agriculture, mining, fishing, and hunting. Secondary activities involve the transformation of primary products to more useful forms via manufacture. Repair activities are also included, since, during the colonial period, persons skilled in repair were also capable of making the item from raw materials. Tertiary activities involve the provision of services or goods, such as marketing, religious, political, and educational activities. Lastly, consumption activities are those in which the products of other activities are used and consumed; the items are non-income producing.

With these definitions in mind, the next procedure entails examining every inventory and assigning each item and its sterling value to one of the four activity groups. Most of these inferences are straight-forward, as are those assignments appearing in Table 21. I continue to be uncertain on the assignment of crops, cloth, and metal. The inference, in these cases, is based on the composition of the entire inventory. The assignment of wool can serve as an example. A quick check of the inventory determines the presence or absence of sheep, sheep shears, cards, and spinning wheels. If the first two appear, then the wool is assigned to the primary group; if cards or spinning wheels, then to secondary; if none appear, then to consumption. When two or more assignments are possible, the general rule is to assign to the earliest activity in the production-consumption chain.

TABLE 21

SELECTED INVENTORY ITEMS AND
THEIR ACTIVITY ASSIGNMENTS

Primary	Secondary	Tertiary	Consumption
Crops	Craft tools	New goods, merchandise	Furniture, pots & pans, household items
Fishing gear	Cider casks	Cloth	Metal
Livestock	Mills	Scales & weights	Wigs
Meat	Grindstones	Surveyor's equip.	Books
Hides, tallow	Mortars & pestles	Medicines	Fireplace tools
Plows, harrows	Churns, powdering tubs	Silver Plate	Guns
Hoes & axes	Saws, nails	Cash	Clothing
Skins	Tobacco hogsheads		

A few inventoried items are never assigned to the four groups. Credits are ignored because they are more properly a measure of interaction which is considered in Chapter VI. Labor and transport items are assigned to their own categories because inferring their activities is subject to a wide margin of error. A slave, for example, could be assigned to one or all of the four activity groups. The same applies for transport equipment. Should a wagon be assigned to the farm (primary), the factory (secondary), to trade (tertiary), or to household use (consumption)? A few other items are unassignable and necessitate a miscellaneous category, including sugar, soap, plank, leather, salt, wine, and other imported beverages. These commodities constitute a very small value of estates, with the exception of wealthy planters. After the assignments are made, each inventory is given four activity scores, being the relative investment in each of the four activity groups.

The specialization index measures the plantation's relative mix of primary, secondary, tertiary, and consumption activities. The index ranges from complete specialization in one activity group to complete diversification, in which investment is equally divided among all four groups.[1] The polar case of specialization occurs when 100 per cent of estate investment is in one activity group. Complete diversification results when each group has 25 per cent of the investment. The specialization index is the sum of the percentage changes in each activity group which are necessary to reach maximum diversification. Thus, the most specialized site, with 100 per cent, receives a score of 150; 75 points must be deleted from the specialized activity, and 25 points added to each of three other activities. Maximum diversification equals zero.

The labor variable is equivalent to the total investment in servants and slaves. Scale of plantation equals the gross value of estate assets.

The last variable, the index of potential self-sufficiency, measures a plantation's "ability" (potential) to satisfy the needs of its personnel and therefore function independently of other sites. The plantation's potential for independence is, of course, quite distinct from its actual interaction (exchange), which constitutes a separate dimension. Stated differently, a potentially self-sufficient plantation may rank high or low on exchange. The index also differs from the index of specialization. The latter measures the relative mix of investment; the former, the absolute potential for self-support.

Potential self-sufficiency is crudely measured by the presence in an inventory of forty-five selected material items which could be used for domestic production. These items all fall within the primary and secondary activity groups, except for pewter and iron (Table 22). The index of potential self-sufficiency, ranging from zero to forty-five, increases with the number of these items in an inventory. High scores denote flexible plantations having an alternative to exchange; low scores identify rigid plantations, having no alternative but to exchange.

---

[1] For measurements of a similar nature, see John W. Webb, "Basic Concepts in the Analysis of Small Urban Centers in Minnesota," Annals of the Association of American Geographers, XLIX (March, 1959), 55-72.

TABLE 22

INVENTORY ITEMS IN THE INDEX OF POTENTIAL SELF-SUFFICIENCY

Cattle	Spinning wheels
Horses	Cards
Hogs	Weaving tools
Sheep	Carpenter's, Cooper's, Joiner's, Turner's, Sawyer's tools
Tobacco	Blacksmith's tools
Corn	Shoemaker's tools
Wheat	Tailor's tools
Peas or Beans	Tanner's tools
Barley, Oats, Rye	Brewer's tools
Flax	Spoon molds
Beehives	Brick molds
Skins	Bullet molds
Fishing	Candle molds
Cider mills, presses, troughs	Wedges, Mall rings
Stills	Mills, millstones
Plantation tools	Saws
Steelyards	Grindstones
Scythes	Mortars & pestles
Plows, Harrows	Milk pans, powdering tubs
Sheep shears	Butter Pots, butter
	Churns
	Cheese press
	Iron, Pewter
	Medical items

Aggregate Changes in Plantation Variables

In the aggregate, the plantations of All Hallows Parish changed substantially between the 1660's and 1769. Over the long-term, the scale of operation grew larger, and diversification and potential self-sufficiency increased. By and large, the most substantial changes occurred during depressions in the tobacco economy.

The changes in the eight aggregate plantation variables appear in Table 23. The variables are grouped into periods of boom and bust in the tobacco economy. Due to the brevity of the cycle after 1749, the three booms are collapsed into one period, and the three depressions into another.

The scale or size of plantations generally increased during the colonial era. But the pattern and rates of increase were uneven, with the greatest growth occurring amidst depressions (Table 23). The scale of plantations rose from an average value of £132 in 1660-1679 to £455 during post-1750 depres-

TABLE 23

MEAN VALUES OF PLANTATION VARIABLES, 1660-1769

	Primary (£ ster.)	Secondary (£ ster.)	Tertiary (£ ster.)	Consumption (£ ster.)	Labor (£ ster.)	Scale or Total estate value (£ ster.)	Spec. Index	Pot. Self-Sufficiency
1660-79	37.21	2.45	13.42	17.18	17.54	132.01	97.66	5.00
1680-97	64.03	4.46	23.56	24.15	38.42	206.12	89.64	7.88
1698-1704	59.94	2.71	20.41	23.96	45.41	164.29	85.77	8.24
1705-18	70.22	4.34	27.01	30.88	70.06	287.41	91.83	9.48
1719-26	57.48	3.85	14.51	23.50	73.08	219.78	81.48	9.55
1727-33	71.38	6.62	83.95	32.17	96.74	417.44	84.86	12.69
1734-39	72.15	8.75	30.88	41.34	115.64	312.36	76.28	9.62
1740-49	73.06	7.61	16.69	31.82	102.56	268.77	83.47	15.95
1750-53 } 1757-61 } 1767-69 }	70.83	7.62	19.34	34.37	140.93	400.95	79.96	15.79
1754-56 } 1762-66 }	59.63	21.70	22.17	34.96	180.81	455.72	84.94	12.69
Total	64.49	7.17	25.52	29.39	88.44	287.55	85.98	10.92

sions. However, growth was not linear, as plantation size increased during depressions and fell during booms. This recurrent pattern held for every boom and bust except the 1740-1749 depression. In the aggregate, planters prospered when tobacco prices were low. Depression growth is surprising, and encourages a suspicion that the inventories may be biased by the death of wealthy men during depressions. But as noted before, inventories closely approximate the characteristics of the total parish population. In addition, it seems reasonable to assume that poor men died in greater numbers during hard economic times. Finally, the phenomenon of depression growth can be adequately explained.

The fluctuations of plantation scale until the 1740's correlated perfectly with increases in credit extension. During depressed periods, credits, or accounts receivable, expanded as a substitute for shortages of cash or English bills of exchange. Thus, a portion of the increment in plantation scale was tied up in the form of debts owed to the estate, some of which were "desperate" or uncollectible. However, the increase in scale was not simply a paper or accounting increase. The growth of material assets followed the same recurrent pattern as scale and credit extension. The value of personal material assets rose in every depression until 1740. The increase was 58 per cent during the 1680's and 1690's; 36 per cent between 1705 and 1718; and 71 per cent in 1727-1733 (Table 24). The pattern persisted in the 1730's boom, when both credits and growth in material assets declined by 36.1 per cent and 9.7 per cent, respectively. Nor were these depression-won assets wiped out by planter indebtedness. The net worth of planters, defined as the mean total estate value minus debts, also increased dramatically (Table 24). Depressions in the tobacco economy resulted in the growth of unencumbered material assets on the plantation.

The pattern of depression growth on the plantations fell apart in the 1740's. Plantation scale and material assets plummeted when they should have risen. The probable cause of this about face was the collapse of local credit extension, which, in earlier and later depressions, revived and revitalized the economy. The anomaly of the 1740's credit failure, in turn, seems rooted in the colony's emission of paper currency in 1733. Before passage of this currency legislation, paper money was not used in Maryland; and scarcity and difficulties with other forms of money, such as tobacco, foreign coins, land warrants, and bills of exchange, made short-term credit, or book debt, the chief instrument of trade. But the scarcity of currency proved a continuing source of

TABLE 24

MEAN VALUE OF DEBTS, NET WORTH, AND MATERIAL ASSETS, 1660-1769

	Debts per estates with accounts (£ ster.)	Net Worth (TEV-debts) (£ ster.)	Material Assets (TEV-credits) (£ ster.)	% change in assets	Credits (£ ster.)
1660-79	64.94	67.07	91.60		40.41
				58.0	
1680-97	72.74	133.38	144.71		61.42
				6.8	
1698-1704	58.86	105.43	154.56		9.73
				36.2	
1705-18	73.65	213.76	210.52		76.89
				-17.3	
1719-26	70.34[a]	149.44[a]	174.06		45.72
				71.3	
1727-33	180.80	236.64	298.13		119.31
				- 9.7	
1734-39	81.73	230.63	269.26		43.10
				-11.6	
1740-49	32.58	236.19	238.11		30.66
				+23.1	
1750-53} 1757-61} 1767-69}	156.18	244.77	293.20		107.75
				+17.1	
1754-56} 1762-66}	197.65	258.07	343.20		112.52

[a]The account of William Nicholson in the period 1719-26 is unusually high, showing debts of £3522 sterling; it is excluded from the above calculations. If included the mean for debts goes up to £189.36, and net worth falls to £30.42.

complaint, particularly in depressions; and so, in 1733 the colony emitted into circulation paper money which passed at a sterling exchange of $33\frac{1}{3}$.[1] As the depression of the 1740's approached, the planters who formerly borrowed on credit, were faced with creditors demanding paper. Increased currency demands coupled with hoarding forced up the exchange rate from $33\frac{1}{3}$ to 100 per

[1]Generally, Maryland scholars have noted the favorable effects of paper currency, while failing to see its impact on credit, economic growth, and welfare. See Clarence P. Gould, Money and Transportation in Maryland 1720-1765, Johns Hopkins University Studies in Historical and Political Science, 33rd Series, No. 1 (1915), Chapter V; and Kathryn L. Behrens, Paper Money in Maryland, 1727-1789, Johns Hopkins University Studies in Historical and Political Science, 41st Series, No. 1 (1923).

cent. Paper was driven into hiding and the economy stagnated. The anomaly of the 1740's soon passed, and credit reassumed its decisive role as a depression lubricant, facilitating exchange, economic growth, and the elaboration of material culture on the plantations.

Parish plantations in the aggregate became more diversified during the colonial era. The long-term downward trend in the parish specialization index (Figure 17) paralleled a similar decline in tobacco prices, but this relationship did not always apply in the short-run.[1] It did apply during the 1680's and 1690's depression when the specialization index fell to a low of 83.5 in 1702. But in the very next depression the index rose to over 94 in 1714. Thereafter, specialization decreased (diversification increased) in the bust of the late 1720's and the boom of the 1730's, when in 1737 the index fell to its lowest point ever (79.2). Two points require emphasis: the correlation between specialization and the state of the economy is complex and the middling indices of specialization suggest that parish plantations are neither overly specialized or diversified in their investments.

The components of the specialization index changed with greater regularity and predictability (Figure 18). In every period of low prices, relative investment in primary activities increased at the expense of consumption investment. And the reverse occurred in boom periods. Secondary investment was generally stable, except for slight peaks in the 1720's and 1740's.

Tertiary investments largely determined the long-term trend toward diversification. While investments in primary and consumption activities alternated with the state of the economy and secondary investment remained relatively static, the expansion of the tertiary sector acted to drive down specialization, especially between 1683 and 1702 and 1725 and 1737. That expansion overlapped the boom-bust cycle, thus obscuring a clear-cut correlation of tobacco prices and the index of specialization. What seems to have happened is this: in the middle of bust periods, some planters, anticipating a boom, laid in a stock of mercantile goods. When the boom arrived, they sold their goods, which had the effect of driving down their tertiary investment and raising aggre-

---

[1]The graph of the specialization index uses a seven-year running average, with three years on either side of the date of entry. A running average is used to increase the number of observations per year in the seventeenth century, when parish inventories are fewer. The intent is not to smooth out short-term changes, though this might occur after 1749 when the length of booms and busts decrease to three to four years. The same grouping procedure is used for the time series of potential self-sufficiency (Figure 17) and for the components of the specialization index (Figure 18).

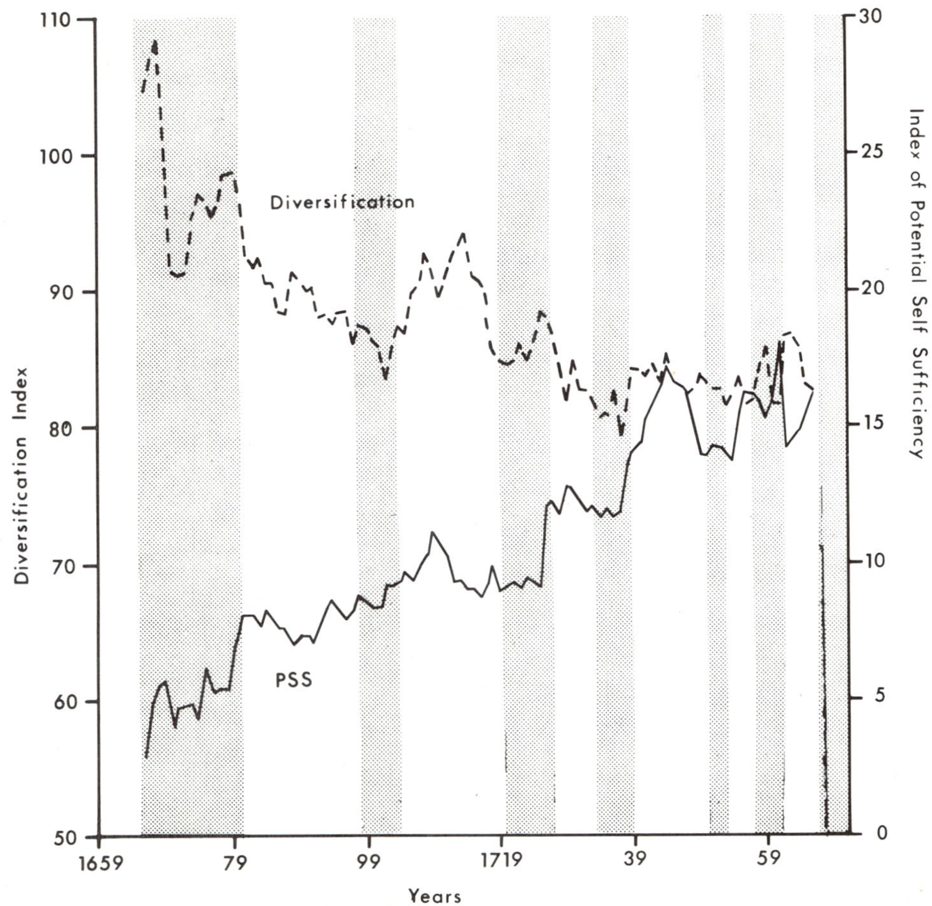

Fig. 17.--Aggregate Diversification (Specialization) Index and Index of Potential Self-sufficiency, 1666-1766. (Shaded areas indicate boom years.)

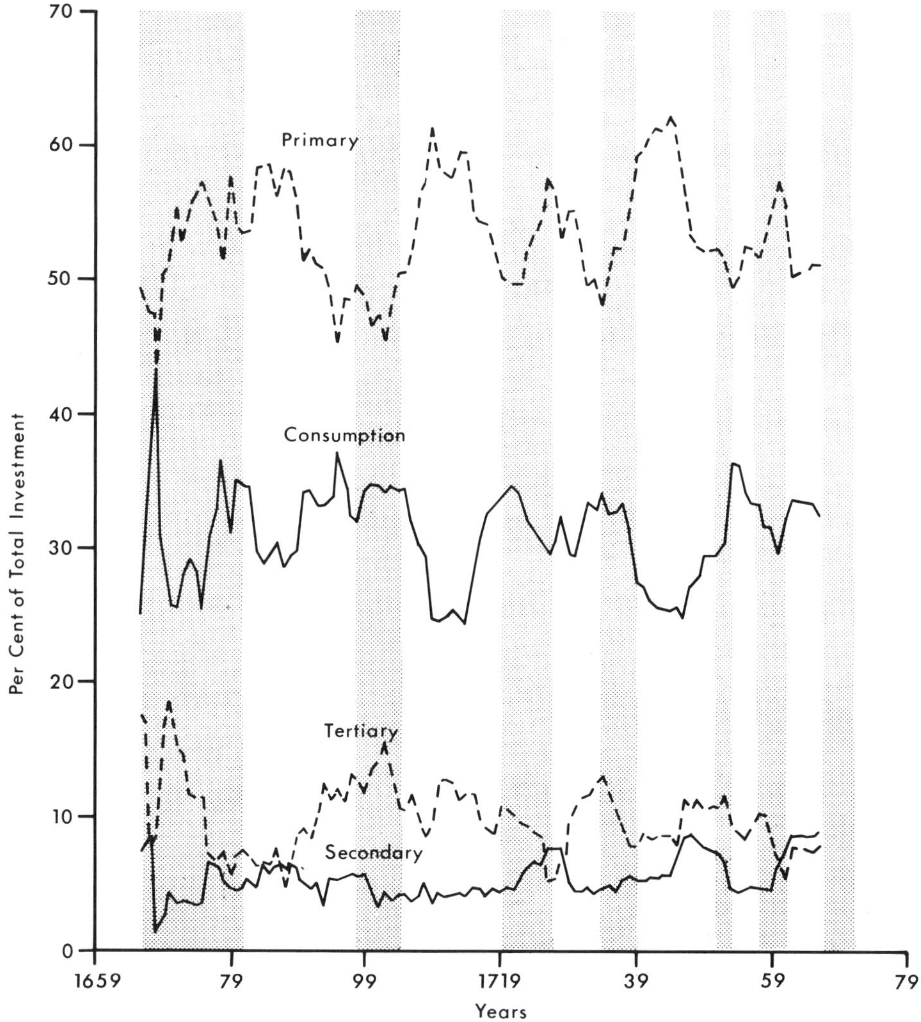

Fig. 18.--Components of the Specialization Index: Primary, Secondary, Tertiary, Consumption, 1666-1766. (Shaded areas indicate boom years.)

gate consumption investment in the parish. Midway through the boom, the trading planters, anticipating now a bust, diminished their tertiary investments and assumed a depression stance.

This flexible investment behavior, finely tuned to long economic swings of fifteen years or more, worked well until 1749; but when the economic cycle telescoped to about eight years, the planters' adjustments were always one step out of phase. During the boom of 1750-1753, planters behaved as they had in the past. Anticipating a boom period of a decade or more, they decreased primary investment and increased consumption and tertiary activities. Unfortunately, they completed these adjustments in 1753-1754, when the price of tobacco had fallen. Hastily, the parish planters resumed the traditional depression stance of high primary, low consumption, and low tertiary investment. Naturally, the boom of 1757-1761 commenced. In conformance with long-standing habits and with the belief that the preceding two short phases were probably an aberration, planters dauntlessly assumed a boom investment posture about 1762. Again they were foiled, as a depression ensued. The realities of a volatile economy dawned slowly and painfully on parish planters. Although they endured four phases of accelerated boom and bust after 1750, their plantation adjustments always lagged one phase behind the swings in tobacco prices.

Recurrent depressions triggered one additional planter response--the acquisition of items of potential self-sufficiency. Substantial increments occurred between 1706-1709, 1725-1729, 1738-1744, and 1754-1756, all of which came in the early years of the bust phase of the economic cycle (Figure 17). The index achieved a maximum of nineteen during the 1740's depression when tobacco prices were lowest, and credit and currency shortages severely hindered the importation of European goods. After these growth spasms in the early part of depressions, the index levelled off until the onset of the next depression. Thus, as depressions set in planters added items that enabled them to replace imports with household production. These increments in potential self-sufficiency were maintained and passed along to the next generation of planters, who behaved similarly.

Summary

During the course of a full economic cycle in the Chesapeake, varied and complex changes occurred in plantation activities and investment. In order to simplify these changes, a schematic model is provided in Table 25. The model is essentially a time-line which indicates the sequence and timing of plantation

TABLE 25

SEQUENTIAL MODEL OF SITE CHANGES
(Prior to 1749)*

Time	Bust 1	Boom	Bust 2
	(1) Tertiary Investment Increases	(3) Tertiary Investment Decreases	(1) Tertiary Investment Increases
	(2) Consumption Increases	(5) Consumption Decreases	
	(2) Primary Investment Decreases	(5) Primary Investment Increases	
		(4) Pot. Self-sufficiency Increases	
			(6) Pot. Self-sufficiency levels off
	(1) Specialization Index Decreases		
		(3) Specialization Increases	
	Credit Contraction	Credit Expansion	

*The numbers indicate the sequence of changes after the onset of a depression.

adjustments during an economic cycle. The cutting point into the cycle is the middle of a bust phase when tertiary investment begins to increase, in anticipation of the boom to follow. The model describes the pre-1749 period most accurately; to make it applicable to the accelerated cycles after 1749, the adjustments must be lagged for one phase.

The Range and Variety of Plantations

Aggregate analysis of parish plantations identified a cluster of changes which took place on the plantations during depressions. These changes included growth in scale, net worth, material assets, and credit. But did all planters and plantations behave similarly and enjoy this paradoxical prosperity? Or were the increases in scale and material assets concentrated among a small group of plantations?

Depression prosperity was an illusion to most planters. These advances in scale and material assets accrued almost exclusively to the great planters, perhaps 10 to 20 per cent of the total. Their spectacular gains widened the scale gap between themselves and the small and middling planters. The gap narrowed in the booms when prosperity shifted away from the large planters. A graphic illustration of this changing concentration of plantation scale with booms and busts is provided by the Lorenz curves, appearing in Figures 19 and 20. On these graphs, a 45° diagonal indicates a perfectly equal distribution of plantation scale; the further the line falls below the diagonal, the greater is the concentration of plantation scale. The lowest lines, indicating inequality, occur in the depressions of 1680-1697 and 1727-1733 when the largest 10 per cent of the plantations possessed over 60 per cent of the cumulative value of all plantations. The line comes closest to the diagonal in the boom of 1698-1704 when the top 10 per cent held 32 per cent of the plantations' value. Indeed, plantation prosperity depended on the rise and fall of tobacco prices, as Charles Carroll claimed. Large planters prospered when prices fell; the rest did so when prices rose. These unexpected relations of economic cycles and plantation scale need to be considered at somewhat greater length.

Plantations were more nearly equal in scale during the boom years of 1660-1679, when the Lorenz Curve was closest to the 45° diagonal (Figures 19 and 20). But in the following bust from 1680 to 1697, the entire curve shifted downward and toward greater disparity in plantation scale. The share of the top 10 per cent rose from 45.3 per cent to 60.4 per cent. The ensuing boom from 1698 to 1704 shifted the curve back to a more equal distribution, very similar to the initial boom. There was, however, a notable difference; the smallest plantations, nearly half of the total, possessed a smaller share than they had in the earlier boom of 1660-1679. In other words, the apparent egalitarian shift favored middling and large plantations. The next three phases of bust-boom-bust from 1705 to 1733 exhibited considerable plantation inequality, with the top 10 per cent retaining over 58 per cent of total plantation value. This twenty-nine year equilibrium persisted through the boom of 1719-1726, which failed to reduce inequality as had earlier booms. The boom of the 1730's reverted to this earlier pattern, as the curve shifted toward a more egalitarian position. The 1740's depression, contrary to expectations, continued this trend toward equality, and its curve resembled the first boom of 1660-1679. After 1750, the concentration of plantation scale changed as it had for most of the colonial era; inequality increased in depressions, and decreased in booms. The exceptions to this pattern, 1719-1726 and 1740-1749, are deserving of brief comment.

The first exception, 1719-1726, may have been caused by demographic

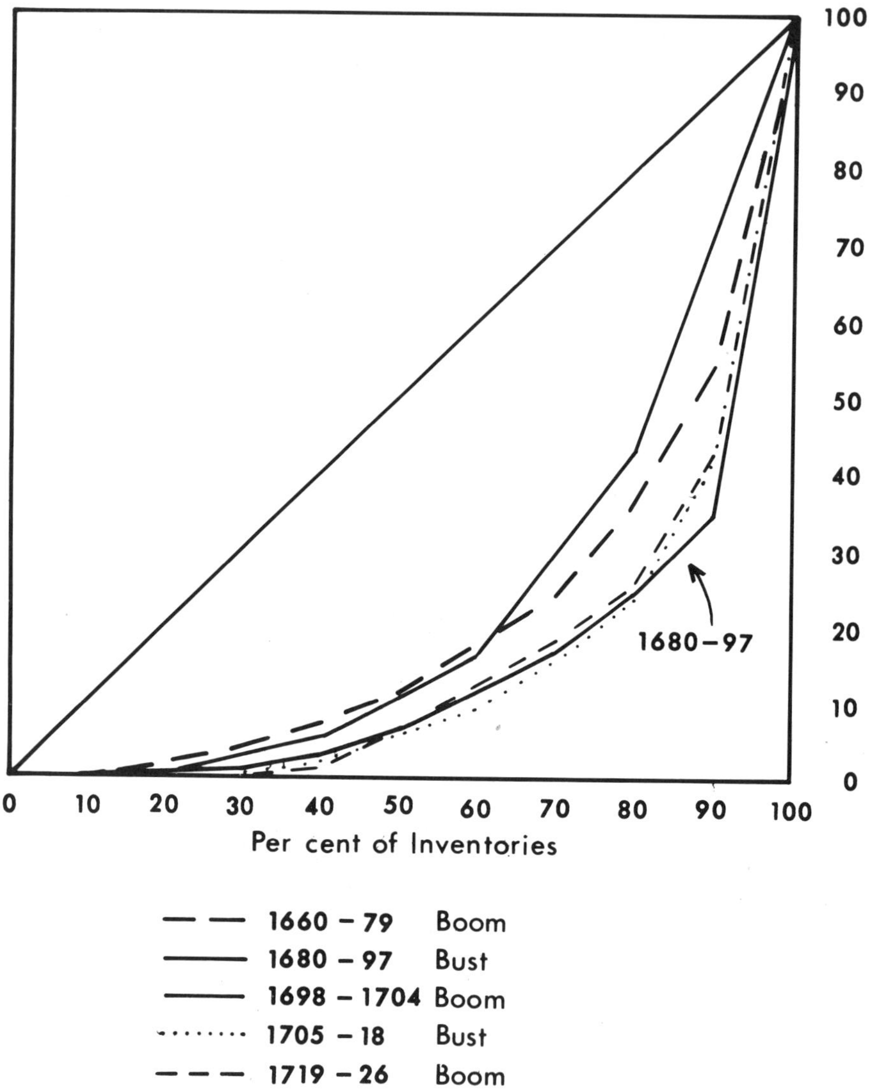

Fig. 19.--Lorenz Curves of Scale of Inventories, for Booms and Busts to 1726.

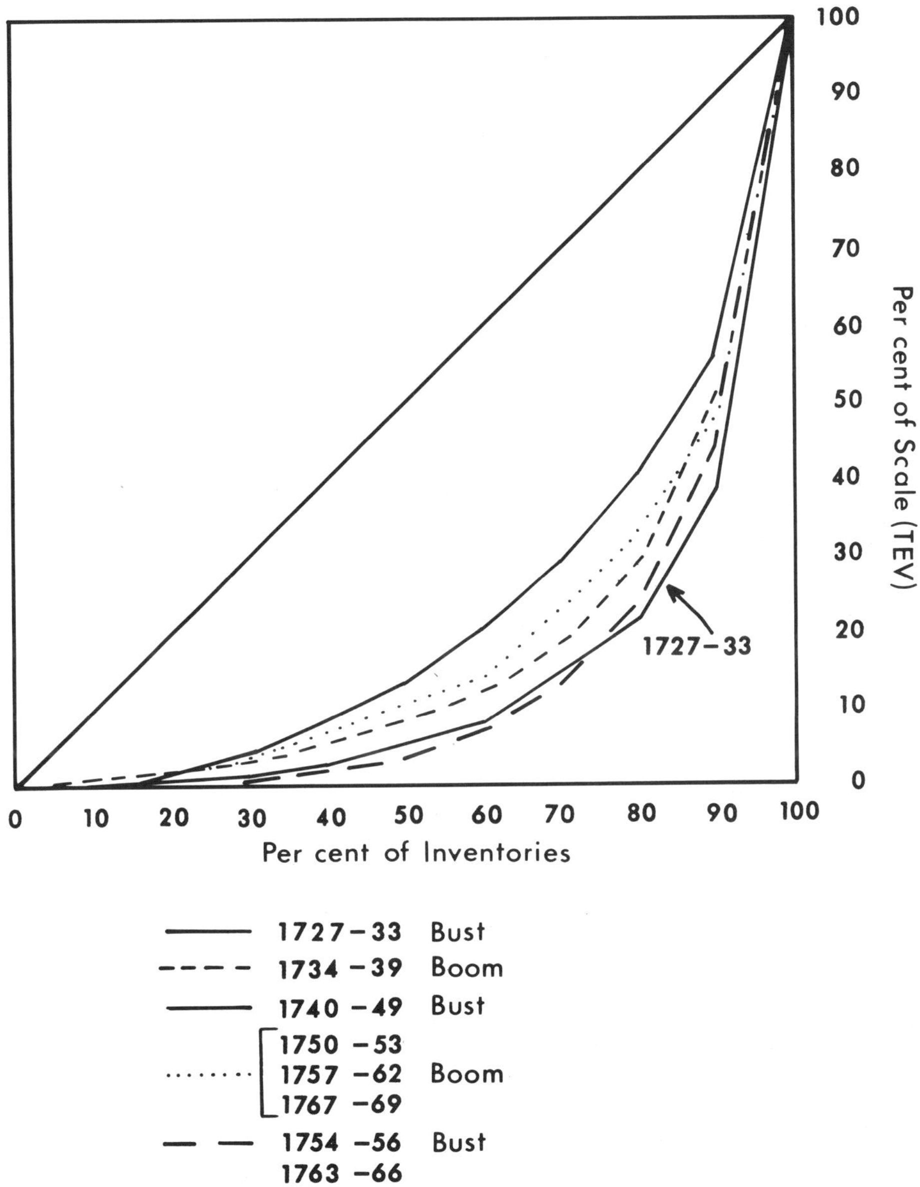

Fig. 20.--Lorenz Curves of Scale of Inventories, for Booms and Busts 1727-1769.

change. The effects of a naturally increasing population were first manifested in the late teens and early twenties. Such growth swelled the ranks of small and middling planters, diminished their opportunities for advancement (Table 26), and maintained plantation scale inequalities at depression levels. Economic factors lay behind the second exception, 1740-1749, when plantation scale became less concentrated during a depression. The shift to paper currency back-fired on large planters who formerly would have extended depression credit and, accordingly, increased the size of their plantations. The credit mechanism simply did not work effectively in the 1740's, to the detriment of wealthy planters.

TABLE 26

MEAN SCALE OF LARGE, MIDDLING, AND SMALL PLANTATIONS, 1660-1769

	Large (Top 30%)		Middling (Middle 40%)		Small (Bottom 30%)
	£ ster.	% Change	£ ster.	% Change	£ ster.
1660-79	341.69		67.99		33.18
		+69.77		+21.58	
1680-97	580.57		82.66		16.37
		-27.02		+42.15	
1698-1704	423.72		117.50		16.24
		+100.09		-19.62	
1705-18	847.82		97.88		18.56
		-24.98		-17.35	
1719-26	636.05		80.90		11.83
		+96.14		+56.30	
1727-33	1247.53		126.45		21.65
		-25.59		- 6.79	
1734-39	928.24		117.87		37.08
		-21.95		+59.02	
1740-49	724.48		187.44		35.77
		+47.40		+ 2.00	
1750-53} 1757-61} 1767-69}	1068.20		191.25		51.15
		+26.60		-27.20	
1754-56} 1762-66}	1353.19		139.12		15.15

More insight into the plantations' changing scale may be gained by dividing them into three groups--small, middling, and large. Large plantations expanded their scale during depressions. In the succeeding boom their mean scale dropped, but at a lesser rate than the depression gains (Table 26). During the first three depressions to 1733, the scale of large plantations increased by 69.8 per cent, 100.1 per cent, and 96.2 per cent. By contrast, their mean scale fell by 25 to 27 per cent during the three booms between 1698 and 1739. Thus, when tobacco prices were low, the large plantations grew spectacularly. In light of this growth, the failure of the Maryland Assembly to pass effective legislation to improve tobacco prices seems entirely rational. But conditions changed for large planters in the 1740's. During these depressed years, their mean scale fell by a disastrous 22 per cent, compounding the 25 per cent drop during the previous boom. In effect, the large planters had endured fifteen hard years from 1734 to 1749, when their scale fell from over £1200 to £724. Like an ascending roller coaster with high peaks and gentle dips, the large planters and their plantations sped upward, until their plummeting descent in the 1740's.

Far less sensitive to the economic cycle were the middling plantations, comprising the middle 40 per cent of all plantations. Their value increased between 1660 and 1704 (two booms and a bust); decreased for twenty-one years until 1726 (one boom and one bust); and then rose continuously to a peak of £191 in the post-1749 booms. Interestingly, middling planters were the only group to prosper during the 1740's depression. Their mean scale rose by 59 per cent, thrusting the Lorenz curve toward equality. Actually, this was an exceptionally large improvement for the middling plantations. The majority of scale changes were on the magnitude of plus or minus 30 per cent and less.

The most critical fact about the smallest plantations (the lower 30 per cent) was their extremely small size. Their mean value did not exceed £37.1 before 1750, though it rose in the succeeding booms. Small plantations fared best during the booms of 1660-1679, 1734-1739, and post-1749.

Differential Expansion of Plantation Activities

As the plantations grew in size, so did the variety of plantation goods and equipment. By the 1740's plantations contained a wide range of activities unknown or uncommon among seventeenth century planters. These additions came in response to the erratic economy. The plantations took on a new look or added new functions after nearly every depression. A new and more flexible settlement institution was evolving--an institution that resembled a small hamlet and housed family, labor, livestock, craft tools, and agricultural implements.

In this process of settlement evolution, some plantations led the way; others lagged; the majority adopted in a mass or swarm. This swarming of adoption is readily apparent in Table 27, which presents time series of selected items from the index of potential self-sufficiency. Discussion of these items is directed toward illuminating the process of plantation change.

Livestock

As planters moved toward potential self-sufficiency, an essential first step was the agricultural diversification of a staple economy. Fortunately, the planters had some experience with diversification because their economy had always included livestock and corn as integral parts.

All Hallows Parish had an abundance of cattle. Ten or more cattle appeared on the average plantation, and 70 per cent or more of the plantations owned at least one cow, with the exception of the decade of the 1690's when several severe winters drove the proportion down to 67 per cent.[1] For the first eighty years of settlement, cattle exceeded the number of any other single form of livestock, unless we include the lowly dunghill fowls (chickens) which were too numerous to count.

In the seventeenth century, cattle were rarely penned or housed; they were free to graze in the woods, or they were let loose upon harvested corn fields to feed upon the blades and tops of maize. The freedom given cattle occasionally created problems. In 1675, Ralph Williams lost one yearling by drowning in a well, two cows and a steer by miring in wetlands, and another cow by falling down a bank.[2] Estate appraisers in the seventeenth century often concluded the inventories with the number of cattle outlying "which cannot be brought to appraisement."[3] The incidence of cattle "in the woods" decreased in the eighteenth century, as woodland grazing areas dwindled in the face of dense population and with the depletion of woodland. Planters then substituted fodder or feeding on harvested corn fields.

Cattle were rarely recorded by size, breed, or function. Color distinctions began only late in the colonial period. The typical inventory entry noted age and/or sex of the animal. However, the inventories make it clear that "cat-

---

[1]Gray, History of Agriculture, I, 200.

[2]Inventories & Accounts, 2, f. 238.

[3]Testamentary Proceedings, 2, f. 283. Open range was practiced for hogs and horses, too; see Inventories & Accounts, 8, ff. 391-93; ibid., 9, f. 111; ibid., 18, ff. 89-108.

tle were multi-functional animals, which were used for draught, milking, meat, tallow, and hides." Although draft oxen were rare, steers were able to pull the plows, which appeared in abundance after 1720 (Table 27). For plowing, steers were probably preferred over horses. Despite the abundance of cows, planters made sparing use of dairy products. Liquid milk spoiled easily in the summer, and perhaps for this reason, apple cider became the preferred drink by the early eighteenth century.[1] Butter appeared infrequently in the parish inventories until the 1730's and 1740's, and even then, less than half the inventories possessed it (Table 27). Cheese was even less common. Beef proved more popular. The slaughter of cattle, and hogs, typically took place in late fall and winter, "for att the fall of the Leaffe they have fatt Beefe and fatt Pork."[2] Some animals may have been slaughtered in the summer, but the chances of spoilage were great if the meat were not consumed quickly:

> In summer when fresh meat will not keep, seeing every man kils of his own, and quantities are inconvenient, they lend from one to another, such portions of flesh as they can spare, which is repaied again when the borrower kils his. . . .[3]

When Dr. James Walker of Anne Arundel County slaughtered his five steers in 1761 they yielded 2, 187 pounds of beef, or an average of 437. 4 pounds.[4] This was less than half the weight of northern Virginia cattle claimed by George Washington, but nearly equalled the dressed weights in southeastern Pennsylvania.[5]

Slaughter by-products included tallow, used for making soap and candles, and raw hides which were sent to the tanner for conversion into leather. Apparently, hides were not abundant in the 1660's, for an ordinance prohibited the export of untanned hides, and stipulated that quit-rents for land could be paid in hides.[6] The situation was quite different one hundred years later, when dying cattle and hides were plentiful.

---

[1] Gray, History of Agriculture, I, 205. See Table 27 in this Chapter.

[2] "Narrative of a Voyage to Maryland, 1705-1706," p. 329.

[3] John Hammond, "Leah and Rachel, or, the Two Fruitful Sisters Virginia and Maryland, 1656," Narratives of Early Maryland, p. 298.

[4] Inventories, 80, f. 55.

[5] Gray, History of Agriculture, I, 204-5; Lemon, The Best Poor Man's Country, p. 163.

[6] Archives of Maryland, III, 457-58.

TABLE 27

PROPORTION OF PLANTATIONS POSSESSING ITEMS OF POTENTIAL SELF-SUFFICIENCY, 1660-1769

	Cattle	Horses	Hogs	Sheep	Corn	Wheat	Peas & Beans	Barley, Oats, or Rye	Flax
1660-79	71	47	56	3	24	3	9	9	0
1680-89	79	81	70	21	32	8	2	2	0
1690-99	67	77	72	10	23	10	8	3	0
1700-09	75	84	75	23	32	9	14	2	0
1710-19	80	85	78	48	43	15	19	7	0
1720-29	83	90	75	44	54	23	19	2	0
1730-39	78	91	83	54	72	28	30	13	6
1740-49	91	97	92	72	73	48	48	25	11
1750-59	83	96	77	58	60	48	25	27	10
1760-69	89	90	85	63	66	26	21	15	8

	Beehives	Skins	Fishing Items	Cider Items	Steel-yards	Plantation Tools	Plows, Harrows	Spinning Wheels	Cards
1660-79	0	6	12	27	35	29	3	0	3
1680-89	0	11	9	30	36	38	2	4	2
1690-99	3	10	10	39	21	49	8	10	5
1700-09	0	18	11	41	39	45	7	9	14
1710-19	0	17	15	56	28	30	20	15	9

1720-29	4	15	4	48	31	60	40	33	8
1730-39	2	6	13	54	31	52	43	39	26
1740-49	8	9	28	75	50	80	66	63	47
1750-59	15	8	15	67	42	77	44	50	40
1760-69	13	3	19	66	29	71	61	69	39

	Wood-working Tools	Blacksmith Tools	Shoe-maker's Tools	Tailor's Tools	Wedges, Mall Rings	Mills, stones	Powdering Tubs, Milk Pans	Butter Pots, Butter	Churns
1660-79	24	3	0	0	32	35	0	6	0
1680-89	26	0	2	0	30	53	21	4	8
1690-99	15	3	3	8	31	51	18	8	10
1700-09	39	5	2	7	34	59	7	7	0
1710-19	30	4	4	2	35	46	4	2	0
1720-29	23	2	2	0	27	52	15	2	2
1730-39	35	2	6	6	26	56	11	13	6
1740-49	61	2	19	8	38	58	30	25	6
1750-59	46	2	21	10	40	54	19	46	6
1760-69	50	5	16	2	39	44	11	29	5

Hogs were also essential in plantation agriculture. In most decades, over 70 per cent of the plantations had them. Yet cattle outnumbered hogs until the 1730's. In that decade, the number of hogs on the average plantation suddenly rose from 21 to 40, while cattle increased slightly from 22 to 26 (Table 28). Hogs maintained their numerical dominance to the end of the period.

TABLE 28

MEAN NUMBER OF LIVESTOCK PER INVENTORIED ESTATE, 1660-1769

	Cattle	Hogs	Horses	Sheep
1660-79	14.88	11.85	1.68	.62
1680-89	19.47	16.45	2.67	3.63
1690-99	17.00	12.93	2.15	1.48
1700-09	17.22	16.53	2.55	3.96
1710-19	23.55	22.24	4.72	11.50
1720-29	22.56	21.58	4.48	8.04
1730-39	26.78	40.68	5.54	12.80
1740-49	25.85	38.56	5.34	15.27
1750-59	22.33	35.50	5.44	15.75
1760-69	12.20	18.93	4.23	10.56

Hogs may have been predominant after the 1730's, but their numbers, along with cattle, and to a lesser extent sheep and horses, experienced an extraordinary reduction in the 1760's. The cattle and hog populations of All Hallows fell by nearly one-half. Similar reductions in other parts of the Chesapeake would help explain the marked decline in beef and pork exports between 1755 and 1768.[1] This decimation of cattle and hogs during the 1760's seems to have been the result of exceedingly scanty grass and fodder, caused by cold winters and prolonged drought. In the spring of 1768, an item in the Maryland Gazette proclaimed that the Winter was remarkably cold and "as yet we have but little Appearance of Vegetation," which caused much distress among farmers and planters whose hay and fodder was exhausted.[2] The Spring and Summer of 1769 were quite dry, and as of August third "many Parts of the Province . . . have scarcely had a Drop of Rain since May."[3]

---

[1]The agricultural historian L. C. Gray observed that Virginia exports of beef and pork declined from 30,000 barrels in 1755 to 4,573 in 1768. Gray questioned the accuracy of these figures, but they are buttressed by the evidence presented here. Gray, History of Agriculture, I, 209-10.

[2]Maryland Gazette, April 7, 1768. [3]Ibid., August 3, 1769.

Yet, considering the magnitude of livestock losses in All Hallows, the Maryland records are surprisingly silent. Neighboring Virginians were more vocal. On March 25 of 1766 Landon Carter wrote the following entry into his diary:

> Cattle are now dying with poverty and how should it be other wise? All the winter food gone and no grass yet on the earth.. . . This is the general time of the year when cattle yeild to their poverty; And I cannot see how it can be avoided, as it is impossible to provide food enough for any number of Cattle after such prodigeous drye years . . .[1]

On April 29 of that same year, he put the 1760's in perspective:

> I fear the summer will turn out much like the last; many good shows for rain wear away with only a drop or so. God be merciful to us, we shall all perish with such an other drye year. No one can forsee the consequences of it; but they become evident in the whole creation. Few calves, very few lambs, old creatures and young died, nothing to fatten nay not to feed with, and of Course very little labour to be carryed, so that many shortages will be produced by one drye summer. What then will not 7 do? This is my 7th drye year.[2]

Hogs were fit for little but food, in the form of bacon, pork, and ham, or for lard. Hog meat, however, seems to have been the meat dietary staple. Like cattle, hogs foraged freely in the seventeenth century woods, but as population densities increased:

> the people that live upon the River sides and the plantations being thick together they are forced to give there Hogs a great Deall of Corne to fatt 'em. . . .[3]

Despite corn-feeding and orchard scavenging, hog weights did not improve markedly. Slaughter weights remained at about 100 pounds for hogs of "killable age," which was probably over two years.[4]

In 1656, John Hammond noted that there were "not many sheep; so that mutton is somewhat scarce."[5] In All Hallows, this was especially true before

---

[1]Jack P. Greene, editor, The Diary of Colonel Landon Carter of Sabine Hall (2 vols.; Charlottesville: The University Press of Virginia for the Virginia Historical Society, 1965), I, 290. See also Ben Howard to [Samuel Gist], August 25, 1766, Great Britain, Public Record Office, Audit Office, 13/30, Folder GII.

[2]Greene, The Diary of Colonel Landon Carter, I, 293.

[3]"Narrative of a Voyage to Maryland, 1705-1706," p. 329.

[4]Slaughter weights in the seventeenth century are found in Inventories & Accounts, 6, f. 513; for 1702, Inventories, 22, f. 35; for 1703, AACo Judgments, G, f. 205; for 1737, Inventories, 22, f. 444; for 1759, *ibid.*, 71, f. 60. The weight range was from 80 to 115 pounds. For "killable" ages, see Wills, 21, f. 804.

[5]Hammond, "Leah and Rachel," p. 291. Alsop explained the lack of sheep

1679 when only 3 per cent of all plantations had sheep. The swarm of adoption did not take place until 1710-1719, and the peak of 72 per cent came later in the depressed 1740's (Table 27). This increase in sheep was paralleled by wool cards, spinning wheels (Table 27), and an occasional fulling mill. Planters who lacked access to a fulling mill were treated to do-it-yourself instructions by a correspondent to the Maryland Gazette. He recommended that planters:

> May very easily thicken their Woollen Cloth without much trouble, or any Expence. The way is, when the Cloth comes from the Weaver's to wet it well with stale Urine warm'd, and put into a Trough and trample it a Considerable Time with bare Feet, turning the Cloth often. It will not be amiss to rub the Cloth over with a small quantity of Fullers earth. . . .[1]

"Country cloth" was a frequent entry in the inventories following the depression of 1705-1718.

During the 1760's when cattle and hogs decreased by 46 per cent, sheep declined only by about a third (Table 28). Thus, the average plantation in the 1760's possessed nearly as many sheep as cattle.

Sheep seem to have been penned more regularly than other livestock; and in 1773, William Eddis declared that the severity of Maryland winters compared to Great Britain required the housing of sheep, and was "extremely prejudicial to the growth and improvement of wool," rendering it coarse like a goat's.[2]

Horses rounded out the major animals on the plantation. After 1680, more plantations possessed horses than cattle, hogs, or sheep (Table 27). However, the mean number of horses per plantation was the lowest of the four animals, never exceeding six horses per plantation. In the fall of 1767, a horse distemper was rife in Maryland, and may have accounted for their slight decline.[3] While horses were sometimes used for plowing, their overwhelming function was for transportation, which is considered in the next chapter.

---

in the seventeenth century; they were easy and delectable prey for the wolves; and worse, sheep drew wolves down among the plantations. Otherwise, sheep would thrive in Maryland as well as any place else. Alsop's explanation seems very reasonable, especially with the policy of open range. Later, when wolves were no longer a problem, sheep were reintroduced, but by then the taste for mutton had diminished. George Alsop, "A Character of the Province of Maryland, 1666," Narratives of Early Maryland, p. 347.

[1] Maryland Gazette, November 2, 1746.

[2] Eddis, Letters from America, p. 74. For sheep-penning, see AACo Deeds, RD#2, f. 138; and Prince George's County Inventories, BB#1, f. 231.

[3] Maryland Gazette, October 8, 1767.

Crops

Plantations were not simply tobacco monocrop operations. Planters conducted a mixed farming system that included the omnipresent livestock and a variety of crops such as corn, wheat, peas, and beans in addition to tobacco. The crop and livestock combinations were less diverse in the seventeenth century, when the plantations produced tobacco, livestock, and corn. Afterward, crops became more diversified.

Parish life was tuned to the seasonal rhythm of tobacco culture, but the seventeenth century parish planter subsisted on "Indian corn."

> The Corne of that Cuntry Comonly Called Indian Corne or maise which grows in great Eares as thick as ones wriste and 7 or 8 inches in length with severall rowes of large grains round itt as big allmost as horse beanes grows upon high stalks 7 or 8 foot high joynted like a large banboo Cane with large Broad long leaves like flags groweing out of each joynt and a high tassell att the top beareing four five or six eares a peice of this same Corne itt being I beleive the greatest increase of any grain in the world there comeing five or six hundred from one grain. itt is a pleasant sight to see a feild of this growing before itt become to high itt being planted att an exact distance one way from another in rowes about six foott distance one way and about 5 foott distance the other way. . . . itt is the cheifest Diett they have in the Cuntrey espeshally where there are great ffamilies of Negroos for they Beat itt in a Mortar and gett the husks from itt and then Boyle itt with a Peice of Beefe or salted Pork with some Kidney Beanes . . . they Call it hommony. itt is very harty and what the servants make there Constant food on. . . .[1]

Corn was also fed to hogs, and portions of the stalk were given to cattle. Despite the dietary reliance on corn, less than 35 per cent of the seventeenth century plantations possessed it; evidently, the remaining households relied upon the surpluses of their neighbors. This was certainly possible, since corn yielded magnificently. In 1775, one writer declared that 50 and sometimes 80 bushels could be gleaned from an acre. He exaggereated, and Bordley's estimate of 12 bushels was closer to the truth.[2] Yields per laborer probably averaged about 80-100 bushels. About 1635, a hand was said to produce 100 bushels of corn, 20 bushels of peas and beans, and a crop of tobacco.[3] In 1669, a figure of 50 barrels or 250 bushels was cited.[4] In Anne Arundel County in 1736, four hands and an overseer produced 80-90 barrels of corn or 400-450 bushels, plus

---

[1]"Narrative of a Voyage to Maryland, 1705-1706," pp. 335-36.

[2]American Husbandry, p. 188. John Beale Bordley, A Summary View of the Courses of Crops in the Husbandry of England and Maryland; with a Comparison of their Products; and a System of Improved Courses Proposed for Farms in America (Philadelphia: n.p., 1784), p. 11.

[3]Gray, History of Agriculture, I, 27. [4]Ibid.

a good crop of tobacco;[1] each hand thus averaged 80 to 90 bushels of corn. While corn production per laborer was about 80 to 100 bushels, annual corn consumption per person, came to 15 bushels or less.[2] Consequently, the labor of one person produced the subsistence for five to seven persons; and the corn-producing plantations, constituting only 20 to 35 per cent in the seventeenth century, met subsistence needs and may have produced a small surplus.

The production of corn for subsistence and trade used more acreage than tobacco production--an ironic twist in a region we have come to know as the "tobacco coast." Each laborer raising maize cared for six to seven acres, that is if we assume per labor yields of 80 bushels and per acre yields of 12 bushels. Tobacco, by contrast, took up three to four acres per laborer.

Tobacco, corn, cattle, hogs, and horses--these were the mainstays of parish plantations down through 1710. But sweeping changes soon transformed this agrarian complex. Crop and livestock diversification and the addition of household manufactures and repair activities were the main ingredients of change.

Wheat cultivation increased markedly between 1700 and 1740. Before 1710, wheat appeared in 10 per cent or less of the parish inventories. By 1740-1749, nearly half listed wheat (Table 27). Wheat, sown broadcast and not in hills, demanded new tillage implements; and plows and harrows increased among plantations, especially after 1720. Harvesting scythes appeared on 12 to 15 per cent of the plantations between 1730 and 1749.[3]

The addition of wheat to the agrarian complex unfolded in two stages. The more dramatic shift occurred during the 1730's and 1740's, when brisk markets in the West Indies and southern Europe translated into widespread adoption of

---

[1] AACo Judgments, IB#1, f. 488.

[2] David C. Klingaman, "The Significance of Grain in the Development of the Tobacco Colonies," Journal of Economic History, XXIX (June, 1969), 273. Klingaman's consumption estimate is about 11 bushels of corn per capita for the 1760's and 1770's. In the seventeenth century, servant freedom dues included 5 barrels, or fifteen bushels of corn; this would maintain him for a full year. Abbot E. Smith, Colonists in Bondage: White Servitude and Convict Labor in America 1607-1776 (Chapel Hill: University of North Carolina Press, 1947, reprinted by Peter Smith, Gloucester, Mass., 1965), pp. 239-40. Alsop, "A Character of the Province of Maryland," p. 358.

[3] Gray seems to suggest, incorrectly, that the scythe was virtually unknown before the American Revolution, and the sickle was the implement used for wheat harvest. Gray, History of Agriculture, I, 170.

wheat farming in All Hallows and the Chesapeake generally.[1] Yet this second stage of mass adoption built on earlier efforts to cultivate wheat. The initial shift, prompted by ecological concerns, occurred ten to twenty years before. By 1700, the system of intensive shifting cultivation had been practiced for nearly half a century. The virgin forests, so esteemed by tobacco planters, had been pretty-well cleared away, and they had little choice but to cultivate the "old fields."[2] Such was the case for the typical 100-acre plantation, occupied and continuously cultivated by one laborer since 1650. The laborer, rotating fields every three years, would have used up over two-thirds of his land ("old fields") by 1720. Adding more labor to the plantation simply accelerated the creation of old fields. Some planters, thus, had to recultivate their old fields, some of which contained second growth forest, others shrubby vegetation, and others still, a thick grass cover. To prepare these old fields for cultivation, the planters made greater use of the plow as a supplement to the traditional plantation tools of hoe and axe. The traditional tools proved ineffective where wild grasses were dense. Even in a young second growth forest, planters more and more used plows. There, large trees were fewer, and as a consequence tree stumps did not greatly impede plowing. Plowed fields, encouraged by old field vegetation, gave the planter more cropping options: he could cultivate hilled Indian plants, such as tobacco and corn, or sow the broadcast English grains as wheat. Some did the latter in the first two decades of the eighteenth century.

Wheat had another ecological asset; its seasonal regime harmonized with that of tobacco. Wheat was sown in September and October, after the harvest of tobacco and before the harvest of late corn. Wheat required little care over the winter and spring, and the June-July harvest came after tobacco's transplanting and before its harvest. By cultivating wheat along with his tobacco, the planter spread his labor more evenly over the year.

Wheat was a more extensive crop than tobacco or corn. One acre of the small grain produced six to twelve bushels.[3] While a family farmer specializing in wheat may have produced 100 bushels, few parish planters came close to this

---

[1] Ibid., p. 167; Klingaman, "The Significance of Grain," pp. 270-71.

[2] "Narrative of a Voyage to Maryland, 1705-1706," p. 329; CSPCS, 1706-08, XXIII, 194.

[3] Bordley estimated 6 bushels of wheat per acre; Bordley, A Summary View of the Courses of Crops, p. 11.

figure. The largest wheat entry in parish inventories measured 241 bushels in 1757.[1] This estate possessed twelve Negro men, each producing about 20 bushels on two to three acres.

The addition of wheat and sheep to many plantations contributed to a thoroughly mixed farming system, yet one that continued to rely on the commercial staple of tobacco. Some plantations went even further down the road of agricultural diversification. Fruit orchards, cider, oats, rye, barley, and flax appeared with greater regularity.

During the fifth and sixth decades of the eighteenth century, about one-fourth of the planters raised the small grains of oats, barley and rye (Table 27). Oats were fed to horses, but their small numbers probably placed limits on the cultivation of this small grain.

Nor was barley production widespread, perhaps because the manufacture of beer from barley made little headway, "for few of them are come to malting their Corn [grain] of any kind. . . ."[2] The chief competition for barley beer came from cider and brandy, produced from the ubiquitous orchards of apples and peaches.[3] After 1700, cider, cider casks, and cider-making apparatus were represented in over 40 per cent of all inventories (Table 27).

The diffusion of flax was less successful. A maximum of 11 per cent of the planters produced flax in the 1740's, and this despite great publicity and encouragement of its growth and of linen manufacture. The county court awarded prizes for the best linen manufactured within the county.[4] Books were imported from Ireland on the art of flax-making and linen manufacture, some of which were excerpted in the Maryland Gazette.[5] Despite the notoriety and the cash reward from the county court, All Hallows planters generally ignored this crop.

---

[1]Inventories, 64, ff. 226-49.

[2]"Itinerant Observations in America, 1745-1746," Collections of the Georgia Historical Society, IV (1878), 34.

[3]Ibid.; Jones, "Maryland in 1699," p. 370. On Anne Arundel Manor in 1767, 45 of 70 parcels contained apple trees; Audit Office 12/79, ff. 134-35.

[4]AACo Judgments, IB#2, f. 173; ibid., IB#1, f. 242; ibid., IB#4, f. 162.

[5]Maryland Gazette, March 3, 1748. Ibid., July 26, 1745; ibid., March 9, 1749.

Crafts

Parish planters complemented agricultural diversification with improved capabilities in home manufacture and repair. They manufactured "country cloth," made possible by the abundance of spinning wheels, cards, sheep, and flax. Planters, though continuing to rely on weavers, conducted many operations in woolen manufacture, including fulling, at home. Wood construction and the repair of wood products also fell within the domain of most planters, who after 1740 owned carpenter's and cooper's tools, saws, wedges, and mall rings (Table 27). Many planters, too, ground their corn and wheat in small-scale, inexpensive hand mills, costing usually less than £1.5.

Summary

The typical plantation after 1740 contained a variety of crafts, crops, and livestock. The planters and their slaves had the equipment and the skills to fashion wood, textiles, leather, shoes, and in some cases, metal. They could repair them also. Similarly, the planters diversified their food supply through the addition of sheep, wheat, other small grains, beehives, and fishing gear. What the planters could not provide for themselves, they found in the community of plantations.

Somewhere between the 1720's and 1740's, parish planters silently, and perhaps unconsciously, slipped from an era of parasitism. Dependence on English imports and European markets diminished. The manifold adjustments taking place on many individual plantations had created a more flexible settlement --one which successfully coped with the vicissitudes of a trans-Atlantic economy.

Types of Plantations

Parish plantations went through three phases between 1660 and 1769. The specialized, more rigid plantations of the seventeenth century (to 1710) produced mainly tobacco, corn, cattle, and hogs. A period of experimentation between 1710 and 1739 introduced new crops, animals and crafts. Some took hold and became integral parts of the evolving plantations; others were abandoned. Experimentation had largely ended by about 1740. Subsequently, planters adopted the successful experiments of an earlier generation. Large numbers of plantations became diversified, flexible, and large in scale.

Two causes appear to have been decisive in the tripartite evolution of the plantation. Fundamental is the depression stimulus toward potential self-sufficiency. The very severe depressions of 1705-1718 and 1740-1749 correspond closely with the major turning points in plantation evolution. Another factor in this evolution is the growth of the labor force on plantations. Servants and slaves often provided the manpower to perform the new activities; however, the role of labor can be overemphasized. Bond labor was not a prerequisite for these activities; indeed, many potentially self-sufficient plantations had neither servant nor slave. But others did, and it is this variety among plantations that now deserves attention.

Within each phase of plantation evolution, there existed great variety among the rural settlements, their labor force, and their activities. As the plantations evolved, this diversity expanded, plantation types proliferated, and representatives of these types diminished. Distinctive plantation types were obscured by this diffuseness.

This variety can be illustrated by classifying individual plantations according to their phase of evolution, their index of potential self-sufficiency, and their servile or bond labor of all ages. The purpose of the classification is the identification of differences in the functions and appearance of plantations; and therefore, it makes little difference whether the plantation dimensions are statistically dependent or independent. In fact, there exists a moderate correlation (.46) between labor and potential self-sufficiency. The classification technique is divisional, which does not require statistical independence. Using the divisional technique, the two dimensions of labor and potential self-sufficiency for all 494 parish estates are arrayed, and division or cutting points are established at noticeable changes in the frequencies. The resulting classes for labor are 0, 1-3, 4-7, 8-13, 14-20, and greater than 21. For potential self-sufficiency, the classes are 0, 1-4, 5-13, 14-20, 21-27, and greater than 28. This produces a six by six table, with thirty-six possible plantation types (Table 29). Four hundred sixty-eight plantations remain in the sample after the exclusion of 24 inventories showing no evidence of primary agricultural investment. Dividing the sample into the three phases, we have 158 inventories, or 33.8 per cent, before 1710; 144, or 30.8 per cent, 1710-1739; and 166, or 35.5 per cent, 1739-1769.

The classification of parish plantations reveals several interesting patterns. In the first place, the variety of plantations from 1660 to 1769 is encompassed by twenty-six of the thirty-six theoretical plantation types. Furthermore, twelve, or one-third, of these types account for 94.9 per cent of all parish plantations. A large number of plantations fall into just three types, II,

III, and IX, scoring from 1 to 13 on potential self-sufficiency and having 0 to 3 bond laborers. These small plantation types account for 49.4 per cent of all the plantations. Next are the middling plantations, types X, XV, and XVI, ranging from 14 to 20 on potential self-sufficiency and 1 to 7 laborers. Together, the three groups contain 19.2 per cent of the plantations. Another 26.3 per cent of the plantations fall into a motley collection of six plantation types, IV, XXI, XXII, XXIII, XXIX, and XXXIV. These tend to be larger plantations especially with regard to potential self-sufficiency.

To describe this variety of settlements, tidewater residents used one term, the plantation. Their failure to conceptualize and denote types of plantations seems to be tied up with the evolution of the plantations themselves. The increase in the number of types and the decrease in their representatives made the attachment of a new term a difficult task. Eighteenth century planters observed fewer clear-cut, identifiable types of plantations, if we define these as types containing at least 10 per cent of all plantations within a specific phase.

Four identifiable plantation types (II, III, IX, and XV) occurred in the years before 1710; and they accounted for 75.3 per cent of the period's plantations. Phase two (1710-1739) had three identifiable types (II, III, and IX) with 54.2 per cent of the plantations. All three of these types were identifiable in the first phase as well. Finally, the third phase (post-1739) included only two identifiable types (III and X), containing 31.3 per cent of the plantations. Put simply, plantation variety increased; concentration among types diminished. Sharp divisions between large and small plantations were further obscured by numerous intermediate plantation types, especially after 1739.

Thus, the differences among plantations were quantitative and not qualitative. The great plantations of more than twenty-one laborers and a corresponding number of activities made up only 2.1 per cent of the plantations after 1739. And they differed only in degree from the middling plantations, and they in turn from the small. This plantation continuum suggests that some ordinary planters could make it to the top; and indeed some did. But the bulk of the small planters and tenants would have recognized that the continuum was nothing more than a statistical illusion, created by the mass exodus of their socio-economic peers after 1720. Had they stayed, the grand plantation and the impoverished tenant farm might have found their way into the parish vocabulary.

TABLE 29

PLANTATION TYPES AND PROPORTIONS OF PLANTATIONS IN EACH TYPE, FOR T) 1660-1769, AND 1) PRIOR TO 1710, 2) 1710-39, 3) AND POST 1739

Potential Self-sufficiency	Number of Laborers		
	0	1-3	4-7
0	1)100 2 2) 0 3) 0 T) .4 I		
1-4	1) 61.0 59 2) 25.4 3) 13.6 T) 12.6 II	1)33.3 9 2)22.2 3)44.4 T) 1.9 VIII	1) 0 3 2)33 3)66.7 T) .6 XIV
5-13	1) 33.3 100 2) 38.0 3) 29.0 T) 21.4 III	1)47.2 72 2)34.7 3)18.1 T)15.4 IX	1)51.6 31 2)19.4 3)29.0 T) 6.6 XIX
14-20	1) 21.0 19 2) 36.8 3) 42.1 T) 4.1 IV	1)15.2 33 2)15.2 3)69.6 T) 7.1 X	1)19.2 26 2)30.8 3)50.0 T) 5.6 XVI
21-27	1) 0 2 2) 50.0 3) 50.0 T) .4 V	1) 0 3 2)33.3 3)66.7 T) .6 XI	1)14.3 7 2)57.1 3)42.9 T) 1.5 XVII
28+			
Total	38.89T	25.00T	14.32T

Note: The number in the northeast corner is the plantation frequency for each type. The Roman numeral on the lower right is the identification number for each type. The numbers 1, 2, and 3 on the left indicate the proportion of plantations contributed by the three phases, pre-1710, 1710-39, and post-1739 respectively, to that type.

T indicates the proportion of all plantations contained within the type.

TABLE 29--Continued

Number of Laborers						
8-13		14-20		21+		Total
						.42T
						15.39T
1) 55.6 2) 33.3 3) 11.1 T) 3.9	18 XXI	1) 0 2) 50.0 3) 50.0 T) .4	2 XXVII	1) 16.7 2) 16.7 3) 66.6 T) 1.3	6 XXXIII	48.93T
1) 14.3 2) 35.7 3) 50.0 T) 3.0	14 XXII	1) 25.0 2) 25.0 3) 50.0 T) 1.7	8 XXVIII	1) 30.8 2) 53.9 3) 15.4 T) 2.8	13 XXXIV	24.15T
1) 0 2) 23.1 3) 76.9 T) 2.8	13 XXIII	1) 0 2) 30.8 3) 69.2 T) 2.8	13 XXIX	1) 0 2) 12.1 3) 88.9 T) 1.9	9 XXXV	10.04T
1) 0 2) 0 3)100 T) .6	3 XXIV	1) 0 2) 0 3)100 T) .2	1 XXX	1) 0 2) 0 3)100 T) .2	1 XXXVI	1.07T
10.47T		5.13T		.21T		100T (n=468)

Plantation Structures

The focus of daily life was the assemblage of plantation buildings which sheltered residence, work places, and crops. The typical planter required a dwelling house for the family; perhaps an austere residence for his several servants or slaves; a few outbuildings housing craft and agricultural implements; and one or more tobacco houses. Schoepf graphically captured the scene in the 1780's:

> A plantation in Virginia, and also in the lower parts of Maryland, has often more the appearance of a small village, by reason of the many separate small buildings, which taken all together would at times hardly go to make a single roomy and commodious house. Here are living-rooms, bed-chambers, guest-chambers, store-rooms, kitchens, quarters for the slaves, and who knows what else, commonly so many small, separate, badly kept cabins of wood, without glass in the windows, of the structure and solidity of a house of cards. This plan is not so much the consequence of any particular taste, as of necessity. In the settlement of a new plantation there is concern for only the most indispensable buildings, and a hastily built block-house is all that is needed at first; but by degrees, the family increasing and more land brought into cultivation, greater convenience becomes an item. And thus are built gradually a good many small houses and cabins, commonly without the assistance of carpenters, patched together by the people themselves and their negroes. This being an easier method than to put together a large house all at once, one often sees such little houses growing up where there is neither material nor capital for bringing them together in one solid house. In such cabins . . . all the evidences of negligence are to be remarked. . . .[1]

At the center of this cluster of plantation buildings was the dwelling house. Seventeenth century houses were described as "Pleasant in their building, which although are but one story besides the loft, and built of wood, yet contrived so delightful, that your ordinary houses in England are not so handsome . . ."[2] But, in 1678, Lord Baltimore denigrated them as "very meane and Little, and generally after the manner of the meanest farm houses in England."[3] The occasional room lists in the inventories confirm the small size of houses. The inventory of William Burges, a planter-merchant with an estate of over £3000 sterling, listed the largest number of rooms and buildings; included were a "new room," a closet, a parlor, and a chamber. Probable outbuildings were a cellar, cider house and store, milk house, and a kitchen.[4] Altogether, eleven

---

[1]Johann D. Schoepf, Travels in the Confederation, 1783-1784, II, 32-33.

[2]Hammond, "Leah and Rachel," p. 297.

[3]CSPCS, 1677-80, X, 226.

[4]Inventories & Accounts, 18, ff. 89-108.

inventories, taken before 1690, listed an average of 2.7 house rooms and 2.2 outbuildings per estate. The outbuildings consisted of milk houses, cider houses, quarters, kitchens, stores, and cellars. These plantations, belonging as they did to the more prosperous sort, contained a dwelling house and a couple of outbuildings. The majority had even less.

The rudeness and paucity of plantation structures endured into the eighteenth century, a fact well-illustrated in the 1767 survey of Anne Arundel Manor.[1] The manor encompassed 10,898.5 acres, divided into seventy tenant parcels. On these parcels, there were 416 buildings, or an average of 5.94 on each. One parcel contained 17 buildings, the maximum number in the parish. Dwelling houses, constructed of clapboard, log, or frame, comprised 18.9 per cent of all buildings. Of these, 22.8 per cent were of "log'd" construction. Rectangular shapes prevailed with the typical length being 20 to 24 feet and width, 12 to 20 feet. The largest house measured 36 feet by 28 feet. Only a few of them had either chimneys or planked floors.

The manor also contained twenty-one quarters, which a contemporary described as "a Number of Huts or Hovels, built at some distance from the Mansion House; where the Negros reside with their wives and Families, and cultivate at vacant Times the little Spots allow'd them."[2] The small quarters of the manor ranged from 12 feet by 15 feet to 16 feet by 16 feet, which made them invariably smaller than the dwelling houses on the same holding. Squarish shapes of the quarters contrasted with the more rectangular arrangement of the dwelling houses of the white population; however, one quarter measured 25 by 10 and this rectangular structure may have functioned as a narrow barracks.

The manor contained 190 outbuildings with greatly varied functions. One hundred of these were simply designated as "outbuildings." The rest included 34 kitchens, 18 corn houses, 4 meat houses, 3 hen houses, 6 milk houses, 2 stables, 1 shack, 2 cellars, a bake house, and a grist mill. The average dwelling house, 79 in all, had 2.4 outbuildings nearby.

After the miscellaneous outbuildings, tobacco houses were the most numerous structures. Indeed, after travelling southward and passing through All Hallows Parish in 1777, Hazard recorded that tobacco houses became more abundant after South River.[3] Thirty per cent of the manor structures were to-

---

[1]Audit Office 12/79, ff. 134-35.

[2]"Itinerant Observations in America, 1745-1746," p. 37.

[3]Shelley, ed., "Ebenezer Hazard's Travels through Maryland in 1777," p. 50.

bacco houses. Invariably rectangular, the dimensions of tobacco houses ranged narrowly in width from 20 to 26 feet, but considerably in length from 30 to 60 feet. The modal size was about 40 feet by 22 or 24 feet. For keen planters, the length of tobacco houses provided a ready-reckoner, with each linear foot equivalent to between 55 and 80 pounds of tobacco.[1] They reckoned a typical tobacco house of 40 feet at 2, 200 to 3, 200 pounds, approximately the output of one to two laborers.

The total parish scene, the buildings, the fields, the landscape, was not pleasing to the eye. Rude dwelling houses with dirt floors and without chimneys; unpainted tobacco houses, some delapidated; a disproportionate share of buildings "old" and "not worth repairs" compared to "new" buildings (15 per cent and 5. 3 per cent respectively on the manor); abandoned old fields; all told of landscape negligence and atrophy, or so it seemed to casual observers. But travellers and not a few historians missed the point: in a mobile agricultural system, the deterioration of buildings and land was integral to the functioning of the system. Unkempt old fields restored soil fertility. In stump-littered tobacco fields, laborers hoed around the hulks and thus saved the expense of rooting them out. Tobacco houses were semi-permanent facilities, relocated with the shifting fields. The planter either abandoned the old tobacco house or dismantled it for reconstruction near the new field. Tobacco houses were as transient as the fields, and painting them, building them to last, or beautifying them was simply irrational.[2] Tidewater landscapes, atrophied and in disarray, sacrificed esthetics for economics and ecology. To infer laziness, slovenliness, and negligence from these landscapes is to build an interpretation with "the structure and solidity of a house of cards."

Plantation Distribution

Parish plantations were always scattered. In seeming defiance of the Indian menace, the seventeenth century planters straggled their settlements along the estuaries. And along none of them were there as many as fifty houses in the space of thirty miles.[3] One-quarter of a mile or more separated near

---

[1]Testamentary Proceedings, 3, f. 225; ibid., 6, f. 164; Prince George's County Inventories, TB#1, f. 225.

[2]A further obstacle was that buildings decayed more rapidly in Maryland than they had in England, and this raised repair cost, or so claimed Governor Francis Nicholson in 1697; CSPCS, 1696-97, XV, 421.

[3]CSPCS, 1677-80, X, 226.

neighbors.[1] The isolation associated with dispersed settlement diminished toward the close of the seventeenth century. Axe-wielding planters attacked the forest and created a more open landscape which exposed neighbors.[2] And plantations along the estuaries were occasionally "thick together" as population densities increased.[3] Nonetheless, settlement dispersal persisted. In 1765 and thereafter, tidewater plantations were described as "scatered"[4] and "widely separated."[5] By the American Revolution, with parish densities exceeding four households per square mile and the woodlands fast disappearing, travellers made no mention of clustering either along the estuaries or the highways.

Two principal factors governed plantation dispersal: a liberal land policy and the evolution of the plantations. The Calverts gave land freely to all transporters of Maryland immigrants up until 1683. Freed servants were also entitled to fifty acres. Virtually every white man had the "rights" to a good-sized parcel of private land, and many of them surveyed their land along the estuaries and located their houses some distance from neighbors. The Calverts encouraged the further spread of settlement and of plantation dispersal by requiring that these landholdings had to be "seated" in order to guarantee the title to the land.[6] Undoubtedly, the proprietor aimed this directive at large land speculators, but it encouraged all to settle on their far-flung holdings, or risk their loss.

The Calverts' liberal land policy withered away in the 1680's, yet plantation dispersal was reinforced by changes among the plantations. The diversification of plantation activities and the expanded potential for self-sufficiency made the planters less dependent on exchange with complementary sites. As the imperative for external exchange diminished the planters worried less about the location of their plantations relative to others. Plantation siting decisions depended more and more on internal plantation constraints, and less on exchange. The essential constraints on siting were tobacco production and the

---

[1]Herrman, Virginia and Maryland. [2]"Maryland in 1699," p. 367.

[3]"Narrative of a Voyage to Maryland, 1705-06," p. 329.

[4]"Journal of a French Traveller," p. 76.

[5]Clayton C. Hall, The Lord's Baltimore and the Maryland Palatinate (Baltimore: John Murphy Company, 1902), p. 202, quoting L'Abbe Robin, Noveau Voyage dans l'Amerique Septentrianale.

[6]Marshall Harris, Origin of the Land Tenure System in the United States (Ames: The Iowa State College Press, 1953), pp. 216-19.

system of shifting cultivation. Planters tried to minimize the movement of labor, materials, and crops between the dwelling house and the fields, which shifted every three to four years; they preferred a central location within the landholding. Distances between plantations tended to increase. The central siting of plantations, by coincidence or design, placed the plantations in salubrious locations. This was so because most of the holdings stretched inland from the estuaries toward the drainage divides, and the central location occurred at higher elevations. Schoepf observed that such sites were initially preferred because they avoided unhealthy, low and swampy areas, and later because of custom and vanity.[1] He failed to consider that these locations gave the best access to all parts of the plantation.

Summation

The planters of All Hallows adapted to an erratic economy of boom and bust. They diversified crops and livestock and added a host of activities and implements that made them less dependent on European imports. The critical period for the evolving plantations came between 1700 and 1740. Ironically, at the same time, the parish merchants moved in the opposite direction when they established a highly specialized, if short-lived, urban settlement. The inevitable was played out in the devastating depression of the 1740's; plantations retrenched leaving the merchants of London Town high and dry.

As the town tottered, the dispersed plantation gained new strength. The scattered pattern of settlement, a legacy of the seventeenth century land system and planter desires for estuarine access, was reinforced by the more self-sufficient nature of plantation activities. Though commerce in tobacco remained as the chief source of income, planters turned inward toward the center of their land, and away from the European entrepôts.

The typical plantation complex was unpretentious and unattractive. Several small, unpainted wooden outbuildings clustered near a modest dwelling house of clapboards or frame. The entire house measured less than two typical living rooms in modern suburban homes. Another residence, or "quarter," housed the several servants or slaves. Tobacco and corn grew on perhaps ten acres of the plantation. The rest of the land was wooded or "old fields" where the livestock ranged freely. Adjacent to the tobacco field stood a narrow, unpainted tobacco house, about forty feet long and holding the tobacco produced by

---

[1]Schoepf, Travels in the Confederation, II, 360-61.

two or three laborers. Nearby, a second tobacco house, "not worth repairs," marked lonely vigil over an unkempt, but recuperating, old field. The scene attracted the scorn and contempt of all who delighted in the sprightly country-sides of England or the colonies northward. But then, they never did understand the fluid agricultural system of the tobacco coast!

CHAPTER VI

ROUTES, TRANSPORT MODES, AND EXCHANGE

As a direct consequence of settlement dispersal and the tobacco economy, parish planters were compelled to make three major adjustments in their travel behavior. First, they adopted the horse and the road as the main means of travel, and they relaxed English standards of travel distance. Second, they meshed their activities and travel with the seasonal regime of tobacco culture. And lastly, the planters adjusted exchange patterns over the long-term in response to the pulsating tobacco economy.

Transport Modes and Routes

The travel behavior of Chesapeake planters made accommodations to the pattern of settlement dispersal. Plantation scattering demanded a willingness to travel longer distances than were customary in England. Stated briefly, the planters' travel behavior became more elastic.

Englishmen were occasionally confounded by these spatial adjustments. One visitor remarked that Maryland planters:

> if they know a Man has a Gallon of Brandy by him they will goe halfe a dozen honest ffellows to pay him a vissitt and never leave him teel all be out tho the[y] goe tenn Miles an end which is no more to them then if itt were butt to the next Tavern here.[1]

In 1726, a hapless Anglican minister, unaccustomed to tidewater spatial realities, was scrutinized by his vestrymen on Kent Island, across the bay from All Hallows.

> Our parishes here differ widely from those in England, where the sound of a bell gives certain notice of the time of divine service, and half an hour or less will suffice to walk: but here we live from the church some fourteen or fifteen miles, so that it is hardly possible to congregate by the time used in England, which some of the principal men in our island had very mildly and with great respect laid before our Minister, but he is so far from being prevailed on by it, that since if there be only himself and his man servant, he will begin the service, not granting people time to ride to Church, from such

---

[1]"Narrative of a Voyage to Maryland, 1705-1706," p. 329.

> an abject distance, by which means to our great grief we are deprived of the benefit of the service of the church.[1]

Accommodation to the settlement system of tidewater thus required a relaxation of distance and time, and a willingness to travel.

The Horse, the Road, and the Ferry

Settlement dispersal in the tidewater Chesapeake encouraged sweeping changes in transport arrangements. One of these changes was the institution of southern hospitality, which was noted by almost every traveller between 1656 and 1775.[2] More far-reaching was the commitment to the horse, the road, and the ferry as the modes and media of transport.

There is a long-standing myth that seventeenth century planters in the tidewater region travelled almost exclusively via water craft, such as boats, canoes, and larger vessels. The evidence from All Hallows Parish does not finally lay the myth to rest, but it does produce a finer sense of proportion.

Boats appeared infrequently in the parish inventories from 1660 to 1769. The peak decade came in the 1680's when 22.6 per cent of all estates possessed either boats, canoes, flats, shallops, or sloops. But this proportion fell to 13.6 per cent for the entire colonial period. These low levels of water craft ownership, never exceeding one-fourth of the plantations, suggest that the parishioners relied on other modes of transport. Indeed, some travellers avoided the bay "highway" even on long-distance journeys. As early as the 1670's estate administrators from Anne Arundel County made the long journey to the prerogative court at St. Mary's City by land and over ferries at South and Patuxent rivers.[3] The existence of these ferries and ferriage rates implies that others followed a similar route to the southern capital.

Water vehicles had several disadvantages compared to their chief competitor, the horse. First, they required access to estuaries; and by the 1670's parish settlement had spread away from the estuaries and up onto the drainage divides. Second, the costs of water transport probably exceeded those for the horse; though for long-hauls, such as to St. Mary's, water transport probably cost less.[4] Compared to the horse, water craft required more skill and more

---

[1]Perry, Papers Relating to the History of the Church in Maryland, p. 257.

[2]Eddis, Letters from America, p. 57. Hammond, "Leah and Rachel," p. 294.

[3]Inventories & Accounts, 2, ff. 228-29; ibid., 5, ff. 279-80.

[4]Travelling from central Anne Arundel County to St. Mary's City and back

work in propulsion. Maintenance costs were greater also, since horses grazed cheaply in the woods. Boats had only one clear-cut cost advantage over horses, and that was in initial capital outlay. In the 1660's and 1670's, an eight- to twelve-foot boat with oars and sails cost about £1.5 to £3 sterling; while a horse averaged between £5.5 and £7 sterling.[1] However, this price differential diminished, and by the 1690's average horse prices had fallen to about £2 sterling.[2] Water transport lost its sole cost advantage for the parish planter.

Horseback riding became the main way of getting about in the parish and in tidewater Maryland. Perhaps the most perceptive remarks on the local transport system issued from men of the cloth, who, travelling to their parishioners for marriages and burials and outlying congregations, came to know it best.[3] The Anglican Reverend Hugh Jones noted in 1699:

> Our soil is generally sandy, free from stone, which makes itt verry convenient for travelling. And we have noe occasion for shoeing our horses except in frosty weather. And what with the goodnesse of our little horses and with the smoothnesse of the roads, we can travell upon occasion fifty miles in a summer afternoon, and sometimes a hundred miles in a day. Indeed, our miles are not soe longe as in England, yet they are measured miles.[4]

For the Catholic priest, Joseph Mosley, in the 1770's, life pivoted on his horse and saddle. "Our rides are constant and extensive . . . I often ride about 300 miles a week, and never a week but I ride 150, or 200 . . ."[5] For such a life, nothing was so important as a good saddle and horse. Thanking his sister for

---

took about six days, either by boat or by horse and ferry. By whichever mode, the traveller was allowed thirty pounds of tobacco per diem; however, ferriage charges could be added in as an expense of the estate. Thus, travelling by land was probably more expensive than by water for this long haul. Inventories & Accounts, 4, f. 359; ibid., 5, f. 280.

[1]For boat values, see Testamentary Proceedings, 5, ff. 343-45, 420; ibid., 2, ff. 24-30; Inventories & Accounts, 1, ff. 92-97. The value of horses appears in V. J. Wyckoff, "Seventeenth Century Maryland Prices," Agricultural History, XII (July, 1938), 308.

[2]Ibid.

[3]For marriages, see Eddis, Letters from America, p. 58. Burial plots on dwelling plantations appear frequently in deeds and wills. Also, the small number of colonial graves in the All Hallows' cemetery is testimony that even in death there was dispersal.

[4]"Maryland in 1699," pp. 367-68.

[5]Reverend Edward I. Devitt, S.J., ed., "Letters of Father Joseph Mosley, S.J. and Some Extracts from his Diary (1757-1786)," American Catholic Historical Society of Philadelphia, Records, XVII (1906), 190-91.

the saddle she had sent from England, Mosley endeared himself:

> It is an excellent one; I've made it groan for many a long day under my load . . . When it is present with me, in my solitary ride, it brings your frequent benevolence . . . to my mind.[1]

But it was the peculiar horses of Maryland which made such journeys possible. Mosley called them "everlasters":

> Our horses in this country go so easy that a ride of 50 miles, perhaps, won't tire a man so much as 20 or 30 with your horses in England . . . they make nothing of travelling 60 miles in a day, which few horses in England can perform . . .[2]

The horse had prevailed over the boat by the 1680's. In that decade, 81 per cent of the parish planters possessed at least one horse on their plantations. And from 1660 onward, saddles and bridles appeared more frequently in estate inventories than did water craft. Horseowners rose sharply from 47 per cent to 81 per cent between the 1670's and 1680's. The increase in saddles and bridles was most marked in the 1690's, with a rise from 28 per cent to 49 per cent. Horses also hauled carts and, much more rarely, wagons. Carts and cart wheels, infrequently recorded in the inventories before 1710, began to appear in larger numbers as agrarian diversification made headway; another substantial increase occurred in the 1740's (Table 30).

TABLE 30

PROPORTION OF PLANTATIONS POSSESSING SELECTED ITEMS OF TRANSPORT, 1660-1769

	Water Craft of all kinds	Horses	Saddles & Bridles	Carts & Cart Wheels
1660-79	15	47	21	9
1680-89	23	81	28	8
1690-99	18	77	49	5
1700-09	11	84	46	9
1710-19	13	85	54	28
1720-29	10	90	58	23
1730-39	4	91	56	28
1740-49	16	97	67	44
1750-59	13	96	56	50
1760-69	15	90	65	63

[1] Ibid., p. 204.

[2] Ibid., p. 191.

The network of parish roads evolved loosely and with little aforethought. Roads were created and maintained with an eye toward immediacy, necessity, and least cost. Not a few planters built their own roads, after submitting a reasonable justification to the county court. The ease of this procedure, plus the low costs of construction, meant a proliferation of roads in a maze-like network.

The best parish roads were those under public jurisdiction. The Assembly in an act of 1696 ordered these roads "cleared and grubbed fitt for Travalling Twenty foote wide" and road intersections clearly marked with tree-notched road signs, indicating the directions to the court house, ferries, churches, and to Annapolis.[1] Administrative responsibility for the public roads fell to the county courts. By 1704, the Anne Arundel County court had delegated the task to appointed overseers of the highways. These political appointees, usually unschooled in road building, supervised road construction and maintenance. They took their orders from the court, and then summoned or "warned" taxable persons in their district to work on the public roads.[2] Evidently, some of the citizenry openly refused to heed the overseers' summons; of 23 taxables "warn'd in" by the overseer for South River Hundred in 1719, only 9 appeared.[3] The public had better things to do than road work, and their attitudes made the overseer's job an unpleasant one. Perhaps the court understood his problems because they admonished him gently when the roads were out of repair. But his failure to keep roads cleared and bridges repaired occasionally produced a presentment from the grand jury.[4]

The road network contained also many private roads. Private citizens constructed and maintained these roads, after the county court gave its approval.[5] At least that is the way it worked in theory; some private roads, however, were cleared by overseers and by summoned taxables. For example, the court in 1707 ordered the overseer to clear a road from John Gresham Sr.'s dwelling plantation to his other plantation or quarter.[6]

---

[1] Archives of Maryland, XXXVIII, 95-97.

[2] For more detail on overseers of the highway, see Gould, Money and Transportation in Maryland, pp. 122-24.

[3] AACo Judgments, RC, f. 553.

[4] Ibid., DG#1, f. 392. In 1758, James Dick, overseer of Lower Rhode River Hundred, was fined 50 shillings current money for not keeping the bridges in repair. Ibid., ISB#4, f. 506. Also see ibid., f. 598.

[5] Ibid., TB#1, f. 533.

[6] Ibid.; ibid., TB#2, f. 373.

Whether public or private, the administrative procedure for creating a new road was extraordinarily simple. To add, delete, improve, or turn a road, the individual petitioned the county court setting forth the reasons for the change. The court accepted hastily most of these petitions; rarely were they rejected. In cases of indecision, two justices viewed the road and reported their findings back to the court. The procedure of viewing and report became more common as the eighteenth century progressed, perhaps because of complaints such as those of Samuel Chambers who strenuously objected to the road ordered through his plantation without his knowledge.[1]

By ignoring some of the interested parties in a road petition or by hastily granting petitions, the court invited private citizens to circumvent the legal process and to construct roads without court orders. These extra-legal roads, about which we know so little precisely because they contravened the law, were numerous. At least two of these roads grieved Thomas Gassaway, who in 1713 discovered two of them running through his plantation.[2]

Roads, legal and illegal, public and private, proliferated. The problems entailed by this proliferation may have outweighed the gains in access and the ability to respond rapidly to changing economic-geographic conditions. One immediate problem of the liberal road construction policy was enormous route duplication. Sometimes, two, three, or more roads cut across the same plantation, as in the case of beleaguered Thomas Gassaway. In 1740, Rachel Welch complained:

> for sometime past three Publick Roads & but a little Distance Asunder have been made thro her plantation Two of them used only in Summer Season being so wet & Low as to render it useless in the Winter Season & neither of them butt is nearly the Same Distance of Ground as the Old Road . . . & it is a good road Winter or Summer. . . .[3]

Further problems were created by the extraordinary latitude given ordinary men. Overseers were untrained in the art of road-building. The court orders that reached their hands usually specified only that a road was to link two points; exact routing was left to the overseer and to his negotiations with planters along the way. Generally the routing was least cost, avoiding gullies, streams and branches, and wet lands.[4] Within these environmental constraints, overseers sought the most direct route between the two points. Their roads,

---

[1] Ibid., TB#3, f. 275a. [2] Ibid., f. 204a.

[3] Ibid., IB#1, f. 133. Also, ibid., G, f. 677; ibid., TB#3, f. 275a.

[4] The court in 1704 specified that gullies and branches were to be avoided. Ibid., G, f. 327.

wending across private plantations, cornfields, and pastures, contained many turnings along the way and--the traveller's bane--frequent road gates and fences.

To protect their fields from careless travellers, planters installed gates and fences along the roadways through their plantations. Several road gates had been erected in the county by 1718; and they impeded the riding post, according to Evan Jones of the Post Office, who hoped they "will be layd aside for the future."[1] His hopes went for nought, for in 1751, the governor of Maryland deplored the ill-consequences of cross-plantation routing:

> While other nations are improving their Commerce, by opening Canals, and shortening and mending their Roads, we are lengthening ours . . . by Windings and Turnings, and obstructing their Passage with Gates and other Incumbrances . . . this is certainly the proper Time to lay them strait and open. . . .[2]

Nor did this distinguished person have effect; the 1774 journal of Fithian noted 32 gates in travelling from Marlborough through All Hallows to Annapolis--a distance of only 20.75 miles.[3]

Unfortunately for the planters, road gates and fences did not always prevent damage. Neglectful travellers left the gates ajar or broke the fences. In this way, John Gresham, in 1718, lost "to the hogs . . . all of the Corn then planted . . . ," amounting to about 150 barrels.[4] Another claimed the loss of her cattle through an open gate and further objected that carts and carriages created new roads in cornfield and pasture.[5]

Frustrated by wayfarers' negligence, the irate planters resorted to "turning" the roads. They removed the gate or "stopt up" the road, and then rerouted it around their fields. Turnings invariably extended road distance and usually placed the road in less desirable terrain. Requests for turnings appeared frequently before the county court; indeed, they comprised one-fourth of

---

[1] Ibid., RC, f. 144.

[2] Archives of Maryland, XLVI, 505-6.

[3] Hunter Dickinson Farish, ed., Journal & Letters of Philip Vickers Fithian 1773-1774: A Plantation Tutor of the Old Dominion (Williamsburg, Virginia: Colonial Williamsburg, Incorporated, 1965), p. 97. Hazard counted the exact same number three years later; Shelley, "Ebenezer Hazard's Travels through Maryland in 1777," p. 50.

[4] AACo Judgments, RC, ff. 236-37.

[5] Ibid., IB#4, f. 297; ibid., IB#2, ff. 305-6. Also, see ibid., AB, f. 479.

all road petitions.[1] But planters occasionally took matters into their own hands. They took down the gates, stopped up the road, and provided no alternative routing. Travellers traced out their own route, at least until the county court received a petition and acted on a new route. Perhaps one-fifth of all road petitions complained of the ill-convenience caused by turnings unauthorized by the court.[2]

Parish roads cut narrow swaths through forest and field. Most roads resembled paths, and only the public roads measured as much as twenty feet across. The unpaved road surfaces consisted of dirt and, on the upland ridges where the main roads ran, coastal plain sand.[3] Dirt, sand, and a hot, sunny day made for a dusty, sweaty journey.[4] Rainy days compacted the deep sand roads and made travelling less tedious.[5] Efforts to maintain the roads were minimal. The overseers and their men cleared away stumps, dead trees, and branches, grubbed the roads, and smoothed out runoff "gutters."[6] Occasionally, on poorly-drained roadways, split or hewed trees were laid down to form a causeway or a corduroy road.[7]

Horses, riders, and roads generally avoided water courses, except at a few crossing places. Yet the ferries and bridges at these places, though few in number, were an integral part of the transport network. Private ferries as early as 1673 crossed both South and Patuxent rivers, though precisely where remains in doubt. The ferrymen there charged twelve to eighteen pounds of tobacco for a man and a horse in the 1670's, but the toll went up to thirty pounds in the next decade.[8] A public ferry crossed South River at London Town

---

[1]Petitions for turnings comprised 27.7 per cent of all road petitions; 14, or 60.9 per cent, of these occurred between 1735 and 1746. Examples are found in ibid., TB#2, ff. 325-26, 375; ibid., TB#3, f. 140.

[2]See ibid., G, f. 677; ibid., TB#1, f. 493; ibid., IB#2, f. 306.

[3]Rochefoucault, Travels through the United States, II, 30.

[4]Farish, Journal & Letters of Philip Vickers Fithian, p. 209.

[5]Shelley, "Ebenezer Hazard's Travels through Maryland in 1777," p. 30.

[6]AACo Judgments, TB#3, f. 406a; ibid., TB#1, f. 412.

[7]Ibid., G, ff. 326-27; ibid., RC, f. 143.

[8]Inventories & Accounts, 2, ff. 228-29; ibid., 5, f. 280.

by 1700 to 1710;[1] this may have been the same ferry operating across that river in the 1670's and 1680's. For trans-Patuxent travellers, growing more numerous as settlement spread into the piedmont, the court in 1721 and 1722 ordered a new ferry to cross the river between Queen Anne's Town and Kilkenny.[2] But the site had some disadvantages, or so claimed Thomas White. In 1722, White extolled a crossing at Mount Pleasant, several miles downstream, which:

> by the computation of Severall Gentlmen is much the nearest way from the City of Annapolis to Marlbrough Town as also the best & nearest way for all comers & goers from St. Marys & Charles County to & from Annapolis. I believe some of your Worships is very Sensible of the Difficulty of Passing & Repassing over at Queen Anne Town, Occasioned by the freshes of the River at Some Seasons, wch is quite the contrary at Mount Pleasant. . . .[3]

A private ferry eventually operated at Mount Pleasant, for there in 1765 a French visitor crossed the Patuxent.[4] A third parish ferry, instituted in the 1740's, offered a brief challenge to the oldest ferry:

> the Subscriber keeps a Ferry over South River, above London Town, where good Attendance is given; and it is a much leveller and nearer Road for Gentlemen passing, and repassing from Queen Anne, to Annapolis, than to go over the Ferry at London Town. The said Ferry is passable in any Wind. . . .[5]

But few travellers heeded these words, and the ferry failed and disappeared from the parish records after the 1740's.

The public ferries in Anne Arundel County, including the South River Ferry at London Town and the Queen Anne Ferry over Patuxent, were maintained out of the annual levy on county taxables. The ferrymen were licensed by the county court, which gave these privileges sparingly. Rarely did an estuary possess two public ferries, and many had none. Since these ferries were publicly supported, tax-paying countians were entitled to ride for free; however, in 1715, the court clarified that this did not include the family of the taxpayer, unless he were a non-resident with a settled plantation in the county.[6] This court ruling, if correct and not the result of syntactical errors, limited considerably the movement of parish servants, slaves, women, and children.

---

[1] AACo Judgments, TB#1, f. 49; ibid., TB#2, f. 231.

[2] Ibid., 1720-1721, f. 514; ibid., 1722-1723, f. 32.

[3] Ibid., f. 50.

[4] "Journal of a French Traveller," p. 71.

[5] Maryland Gazette, December 9, 1747; AACo Judgments, AB, f. 448.

[6] Ibid., VD#1, f. 50.

Free rides were limited to daylight hours, Monday through Saturday. On Sundays and nights, ferrymen charged six pence for a man and a horse.[1] However, Sunday church-goers received special exemption; they paid no tolls between nine and eleven in the morning, and two and four in the afternoon.[2] Further exemptions appeared as ferry policy evolved and became less restrictive to movement. In 1741, jurymen were exempted from the tolls after sunset.[3] Nine years later, the court ordered free passage during regular hours for all countians.[4] And justices, sheriffs, jurymen, and "evidences when attending court" were to pass toll-free at any hour.[5] Some goods and stock were also ferried at no charge. In 1713, pack horses belonging to countians were not charged;[6] the gratis trip was extended to baskets, wallets, hogs, fowls, poultry, geese, turkeys, and dead meat in 1750.[7] Cattle and sheep, however, always had a toll assessed. The court also applied special rates to wheeled vehicles. In 1771, the justices ruled that four-wheeled carriages passed at three shillings; two-wheeled carriages at two shillings; and wagons and carts ferry-free--the last perhaps being a commentary on an expanding provisions and grain trade in the tobacco coast.[8]

The ferries usually operated from sunrise to sunset, with attendance required at all times. But in 1761, the court imposed a more specific schedule, running from sunrise to 7:00 P. M. in winter, and to 9:00 P. M. in summer.[9] South River Ferry received an exclusive and more arduous schedule in 1767. Travellers were given free passage between 4:00 A. M. and 8:00 P. M. between April 1 and September 29; 6:00 A. M. to 6:00 P. M. for September 29 to March 1; and 6:00 A. M. to 7:00 P. M. for the month of March.[10] This scheduling assisted travellers coming to the county and provincial seats at Annapolis, since three of the four annual county court sessions were held in March, June, and

---

[1] Ibid., TB#3, f. 155a; ibid., ISB#1, f. 352. However, the ferriage rate after sunset and on Sunday was lowered to two pence for Queen Anne's ferry in 1743; ibid., IB#4, f. 295.

[2] Ibid., TB#1, f. 49.

[3] Ibid., IB#1, f. 326.

[4] Ibid., ISB#1, f. 629.

[5] Ibid.

[6] Ibid., TB#3, f. 156a.

[7] Ibid., ISB#1, f. 629.

[8] Ibid., EBY, f. 304. But carriages went free over South River after 1773; ibid., 1773, f. 59.

[9] Ibid., IMB#1, f. 377.

[10] Ibid., IMB#2, f. 112.

August. The other was in November. The volume of traffic funneling over the South River Ferry rose considerably during "publick times that is during the Sittings of the Assembly Provincial & county Courts & elections."[1] During these times, the court ordered the ferrymen of South River to keep three boats with good hands in each, otherwise two boats were sufficient.[2]

The business of operating a public ferry was fairly lucrative, judging from the competition for licenses. This was especially true for the South River Ferry which received the largest sum from the county court. Between 1741-1743, the South River ferryman received £80, the highest of the four county ferries, compared to only £12 to £15 for the Queen Anne Ferry.[3] By 1773, the rate for South River had risen to £140.[4] Earlier in the century, competing ferrymen conducted a spirited rivalry for the South River Ferry license. Charges of neglect and ill-attendance were levelled at the incumbent. One Edward Rumney petitioned four times for the ferry between 1712 and 1714. He recounted the verbal promises made by the court, and his investment of over £300 for boats, hands, and a place of entertainment for travellers and their horses.[5] The court acceded and granted the license to Rumney in August of 1715, but rescinded his license by November.[6] The situation became more stable by the 1720's; and thereafter, the ferrymen on South River enjoyed fairly long tenures.

Ferriage or fording slowed down travellers; bridges were more speedy, but they cost a great deal for construction and the overseers seldom possessed the skills to make large bridges over rivers as broad as South and Patuxent. Overseers and county taxables did erect several bridges, but they were of the small variety crossing narrow branches, and creeks near their head.[7] As mills and mill dams sprang up, the dam tops served as bridges or as bases for laying a bridge. In 1721, Beall's and White's mill dams near the head of South River functioned as bridges on the main road.[8]

---

[1] Ibid., 1773, f. 59.

[2] Ibid.

[3] Ibid., IB#1, f. 326; ibid., IB#4, f. 295.

[4] Ibid., 1773, f. 59.

[5] Ibid., TB#3, ff. 102, 108a-109a, 154a-155a, 409a.

[6] Ibid., VD#1, f. 172.

[7] AACo Deeds, IB#2, ff. 45-48; ibid., RB#1, ff. 232-33.

[8] AACo Judgments, 1720-1721, ff. 413-14, 514.

Greater public works were called for, according to the colonial governor in 1719. He entreated the Assembly to provide for bridges over the Patuxent at Queen Anne and over Kent Marshes on the Eastern Shore:

> These two places being the great road, through the Heart of this Country, and also the usuall'and Shortest passage for all travellers to, and from his Majestys plantations on this continent.[1]

The Assembly, in turn, placed the responsibility for bridges on the counties. Apparently, these efforts stalled. The Queen Anne's bridge probably was not built until after 1744, since the Queen Anne's Ferry continued to operate until at least November of 1743, when it disappeared from the county records. In August of 1744, the court agreed with John Fowler for the building of an arched bridge over Patuxent, at Queen Anne ferry. The total cost of £100 was to be shared between Anne Arundel and Prince George's counties.[2] At least three precedents were established in this decision. For the first time the court laid out money from the public levy for a substantial bridge and for its maintenance. Secondly, the court contracted with a private individual to perform the task, rather than using overseer and taxables. Third, there was no provision for tolls on non-county residents. These precedents reinforced other court promulgations which diminished the restrictions on movement, while recognizing the county's responsibility to facilitate transportation.

With these precedents established, bridge-building over the Patuxent became contagious. Between 1744 and 1773, the Anne Arundel court made agreements for the construction of not less than sixteen bridges over the Patuxent, north of Queen Anne's.[3] These bridges aged quickly and thus required frequent repair. At Queen Anne's, a new bridge was needed by 1754, only ten years after the construction of the initial bridge.[4] And thirteen years later, two new bridges were built at Queen Anne's.[5]

The number of bridges constructed after 1744 and their location north of Queen Anne's on Patuxent River underscored critical changes in the relative location of All Hallows and London Town. Colonial Maryland was in the midst of major geographical realignments. After the 1740's, the towns of Frederick, in the back country, and Baltimore, up the bay on the Patapsco, grew by leaps

---

[1] Archives of Maryland, XXXIII, 370.

[2] AACo Judgments, IB#5, f. 14.

[3] See AACo Judgments from 1744 to 1773.

[4] AACo Judgments, ISB#3, f. 44.

[5] Ibid., IMB#2, ff. 2-3, 240.

and bounds. And near the falls of the Potomac, Georgetown and Alexandria emerged to handle the back country trade. "The great road, through the Heart of this Country. . ." was shifting westward, and Baltimore, not Annapolis, soon occupied the pivot.

The Network of Roads, Ferries, and Bridges

But before the 1740's and before the rise of Baltimore and the inland towns, All Hallows and London Town occupied a central position in the tidewater transport system. Their assumption of this central position begins back in the 1690's when the fortunes of the area seemed to take a turn for the worse with the establishment of Annapolis as the county seat and the provincial capital. All Hallows may have lost the capital, but it gained the traffic to it. The parish became a funnel for Anne Arundel countians going to court, for lower Western Shore residents on provincial business, and for intercolonial travellers. These travel patterns were clearly reflected in the parish transport network of 1734.

At the August Court of 1734, the Anne Arundel justices recorded the public roads in the county.[1] Seven of the twenty county roads passed through All Hallows. Six of the seven had one terminus at the South River Ferry at London Town (Figure 21). Roads radiated from London Town to Bell's mill at the head of South River; to Queen Anne's ferry; to Anne Arundel Manor, due south; to Fishing Creek in St. James' via the Bayside Road; and to Pigg Point ferry at Lyons Creek in southwestern St. James'. The last two roads probably followed the same course as the Manor road, but extended further south into the county. The seventh road came out of the Rhode River area, and proceeded to Queen Anne's. Without question, London Town was the most accessible point in the parish, if not in the colony as a whole. Annapolis, the provincial capital, was the terminus for only five public roads.[2]

London Town in 1734 was the focal point of the road network, despite the inevitable delays occasioned by ferry travel over South River. Travellers to Annapolis could have avoided these delays by taking the alternate route around the head of South River, but apparently few did. Perhaps they enjoyed the leisurely ferry ride over the mile broad and beautiful estuary. But time costs were important, too. Travel time by horseback from Annapolis to London Town, a distance of four miles, amounted to forty minutes.[3] And the ferry

---

[1] Ibid., IB#1, f. 78. [2] Ibid.

[3] Estimate of speed based on Fithian's journey of 16 miles between Port

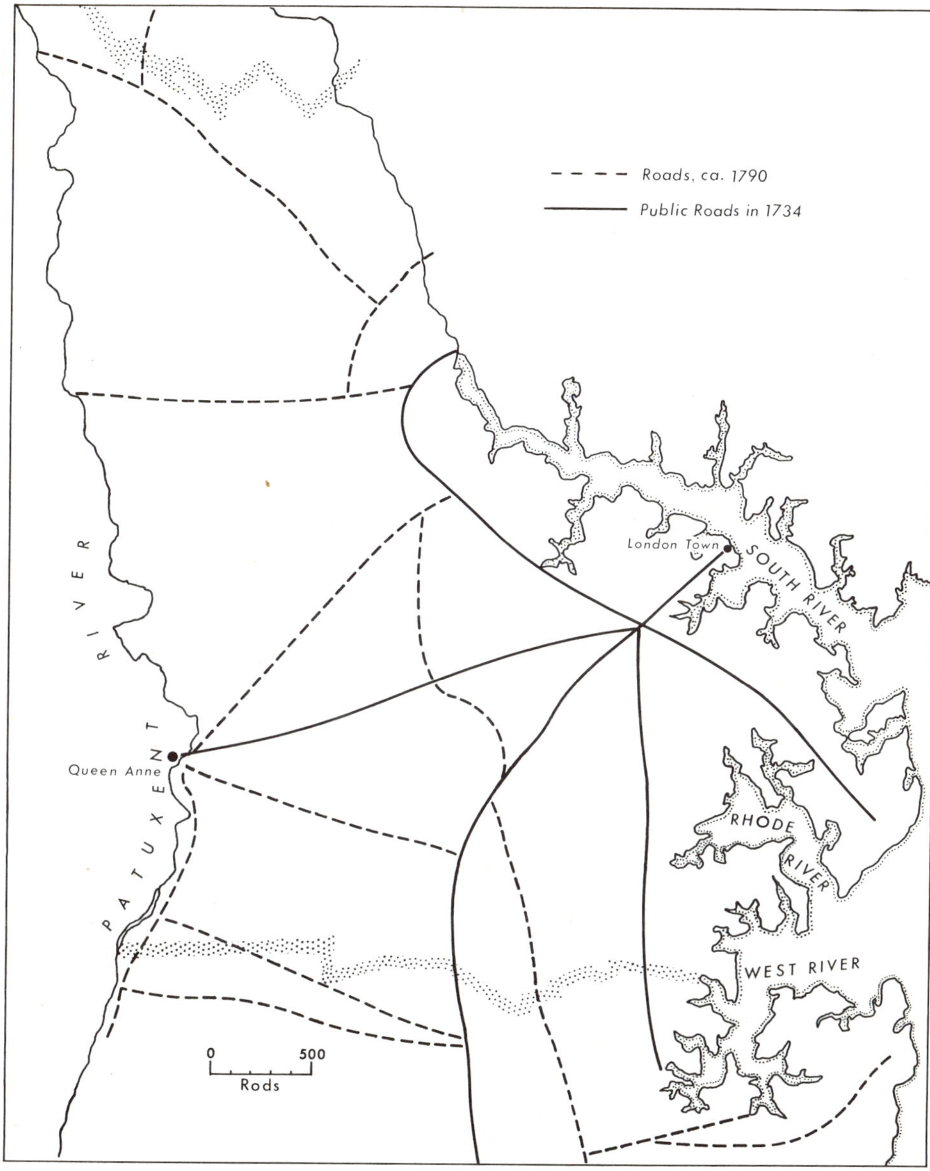

Fig. 21.--Roads in 1734 and 1794 (Sources: for 1734, see text; for 1794, see Dennis Griffith, Map of the State of Maryland . . . , June 20, 1794 (Philadelphia, 1795).

ride across South River, where boats were maintained on both sides, required probably not more than an hour. Total time expended of about one hour and forty minutes compared favorably to the alternative route from Annapolis around the head of South River. This land journey of about seven miles took over an hour of riding. In addition, the traveller headed for the lower Western Shore had to backtrack toward the bay as he followed the "Ridge" road south. His travel time equalled or exceeded that of the London Town ferry route. The latter remained the preferred route, so long as southern Maryland continued as a main destination for Maryland travellers.

But already by 1734, the flow of traffic was shifting to the north and west, reflecting developments in the piedmont and the back country. German settlers penetrated the back country in the Monocacy Valley, forty miles to the west. And north and west up the Patuxent and Potomac valleys, pushed groups of tidewater outmigrants. Urbanization proceeded rapidly in these newly-opened areas. Frederick Town in the Monocacy Valley probably surpassed Annapolis by 1755; so, also, did Baltimore by 1764, and a decade later, that town quartered more than 5,000 persons in over 560 houses. Annapolis at the time had but 260 houses.[1]

These external changes translated into the parish transport network in several ways. New road construction focused on the northwestern edge of the parish. Petitioners in 1740 sought a new public road above London Town and running from Beards Creek over to Queen Anne's.[2] They intended, no doubt, to link this road with the second South River ferry that flourished briefly in the 1740's. Another signal of external change came after 1744 with the numerous agreements for Patuxent bridges. These bridges, all upstream from Queen Anne's, vastly improved access to western Maryland and the Potomac towns. "Governors Bridge," erected by 1760 and located almost due west of the head of South River, offered especially direct access for travel between Annapolis and the western settlements.[3] The older route through Queen Anne's, All Hallows,

---

Tobacco and Upper Marlborough in two and a half hours, or 6.4 miles per hour. Farish, Journal & Letters of Philip Vickers Fithian, p. 209.

[1]Figures on town size from Karinen, "Numerical and Distributional Aspects," pp. 197-206. For the best interpretive essay, see Clarence P. Gould, "The Economic Causes of the Rise of Baltimore," Essays in Colonial History Presented to Charles McLean Andrews by his Students (New Haven: Yale University Press, 1931), pp. 225-31.

[2]AACo Judgments, AB, f. 448.

[3]AACo Judgments, ISB#4, f. 595.

and London Town suffered by comparison.

That old "great road" carried less and less traffic. Of it, a traveller in the 1770's remarked that:

> This route is by no means the nearest or direct route to Baltimore; but Mr. Buchannan having business at these places, I went with him for the sake of Company.[1]

Later, in the 1790's, Rochefoucault was induced to take the old road by an English merchant travelling with him, "notwithstanding the inconveniency of three passages over rivers, which I could have avoided by taking that of Bladensburg" via Governors Bridge.[2] New places of importance had entered the Maryland scene, including Baltimore, Bladensburg, and Frederick. These external changes compelled a few additions to the parish transport network, and though few, they were vital in the unseating of the parish and London Town from their position astride the major intercolonial route.

Yet the declining traffic in the parish had negligible effects on the planters. The network of roads, bridges and ferries served them well as they followed the annual rhythm of tobacco culture.

Annual Rhythms

A distinctive rhythm prevailed in All Hallows Parish. This rhythm of human activities and movements had evolved by the blending of an older religious calendar, reflecting English protestantism and Catholic traditions, with a newer agricultural calendar, reflecting tobacco's highly uneven demands on labor and time. The blending proved harmonious, even reinforcing; sacred times fell usually at slack times for the tobacco planters.

The Christian calendar gave temporal order and meaning to the parishioners of All Hallows. They reckoned time with respect to Christ's birth, "anno Domini." They celebrated during the course of each year the holy days commemorating holy men and events. The calendar year divided into four quarters, beginning with a quarter day. The first of these, and the first day of the year by the old style calendar, fell on March 25 or Lady Day, followed by Midsummer's Day on June 24, Michaelmas on September 29, and Christmas on December 25. On Lady Day and Michaelmas, the Maryland proprietor saw fit to collect the quitrents for land;[3] the dates, while satisfactory for the English farmer,

---

[1] Smyth, <u>A Tour in the United States of America</u>, II, 212.

[2] Rochefoucault, <u>Travels through the United States</u>, II, 288.

[3] See various Libers of Patents.

came too early for the tobacco planters, who sold their crops in October and November. The quarter day of Christmas marked the highest of holidays and planters celebrated by going to church, exchanging gifts, dispensing gratuities, visiting, vacationing, and partying.[1] Nuptials also rose sharply at the Christmas season. December marriages alone accounted for 13 per cent of all Anglican marriages recorded in the parish between 1700 and 1776 (Table 31). More precisely, the marriage "season" peaked in December, but it extended from October to February. This longer "season," as we shall soon point out, corresponded with a slack period for plantation labor. Ministers had many a cold winter ride, as they adhered to the "universal" practice of marrying couples in the home instead of the church. The home weddings were festive occasions:

> The company who are invited assemble early in the evening, and after partaking of tea and other refreshments, the indissoluble contract is completed. The bride and bridegroom then receive the accustomed congratulations; cards and dancing immediately succeed; an elegant supper, a cheerful glass, and the convivial song close the entertainment.[2]

Saints' days, Easter, and Whitsunweek also punctuated the religious calendar. The parishioners, especially the youth, honored the patron saints of England, Scotland, Wales, and Ireland with assembly and celebration.[3] Far more serious and sober were the holy days of Good Friday and Easter Sunday in the months of March and April. But gaiety returned on Easter Monday, as it did on the Carter plantation in neighboring Virginia. There, the master gave a general holiday, and "Negroes now are all disbanded till Wednesday morning & are at Cock Fights through the County. . . ."[4]

Whitsunweek began seven Sundays after Easter. Tradition has it that this day called White Sunday derived its name from the white robes worn by those baptized on this occasion. Parish Anglicans may have practiced this custom because their baptisms between 1700 and 1776 peaked in the Easter months of March and April, fell off a bit in May and rose again in June, the usual month of Whitsunday. Note, however, that baptisms reached an inexplicable maximum

---

[1] Eddis, Letters from America, p. 58; Farish, Journal & Letters of Philip Vickers Fithian 1773-1774, pp. 39-40.

[2] Eddis, Letters from America, p. 58.

[3] Ibid.

[4] Farish, Journal & Letters of Philip Vickers Fithian 1773-1774, p. 91. Cockfighting was also a popular avocation in Maryland. Josiah Quincy, "Journal of Josiah Quincy, Junior, 1773," ed. by M. A. DeWolfe Howe, Massachusetts Historical Society Proceedings, XLIX (1915-1916), 467.

TABLE 31

NUMBER AND PERCENTAGE OF MARRIAGES AND BAPTISMS PER MONTH IN ALL HALLOWS PARISH, 1700-1776

Jan.	Feb.	March	April	May	June	July	Aug.	Sept.	Oct.	Nov.	Dec.
					Marriages						
67	75	31	43	39	37	44	47	40	49	56	79
11.0%	12.4%	5.1%	7.1%	6.4%	6.1%	7.3%	7.7%	6.6%	8.1%	9.2%	13.0%
					Baptisms						
28	73	85	94	73	87	69	101	82	82	42	37
3.3%	8.6%	10.0%	11.0%	8.6%	10.2%	8.1%	11.8%	9.6%	9.6%	4.9%	4.3%

in the month of August (Table 31).[1] Whitsunweek was also a time of leisure, and the Quakers capitalized on the holiday:

> The Yearly Meeting in Maryland now came on which held four days viz three for worship and one for business. Many people resort to it and transact a deal of trade one with the other so that it is a kind of market or exchange where Captains of ships and planters meet and settle their affairs. And this draws abundance of people of the best rank to it, being it is what is called Whitsunweek.[2]

Each week began with the Sabbath--a day of rest, church, and godly thoughts. The mere act of "Grinding Corn on the Sabath day" was cause for indictment by the grand jury.[3] Not even the sheriff could make arrests on Sunday.[4] Whites were expected to attend church, and they were encouraged to do so by exemptions from ferry tolls between 9:00 A.M. and 11:00 A.M. and 2:00 P.M. and 4:00 P.M. This long exemption period of up to seven hours tells us that church meant more than an hour's service and a hasty departure. Both before and after church they mingled, socialized, read and digested the notices nailed to the church door, and visited friends for dinner.[5] Sunday was the one day when the dispersed white planters and their families assembled together. And as they convened at the church, their Negro slaves "meet in great Numbers on Sabbath and other Holy-Days. . . ."[6]

The large meetings and extraordinary mobility of black slaves persisted, despite legislation aimed at curbing their "tumultuous meetings."[7] Whites frequently encountered Negroes miles from their home plantations. Indeed, in the early eighteenth century, two Negroes were given a gun and sent out to retrieve newly-killed turkeys; they stayed out overnight, more than five miles from home.[8] Easter Monday holidays, Whitsunweek, and the yearly meetings of the Quakers also increased Negro travel and assembly. This disturbed the Quakers,

---

[1]All Hallows Parish Registers.

[2]Kelley, Quakers in the Founding of Anne Arundel County, p. 89, quoting Samuel Bownas, "Journal," Friends Library, III, 426, citation incomplete.

[3]AACo Judgments, G, f. 109.

[4]Schoepf, Travels in the Confederation, I, 362.

[5]On notices, see AAco Deeds, IT#5, f. 143.

[6]Archives of Maryland, XXXIV, 731-33.

[7]Ibid.

[8]"Narrative of a Voyage to Maryland, 1705-1706," p. 330.

who in 1747 complained of inconvenience to their yearly meetings at West River, south of the parish, and at Third-Haven on the Eastern Shore. These "tumultuous meetings" were caused by:

> the great Concourse of idle and prolifigate white People, and great Crowds of Negroes that assemble together at the usual Times of their yearly Meetings . . . drinking to Excess, and behaving in a riotous and turbulent Manner . . . where strong and spiritous Liquor can be had. . . .[1]

Negro mobility and freedom also improved after dark. One parish planter in 1744 sorely complained that a nearby road was "a great Inconveniency to him, not only by Negroes and other loose persons going the said Road at all Hours of the Night. . . ."[2] Thus, Negro mobility, activity, and freedom improved at night and on Sundays and holy days when the white men prayed to their god.

Tobacco culture superimposed a new rhythm on the religious calendar round. Tobacco planting began in February when the seeds were sown in a small bed; but labor demands were not excessive until transplanting began in May and June, and then they remained heavy until October. Especially busy were the months from July to September:

> the Time of Housing . . . is so busy, if not the busiest Time of the whole Year, with Planters; there being at that time several other Things which can't well be neglected, as procuring Fodder, and beating of Cyder. . . .[3]

A Quaker youth's meeting scheduled "about the midst of harvest time & a busy time with diverse of the youth" was quickly rescheduled for November.[4]

If Winter in the Chesapeake was the marrying season, late Summer and Autumn were times of death and burial. The parishioners in August and September spent long hours in hot, humid fields harvesting and housing their tobacco. Deaths were more frequent in these arduous months, and the plantation burials kept the minister and kin on the move. The funeral services and the burials took place usually at the plantations, where the better sort of planter wanted his final resting place.[5] After a solemn service, the congregation of kin and friends were entertained with good company, cider, wine, rum, punch, and

---

[1] Archives of Maryland, XLIV, 647. [2] AACo Judgments, IB#4, ff. 394-95.

[3] Maryland Gazette, April 13, 1748.

[4] Annapolis, Hall of Records, microfilmed MSS, Quaker Records, West River and Herring Creek Minutes, July 5, 1710, M548.

[5] For example, see Original Wills, Box L, folder 35. In Virginia, Fithian notes that "'only the lower sort of People are buried at the Church; for the Gentleman have private burying-Yards.'" Farish, Journal & Letters of Philip Vickers Fithian, 1773-1774, p. 41.

sometimes with cakes and meat.[1]

The month of November signalled the arrival of the annual tobacco fleet and a leisurely time for planters. The fleet of usually eighty to one hundred and fifty ships, having left English shores in September, arrived four to six weeks later in the Chesapeake Bay.[2] Maryland waters received one-third to one-half of these ships, which then fanned out to navigable estuaries with safe anchorage, abundant crops of tobacco, and a minimum of competition from fellow ship captains.[3] The captains remained in the Chesapeake and probed the estuaries until their ships were full with tobacco. Not infrequently, the collection of tobacco held vessels over until the following summer.

Anne Arundel County estuaries harbored ten to sixteen tobacco vessels a year between 1705 and 1748. The number dwindled to seven over the next seven years, in all probability because the inspection act substantially pared tobacco production.[4] These vessels entered all of the county's estuaries, but South River proved the favorite. As the anchorage site recorded for 42 per cent of all ships giving freight rates in the county court records, South River easily outdistanced the estuaries of Patapsco, Magothy, Severn, and West rivers, along with Herring Bay.[5] Rhode River, the second important parish estuary, received just one ship.

---

[1]The funeral expences for Thomas Ricketts, a middling planter dying about 1732 with an estate of £132.25 sterling, included seven gallons of rum, ten pounds of sugar, one ounce of cloves, four gallons of wine, eleven and three-quarters gallons of cider, a coffin, and the funeral sermon. Accounts, 6, f. 52.

[2]The number of ships varied. The average for the 1660's was probably thirty to forty; Alsop noted that twenty ships and upwards entered into Maryland in the 1660's. Alsop, "A Character of the Province of Maryland," p. 363. One hundred to one hundred fifty ships came typically in the eighteenth century, but three hundred came in 1706. Middleton, Tobacco Coast, pp. 244-45.

[3]CSPCS, 1689-92, XIII, 578.

[4]John Hemphill identifies this change in ship frequency after 1747, but I suspect that the decrease was due to the inspection act rather than to an increase in purchased tobacco or the geographical shift of tobacco to the piedmont, as Hemphill suggests. Hemphill, "Freight Rates in the Maryland Tobacco Trade, 1705-1762," pp. 54-55.

[5]Calculated from John M. Hemphill II, "Freight Rates in the Maryland Tobacco Trade, 1705-1762: Appendix," Maryland Historical Magazine, LIV (June, 1959), 153-87. This is not a complete list of ships serving Anne Arundel County, since it excludes chartered ships which were filled by Maryland factors of English firms. However, the list probably includes the majority of ships trading in the county, since many chartered vessels had to advertise their rates in order to fill their holds.

The arrival of the tobacco fleet spurred the beginning of the real business of the Chesapeake--selling tobacco. But before the dealing began, the principals came together, socialized, and exchanged market intelligence. The ship captains usually invited several of the leading planters along the estuary out to their ships. There, they discussed the size of this year's crop, tobacco markets, prices, and freight rates, between drafts of wine and rum.[1] On occasion, the exchange of economic intelligence continued on into the evening when the captain entertained the planter and his family as dinner guests.[2] In this convivial setting, vital economic information had been exchanged, and it quickly spread from the captain's table to the lesser planters of the parish.

Planters next struck a bargain for their tobacco. They transacted their business in one of three ways: barter, consignment, and direct sale. The barter trade involved an exchange of commodities between captains or supercargoes and planters; George Alsop in 1666 described the essentials of this trade:

> Between November and January ther arrives in this Province . . . Merchantmen loaden with Commodities to Trafique and dispose of, trucking with the Planter for Silks, Hollands, Serges, and Broad-clothes, with other necessary Goods, priz'd at such and such rates as shall be judg'd on is fair and legal, for Tobacco at so much a pound. . . .[3]

Alsop implied that barter was the chief mode of trade in seventeenth century Maryland, and perhaps it was in Baltimore County where he resided; but in All Hallows and elsewhere, a new consignment trade was flourishing. In this trade, the planter retained ownership of the tobacco. Hiring ship space for his crop, he then consigned his tobacco to an English middleman and merchant who sold the tobacco in Europe and credited sales to the planter's account. The planter used his account balance to pay for European goods sent at his request by his English agent or by a third party. Payment for the goods was made by debiting his English account or by drafting a bill of exchange, the equivalent of a modern-day check, on his account. The consignment trade had a few advan-

---

[1]This reconstruction of contacts between planter and ship captain is based on eighteenth century evidence, but is probably reasonable for the seventeenth century, too. In 1718, a ship captain received the following order from Higginson and Bird: "'Inclos'd you have an ordr on Mr. John Fuller of deale to deliver you thirty Gallons of Brandy to drink our healthe wn . . . you arrive in Maryland; what services you doe us amongst the Gentlemen there wee shall take as a perticular favour. . . .'" Higginson and Bird to Captain Richard Smith, November 10, 1718, Higginson & Bird Letterbook, No. 1706.

[2]"Journal of a French Traveller," p. 72.

[3]Alsop, "A Character of the Province of Maryland," p. 363.

tages over barter. The consigning planter, when faced with falling Chesapeake tobacco prices, stood a good chance of earning higher prices and profits by selling in England or Europe.[1] No less important, he exercised some control over the kinds, quality, and quantity of goods sent from England to the Chesapeake.

The extent of the consignment trade may be estimated roughly by those parishioners whose inventories reveal English accounts in the form of credits or debits. The procedure is not foolproof because planters probably acquired English balances by means other than consignment of tobacco. Nor does the procedure tell us how much of the tobacco crop of the parish was consigned. What it does do is establish the theoretical maximum number of consigning planters; these appear in Table 32. Few planters, it appears, consigned tobacco before 1680; but in the depression that lasted from that year to 1697, the proportion of consigning planters rose to 20 per cent. The consigning trend continued, rising sharply to 35 per cent in the boom of 1719-1726, and to about 45 per cent amidst the depressions of 1727-1733 and 1740-1749. The trend reversed after mid-century, when 22 per cent to 35 per cent of the planters consigned their crops.

TABLE 32

PROPORTION OF PARISH ESTATES CONTAINING THE NAMES OF ENGLISH MERCHANTS AS CREDITORS AND/OR DEBTORS BY BOOMS AND BUSTS, 1660-1769

1660-1679	8.3	1740-1749	46.9
1680-1697	20.5	1750-1753}	
1698-1704	26.3	1757-1762}	35.4
1705-1718	25.0	1767-1769}	
1719-1726	35.7		
1727-1733	45.7	1754-1756}	22.0
1734-1739	32.3	1763-1766}	

The consignment trade proved efficacious for the planter, and the trade made substantial inroads on the barter trade between 1680 and 1750. Some planters continued to barter with ship captains and supercargoes, but as the eighteenth century progressed, the majority either consigned or sold their crops directly to a resident agent or factor for an English merchant house. These two modes of trade, it should be emphasized, had significantly different

[1]The consignment trade is concisely summarized in Middleton, Tobacco Coast, pp. 104-7.

effects for the settlement system. Direct sales of tobacco to British factors, based in small towns as London Town, focused the movement of people and goods on these small, but significant urban places. The consignment trade had quite the opposite effect. The trade encouraged the combination of planting and mercantile functions, thus decentralizing trade among the planter-merchants. The fact that these two polar trades developed and expanded simultaneously during the first half of the eighteenth century reinforces the view that town and plantations followed divergent courses of development. Even more fascinating is the mid-century decline of both consigning planters and town-based factors and merchants engaged in a direct sale trade. That both should decline simultaneously is rather surprising, and it is a problem to which we shall return.

While planter, merchants, and ship captains did business, the new-arrived sailors, as they were wont to do, flocked to the local taverns, or as they called them, the ordinaries. Several commanders complained of great damages suffered "by their Saylors being entertained by the ordinary Keepers at South River. . . ."[1] The sailors evidently ran up big tabs, and their captains were stuck with the bill. But a sailor needed a few hardy drinks, because back-breaking work remained to be done: collecting and transporting the tobacco from the plantations to the water side, loading the heavy and bulky hogsheads aboard small vessels, transferring these hogsheads from smaller collecting vessels to the seagoing ships, and stowing the hogsheads away. When the hogsheads of four hundred pounds or more were stored on inland plantations, the labor became even more arduous. An acute observer at the beginning of the eighteenth century put it succinctly:

> the sailors . . . fetch itt from Plantations to Carry itt aboard there ships some times being forced to rowle itt by land four or five mile, nay some times I have known 'em Rowle itt seven miles an end befor the could bring itt to there Boates and then p'haps they have forty or fivety Miles to Cary itt to their ships.[2]

In collecting the tobacco, the sailors employed a variety of water craft. Amidst the smaller creeks, they used the smallest vessels called flats. These were:

> large, flat-bottom'd boats, capable of carrying some Tons of Goods, and used in the Tobacco countries to unlade vessels with. They have also a kind of Sloops, clumsily built, which may be called Tobacco Druggers, of 70 or 80 Tons Burden. . . .[3]

---

[1] Archives of Maryland, XXIV, 213.

[2] "Narrative of a Voyage to Maryland, 1705-1706," p. 336.

[3] "Itinerant Observations in America," p. 29. Also, see the advertisement

The typical parish flat carried nine to twelve hogsheads, or the equivalent of two to three tons of shipping space. The tobacco hauled by twenty to thirty flats filled up a sloop or "tobacco drugger." Ships occupied the top of the collection hierarchy, and their capacities ranged from fifty tons burden to over five hundred tons, with an average of about one hundred and seventy tons.[1] Filling the hold of a five hundred ton vessel required perhaps six sloops and one hundred and twenty to one hundred and eighty flats, or the equivalent in vessel trips.

Conducting trade in this fashion was slow and tedious; and occasionally, ships remained for months in Maryland waters. Seeking to minimize these costly layovers, merchant-planters and resident factors by the late seventeenth century began to streamline the transactional end of the tobacco trade. In advance of the tobacco fleet's arrival, they completed the transactions for consignment or purchase of tobacco. Specific instructions to this effect accompanied one English factor destined for the Chesapeake in 1695:

> take care that you Comply with ye time Exprest in your Charter party for ye shipping your tobaccoe, you keeping a small pockett booke of ye Quantity of hogsheads you Receive at Every Place . . . by which meanes you Can readily give noates to ye Master for ye fetching of your tobacco. . . .[2]

Advanced transactions of this sort expedited the collection of tobacco and the turn-around time for the tobacco ships. The efficiency brought about by advanced transaction impressed an observer of the trade at Oxford on the Eastern Shore. The scene he portrayed, just before the 1747 inspection act, applied, though on a smaller scale, to All Hallows.

> Seven or eight large ships, at the same time were frequently seen at Oxford, delivering goods and completing their landing; nor was it uncommon to dispatch a ship with 500 hogsheads of tobacco in twelve days after its arrival. At that time tobacco was not examined or inspected by sworn officers as now. Men skilled in the article were employed by the merchants or store keepers and called Receivers, to view, weigh, mark and give receipts to planters after which vessels were sent to collect it, when it underwent a pressing and packing preparatory for shipping.[3]

---

of a schooner, holding forty hogsheads underdeck, "'fit for Tobo Droguer.'" Maryland Gazette, September 30, 1746.

[1]Middleton, Tobacco Coast, pp. 244-45. A ton was a measure of space allotted rather than weight. One ton was equivalent to four hogsheads.

[2]Annapolis, Hall of Records MSS, Jno Purtis to Charles Jones, January 21, 1696, Charles County Land Records, Q#1, ff. 117-18.

[3]Oswald Tilghman, History of Talbot County Maryland, 1661-1861 (2 vols.; Baltimore: Williams & Wilkins Company, 1915), II, 357. The turn-around time was expedited also in Anne Arundel County. The ship "'Britannia'" loaded 1,064 hogsheads in less than two months in the Severn River. Maryland Gazette,

Some merchants further expedited the tobacco trade by collecting the purchased or consigned tobacco in a central place. For example, Patrick Sympson of London Town received instructions to send goods up the bay to one of his assistants, but to "Contrive it so that a sloop or sloops that transport sd goods may bring back Tobo to put on board the Murdock, which may prove of service to his dispatch. . . ."[1] In this case, Sympson functioned as a wholesaler of goods and a collector of distant tobacco; through Sympson, London Town acquired a higher-order urban function.

Further streamlining of the tobacco trade occurred through ship charter and preferential freight rates. When Patrick Sympson collected tobacco from his assistant up the bay, he knew that the ship "Murdock" would shortly put in at London Town for loading. He knew this because his English employers had probably chartered that vessel for their exclusive use. The captain and his vessel operated under the instructions of the English merchant or merchants in the "charter party." The merchants, in turn, told their Maryland factors of the time and place of the ship's arrival so that tobacco could be purchased and ready.[2] Ship chartering by a single English merchant house became very common in the eighteenth century. Not infrequently, the tobacco purchased by Maryland factors did not fill the vessels. When their purchases came up short, the ship captains solicited more tobacco. They recorded their freight rates in the county court, along with anchorage sites and the English merchants to whom their ships were chartered.[3] These court entries, beginning in 1704, usually listed a single English merchant as consignee; thus, the planters had to consign to these merchants, though occasionally the captains gave liberty of consignment.

Ship captains also expedited collection by offering preferential rates for "delivered" versus "fetched" tobacco. Planters who delivered usually saved a pound sterling or current money for every ton of tobacco freighted.[4]

March 24, 1748. And in 1747, the "'BridgTown'" loaded 441 hogsheads at London Town, "'having been but 22 or 23 days taking it in.'" Maryland Gazette, October 14, 1747.

[1]Higginson and Bird to Patrick Sympson, January 3, 1719, Higginson & Bird Letterbook, No. 1887.

[2]Charles County Land Records, Q#1, ff. 117-18.

[3]Hemphill, "Freight Rates in the Maryland Tobacco Trade, 1705-1762: Appendix," pp. 153-87.

[4]Ibid.

The ultimate in speed of collection was achieved after the inspection act of 1747, when all Maryland tobacco was assembled in a limited number of inspection houses.[1]

As the planters busied themselves with tobacco selling, consigning, and shipping, they also examined the goods and fineries brought by the annual tobacco fleet.[2] Local merchants and factors enticed the planters with the variety and novelty among the "new goods" and with reasonable prices, at least at the outset. For example, one factor was instructed to sell "your goods at ye beginning for ye Encouragement of trade as they are Valued in your Invoyce, and afterwards make yor advance on your goods as you shall have opportunity. . . ."[3] The brisk sales of mundane and exotic goods took place usually at the stores of Maryland merchants and factors and, less often, on shipboard. The period of shipboard sales was, of course, very brief, owing to the increasingly rapid turn-around of the tobacco ships.

Chesapeake planters received the latest European goods via the tobacco fleet. The "quick importation of fashions from the mother country" astonished William Eddis in 1771:

> I am almost inclined to believe that a new fashion is adopted earlier by the polished and affluent American than by many opulent persons in the great metropolis. . . .[4]

Eddis's claim applied just as well to All Hallows as it did to his Annapolis community. After the arrival of the fleet, news of these fashions spread rapidly by word-of-mouth and in the columns of the Maryland Gazette. The parishioners' acceptance of the "new fashion" of tea-drinking may serve to illustrate the speed at which innovations diffused within the tidewater settlement system. Before 1741, three or four scattered inventories contained tea or teaware. Between 1742 and 1752, precisely one-third of the 63 inventories listed these items; between 1753 and 1762, 24 of 45 (53.3 per cent) had adopted the fashion.

---

[1]It was claimed for Virginia's tobacco inspection act, after which Maryland's was modelled, that "'one Factor . . . can purchase, in less Time, and with much less Trouble and charge, more Tobacco than 4 or 5 Factors can do . . .'" in Maryland, and ships were dispatched soon after arrival. Maryland Gazette, December 9, 1747.

[2]For examples, see Margaret Shove Morriss, Colonial Trade of Maryland 1689-1715, Johns Hopkins University Studies in Historical and Political Science, 32nd Series, No. 3 (1914).

[3]Charles County Land Records, Q#1, ff. 117-18.

[4]Eddis, Letters from America, p. 57.

Adoption then levelled off; and between 1763 and 1769, 24 of 46 (52.2 per cent) had tea or teaware. Thus, in the case of tea-drinking, maximum adoption occurred within ten to twenty years of initial acceptance; and the majority of these adopters did so within the first decade. Eddis did not exaggerate; information and goods spread rapidly in the Chesapeake, which warrants the label of "rural cosmopolitan."

Winter signalled a lull in the planter's economic activity. He had sold his tobacco, and purchased his goods. The affluent and the poor, the servile and the free enjoyed celebration, festivity, and marriage. There was abundance of imported liquors and wines, domestic cider, and fresh-killed meat. And on the plantations, little work remained to be done; and servants and slaves could relax,[1] compared to the rest of the year.

Temporal and Spatial Variations in Exchange

Exchange and Potential Self-sufficiency

While tobacco culture imposed a repetitive annual rhythm on the way of life in All Hallows Parish, the economics of tobacco imposed rhythms of longer durations. The rhythm of the economic cycle caused repeated adjustments on the plantations. During depressions, the plantations became more flexible. Planters increased their potential for self-sufficiency, which enabled them to substitute household production for imports. As a consequence, exchange and trade among the plantations and with English merchants diminished. In the inevitable boom that followed, planters readjusted by cutting back household production and resuming imports and local purchases. Thus, the plantations wavered between autarchy and complete commercial specialization, while never achieving either polar position. At all times, the planters marketed tobacco and purchased goods and services, but their emphases changed according to the state of the tobacco economy. Not every plantation achieved a position of flexibility. A substantial number remained rigid and incapable of "rolling with the punches" of the tobacco economy.

These statements constitute a theory of plantation exchange, but before testing the theory, we must make the phrasing more explicit. Plantation ex-

---

[1]In 1666, Alsop claimed that servants did little work between December and February, except cutting wood for fires by which they lay. Alsop, "A Character of the Province of Maryland," p. 357. Over one hundred years later, the cutting and working of wood was still the principal winter occupation of slaves, but perhaps with less indolence than Alsop experienced. American Husbandry, p. 165.

change is a function of a plantation's potential self-sufficiency and the state of the economy. During depressions, flexible plantations (having indices of fourteen or more for potential self-sufficiency) decrease external exchange, as measured by the relative value of inflows to the plantation. In booms, they increase inflows. By contrast, rigid plantations (having indices of four or less for potential self-sufficiency) maintain exchange at high levels regardless of economic conditions. Intermediate plantations (having indices of five to thirteen for potential self-sufficiency) exhibit exchange patterns that are transitional from the rigid to the flexible plantations.

Before examining these hypotheses, we should briefly consider the measurement of plantation exchange, plantation self-sufficiency, and the state of the tobacco economy. The latter two are measured by the index of potential self-sufficiency and by the price of tobacco. The third variable, plantation exchange or inflow, is measured as the relative value of debts owed from the plantation to other parties in payment for goods, services, or capital. A relative measure of debts or inflows is preferable because it permits the comparison of plantations of widely varying scale. Thus, relative inflows are defined as the proportion of debts to total estate value (scale). Some peculiar problems arise when debts are used to estimate inflows to the plantation, and these problems require amplification.

Plantation debts were recorded frequently in the probate process. Debts and other liabilities against an estate appeared in an Account, and this document accompanied about three-fifths of the inventories. Occasionally, the executor or administrator filed several accounts as new claims against the estate came to light. Several types of liabilities appeared in the accounts: debts incurred during the lifetime of the decedent; posthumous expenses such as funeral charges, administration fees, and lawyers' fees; legacies; deductions for overcharges and errors in the inventory or because of the death of labor or animals; and deductions for "desperate debts" owing to the estate but uncollectible for whatever reason. For purposes of this study of exchange, debts are narrowly defined as those incurred during the lifetime of the decedent. All posthumous estate liabilities are excluded.

Accounts are less representative than the inventories. More accounts survive for large estates having extensive trading ties. To rectify this bias, we draw no conclusions from the total sample, but instead confine attention to the exchange behavior of three classes of plantation: flexible, intermediate, and rigid.

Another bias is that the accounts may understate the volume of exchange, especially in boom periods. The account debts all involve credit purchases; cash and barter purchases are not recorded. Consequently, cash purchases probably increased in boom periods when more hard money circulated; in these periods, account debts underestimated the volume of exchange. Thus, account debts provide a conservative estimate of plantation inflows, especially during prosperous years. With these provisos in mind, we begin the examination of plantation exchange.

The economic exchanges of parish planters behaved predictably during booms and busts between 1660 and 1769 (Table 33). Flexible plantations adjusted inflows in response to the economic cycle. During all boom periods, inflows rose; more than 25 per cent of the flexible plantations held debts in excess of half their total estate value. In depressions, this proportion fell to 16.2 per cent, as household production replaced imports (Table 33). At the opposite extreme, rigid plantations increased their indebtedness during depressions when more than half of these plantations had debts exceeding 50 per cent of plantation scale. The proportion fell to 39.3 per cent during prosperous years. The rigid plantations, then, increased relative inflows during depressions; these expenditures were necessary because goods and services could not be produced at home. Rigid planters suffered further when tobacco prices fell; their revenues from tobacco declined and they lost parish customers who were more flexible. Intermediate plantations were more stable. Their indebtedness showed only minor differences between boom and bust periods (Table 33).

These overall adjustments of plantation exchange also held true through time, with one exception (Table 34). Flexible plantations behaved consistently both before and after 1734. During boom periods before and after that date, these plantations expanded imports (mean relative inflows). And in depressions, they replaced imports with self-sufficient production (Table 34). However, imports were not completely discontinued; they continued to enter the flexible plantations but at diminished levels. As significant as the cyclical fluctuations in the exchange of flexible plantations, was the long-term decline in their indebtedness. Mean indebtedness fell to 19.2 per cent in the depressions after 1740; and the proportion during booms dropped from a pre-1734 figure of nearly 50 per cent to a post-1734 figure of 34.3 per cent. Flexible plantations became less dependent on exchange with local planters and British exporters.

Rigid plantations were always more indebted than other plantations in the parish. During pre-1734 depressions, however, the direction and magnitude of

TABLE 33

POTENTIAL SELF-SUFFICIENCY AND RELATIVE INDEBTEDNESS ON PLANTATIONS WITH ACCOUNTS FOR BOOMS AND BUSTS, 1660-1769

Relative Indebtedness	PSS			
	0-4	5-13	14+	Totals
		All Boom Periods		
0-50.9%	17	37	35	89
51-100.9%	6	17	9	22
101%+	5	5	3	13
Total	28	59	47	124
% of Plantations with indebtedness ≥51%	39.3	37.2	25.5	28.2
		All Bust Periods		
0-50.9%	9	51	62	122
51-100.9%	7	21	9	37
101%+	3	10	3	16
Total	19	82	74	175
% of Plantations with indebtedness ≥51%	52.6	37.8	16.2	30.3

change were the same for both rigid and flexible plantations. On rigid plantations in these years, average indebtedness fell from a boom mean of 68.2 per cent to 48.7 per cent during the busts. Clearly, the reduction of inflows on rigid plantations was not attributable to import replacement, since self-sufficiency was impossible. The decline almost certainly resulted from voluntary or compulsory austerity. Small planters had a difficult time securing depression credit, because wise merchants and creditors knew they were poor risks. "Runaways" and insolvents were frequent among the small planters, and their debts had to be written off as a loss.[1] In early 1719, Higginson and Bird advised their factor, Patrick Sympson, not to contract debts for goods, "but receive Tobo . . . & tho it may cost something more yett its better than to have

[1] Maryland Gazette, July 14, 1747.

TABLE 34

MEAN VALUE OF RELATIVE INDEBTEDNESS FOR PLANTATIONS WITH GIVEN LEVELS OF POTENTIAL SELF-SUFFICIENCY DURING BOOMS AND BUSTS, 1660-1769

	PSS		
	0-4	5-13	14+
Booms 1660-1679 1698-1704 1719-1726	68.2 (20)	38.2 (26)	49.6 (10)
Busts 1680-1697 1705-1718 1727-1733	48.7 (12)	55.3 (59)	31.0 (30)
Booms 1734-1739 1750-1753 1757-1762 1767-1769	31.0 (8)	46.7 (23)	34.3 (37)
Busts 1740-1749 1754-1756 1763-1766	89.2 (7)	37.3 (22)	19.2 (45)
Total Booms	57.6 (28)	50.0 (49)	37.5 (47)
Total Busts	63.6 (19)	50.4 (81)	23.9 (75)

Note: Figures in parentheses are the number of observations.

the perplexity of getting in debts which are so uncertain."[1] Confronted with tighter credit, smaller planters had little choice but to involuntarily reduce purchase from others. Their dilemma compounded as estate values declined during these depressed years.

After 1734, the pattern of exchange on rigid plantations shifted. During booms, relative indebtedness fell to 31.0 per cent, but rose to 89.2 per cent during the busts. Apparently, credit was accessible during these later depressions. In addition, the range of indebtedness increased, as evidenced by a difference of 60 per cent between the booms and the busts. Finally, these statements should be interpreted as suggestive and not conclusive, since the post-

[1]Higginson and Bird to Patrick Sympson, January 3, 1719, Higginson & Bird Letterbook, No. 1887.

1734 sample of rigid plantations includes only fifteen plantations.

Intermediate plantations were transitional. Their patterns of exchange possessed elements of both rigid and flexible plantations. For all booms and busts, intermediate plantations exhibited inflows of about 50 per cent of total estate value. Thus, the intermediate plantations exchanged more than the flexible plantations (with a mean indebtedness of 37.5 per cent or less) and less than the rigid plantations (with a mean indebtedness of 57.6 per cent or more) (Table 34). Before 1734, the intermediate plantations behaved as though they were rigid plantations. During these early depressions, the intermediate plantations raised their level of indebtedness. Perhaps they siphoned off the pool of credit, thus forcing the rigid planters into austerity. After 1734, the intermediate plantations behaved as flexible plantations. Their inflows fell to 37.3 per cent during depressions and expanded to 46.7 per cent during booms. These changes reflected the transitional nature of the intermediate plantations; as time passed, they became increasingly similar to flexible sites.

How pervasive were these changes toward plantation flexibility--changes that encouraged import replacement or resumption, depending on the state of the economy? Flexible plantations (with potential self-sufficiency of 14 or more) constituted 33.2 per cent of all inventoried plantations; intermediate plantations comprised 47.0 per cent; and rigid plantations (with potential self-sufficiency of 4 or less) comprised 19.8 per cent. The long-term trend was toward increasing potential self-sufficiency, and larger numbers of plantations fell into the flexible or intermediate groups (Table 35). After 1679, these plantations accounted for at least 70 per cent of all plantations; but the proportion increased during depressions, and especially in the 1740's when 95 per cent were intermediate and flexible.

Since the 1690's, keen observers of the tidewater scene captured glimpses of an evolving plantation self-sufficiency and its corollary, import replacement. But these insights, formulated during depressions, were frequently clouded in the predictable boom that followed. A succinct example of misunderstanding came in 1765, when a Frenchman visiting the Galloways of West River attempted to explain what he saw:

> It is Certain that this act [the Stamp Act] has made a great alteration in the americans Disposition towards great britain, . . . it has already set them on raising everything themselves, which they would never have thought of otherwise, for they hithertoo were the greatest spendtrifts in the world, satisfied if at the years End the[y] Could make both Ends meet . . . however they seem already to be intend on raising manufactures, spinning and weav-

TABLE 35

PROPORTIONS OF RIGID, INTERMEDIATE, AND FLEXIBLE PLANTATIONS BETWEEN 1660 AND 1769

	Rigid	Intermediate	Flexible
1660-1679	50.0	50.0	0.0
1680-1697	29.5	59.0	11.5
1698-1704	24.3	62.2	13.5
1705-1718	16.7	56.1	27.3
1719-1726	28.6	47.6	23.8
1727-1733	11.4	37.1	51.4
1734-1739	23.3	50.0	26.7
1740-1749	4.8	27.4	67.8
1750-1753 } 1757-1761 } 1767-1769 }	7.4	35.2	57.4
1754-1756 } 1762-1766 }	13.2	45.3	41.5

> ing . . . In so much that there are great Complaints in England of the few goods taken of their hands this last year. . . .[1]

The naîveté of this interpretation of colonial response to Imperial policy lay in its temporal myopia. The experience of three or more generations of colonial planters bore witness that this was the only way to behave and survive in an erratic trans-Atlantic economy--1765 marked the fourth year in the mid-1760's depression.

London Town Merchants Revisited

The merchants who descended on London Town in the first quarter of the eighteenth century chose two divergent paths in their careers; at least four of them left London Town for other parts of Maryland or London. The remainder chose to stay. For them, the unforeseen result was a decline in personal fortune and eventually, in the fortune of the town which was their home.

Seven London Town merchants died and left inventories between 1733 and 1767, and five left accounts as well. These records captured the plight of the specialist merchants (Table 36). Their flexibility either stabilized or declined, while indebtedness increased. Precisely the opposite trends occurred among the plantations.

---

[1]"Journal of a French Traveller," p. 74.

TABLE 36

THE ECONOMIC STATUS OF LONDON TOWN MERCHANTS AT THEIR DEATHS

Name	Scale	PSS	Debts as a % of Scale
Samuel Peele, 1733	£5792	18	37.3
Richard Moore, 1735	£1317	19	47.3
William Peele, 1750	£ 636	11	80.9
William Chapman, 1762	£1402	11	111.2
William Chapman, 1767	£2031	20	87.3

The problems experienced by London Town merchants were the logical consequences of occupational specialization which ran counter to the general drift of change among the plantations. As the merchants' customers became more flexible, their demands for mercantile services diminished. The merchants served a shrinking clientele composed mainly of high-risk debtors operating small and rigid plantations. During boom years, the merchants won back some of their old customers; but this was little consolation in the tidewater region where the probability of a prosperous year was usually less than 50 per cent. As a result, the economic posture of London Town merchants deteriorated; and, understandably, merchant recruitment was ineffective. As the older merchants died or moved on, the regression of London Town became more apparent.

The Structure of Exchange

Economic exchange in All Hallows Parish was both concentrated and diffused. A very few planters provided the bulk of credit volume. Yet, these leading creditors were rarely the primary or largest creditors for individual parish residents. This paradoxical situation arose for two reasons. First, the leading creditors made many loans, but most were for small sums. Second, many parishioners extended credit, and thus the planters had a multiplicity of credit sources. As a result, planters usually owed their largest, or primary, debt to relatively minor parish creditors, with respect to total volume. The paradox of exchange persisted throughout the colonial period. However, as London Town grew vigorously after 1710, the traffic in credit increasingly focused on the town merchants. As the town decayed after 1750, the geographic focus of credit shattered into multiple foci, one of which was Annapolis.

A few parish residents generated the vast majority of exchange credit. For example, 10 per cent of the inventoried estates provided at least 78 per cent of credit volume between 1680 and 1697, 1705 and 1739, and after 1749 (Table 37). The most pronounced concentration of credit occurred between 1705 and 1733 and in the post-1749 booms, when 10 per cent of the inventories totaled over 90 per cent of the credit. Least concentration existed during the depression of the 1740's when the credit mechanism collapsed; yet even at these times, the top 10 per cent extended one-half or more of all credit.

TABLE 37

THE LARGEST RESIDENT CREDITORS IN ALL HALLOWS PARISH, 1660-1769

	% of Credit Extended by Top 10% of the Inventories	% of the Largest Creditor	Mean Value of the Credits of the Largest Creditor*
1660-1679	61.6	17.8	3.25 (80)
1680-1697	78.8	47.2	14.50 (152)
1698-1704	83.3	27.3	4.28 (23)
1705-1718	94.0	51.7	31.63 (83)
1719-1726	96.9	44.5	213.74 (4)
1727-1733	95.6	58.0	11.98 (202)
1734-1739	86.0	46.4	3.67 (169)
1740-1749	51.9	18.7	3.64 (101)
1750-1753} 1757-1761} 1767-1769}	94.6	31.0	19.76 (93+)
1754-1756} 1762-1766}	82.6	40.9	8.07 (325)

*Figures in parentheses indicate the number of persons who were indebted to the largest parish creditors. A plus behind the number indicates that the inventory is torn or obliterated; and therefore not all of the persons to whom loans were made are ascertainable. Thus, the mean value of credits is inflated slightly in these cases.

Equally typical was the concentration of credit value in one person. When the founder of London Town, William Burgess, died about 1687, his estate listed book debts due to him amounting to £2204.48, or 47.2 per cent of all credits held by inventoried decedents between 1680 and 1697.[1] In the next depression,

[1]See the sources listed in Table 38 for all of the leading creditors.

1705 to 1718, Gabriel Parrott provided 51.7 per cent of parish credits. Between 1719 and 1726, Samuel Galloway held 44.5 per cent. The ultimate in individual concentration occurred in the depression of 1727 to 1733 when Samuel Peele of London Town garnered 58 per cent of the total credit value. Between 1734 and 1739, Thomas Gassaway's £620.10 in credits fell to 46.4 per cent of the total. The 1740's depression, peculiar in most respects, witnessed a dramatic decline in individual credit concentration, as well as in the amount of credit emitted. John Watkins had only £367.59 in credits, which made him the leading creditor with just 18.7 per cent of the total. After mid-century, credit concentration rose, but it never equalled pre-1740 levels. During the post-1750 booms, Joseph Galloway led with £1837.9, or 31.0 per cent; and in the busts, Richard Snowden loaned out £2622.15, or 40.9 per cent.

The location of these leading creditors was not a major factor in their remarkable achievements. Although they did not cluster at specific sites, these creditors usually resided near South and West rivers (Table 38). All but one of the pre-1740 leading creditors lived in the vicinity of South River; however, only Samuel Peele made his home in London Town. During the eighteenth century, South River's primacy diminished at the hands of West River creditors. Some of these West River creditors, such as the Galloways, may have lived slightly south of the parish boundary, which in any case was very vague. Nonetheless, they were very active in the parish credit and land markets. Patuxent River was the home of only one major creditor, namely Richard Snowden who lived in the far northwest corner of the parish. The Snowden family had a long history of mercantile involvement in the parish and they were especially active in the area near the head of South River.

From the standpoint of these leading creditors, success hinged on their contacts with English merchants. Most of the parish's leading creditors were intimately related with London firms. These firms were the source of long lines of credit for colonial investment; however, the dependence of parish creditors on English capital varied enormously. In 1705, Gabriel Parrott's credits totalled £2625.62 and debts, £822.91. Of the debts, more than £500 were owed to the London firm of Micajah Perry and Company. In 1733, Samuel Peele owed his brother John Peele, Merchant in London, £491-15-4 and over £190 to two other London merchants. Such credit lines enabled Samuel to loan out £2420.49 in the Chesapeake. Even more diverse sources of English credit appeared in Richard Snowden's 1767 account. His largest debt lay with Silvanus Grove, London Merchant, for £272-14-2, but five other English merchants

TABLE 38

PROBABLE LOCATIONS OF LEADING RESIDENT CREDITORS, 1660-1769

1660-1679	John Hatton, Merchant	Uncertain, South or West rivers
1680-1697	William Burges	On "Burgh," near London Town
1698-1704	(No creditor extending more than £100)	
1705-1718	Gabriel Parrott, Merchant	Above Flatt Creek, near the head of South River
1719-1726	Samuel Galloway	On West River
1727-1733	Samuel Peele	London Town
1734-1739	Captain Thomas Gassaway	"Hall's Inheritance" on the drainage divide between South and Rhode rivers
1740-1749	John Watkins	On north side of West River
Post-1750 Booms	Joseph Galloway	West River
Post-1750 Busts	Richard Snowden	On Patuxent River in far northwest of parish

Sources: For Hatton, Testamentary Proceedings, 1, ff. 156-62. For Burges, Inventories & Accounts, 18, ff. 89-110; Wills, 4, ff. 242-45. For Parrott, Inventories & Accounts, 25, ff. 89-90; ibid., 26, ff. 219-20; ibid., 32B, ff. 226-28; ibid., ff. 243-45; Wills, 3, ff. 440-41. For Samuel Galloway, Inventories, 4, ff. 313-17; Accounts, 5, f. 2; Wills, 16, ff. 393-402. For Peele, Inventories, 18, ff. 150-76, 518-19; Accounts, 12, ff. 294-96; ibid., 13, ff. 236-39; ibid., 17, ff. 406-9; ibid., 19, f. 192. For Gassaway, Inventories, 24, ff. 421-22; ibid., 25, ff. 399-400; Accounts, 19, ff. 258-63; Wills, 22, f. 97. For Watkins, Inventories, 29, ff. 118-20; ibid., 30, ff. 221-24; Accounts, 21, ff. 271-75; ibid., 26, ff. 134-37; ibid., 36, ff. 348-49. For Joseph Galloway, Inventories, 57, ff. 133-37, 151; Accounts, 36, ff. 426-34; Wills, 28, ff. 412-16. For Snowden, Inventories, 89, f. 203; Accounts, 56, ff. 33-36; Wills, 31, ff. 902-7.

were owed over £600. Apparently Snowden's credit line with Silvanus Grove was tenuous, for many of Snowden's bills of exchange drawn on Grove were returned protested, which meant that there were insufficient funds in the account. Snowden also had an account with the Liverpool merchants Crosbies and Straffred, which was very unusual given the London dominance of parish trade. Thomas Gassaway also depended on London merchants. In 1739, he had £620.10 in credits, and meanwhile he was indebted to London merchants for over £100. Gassaway, along with Parrott, Peele, and Snowden, relied upon English merchants as their chief source of capital. In turn, this credit multiplied in the Chesapeake. For these four leading parish creditors, one pound of English credit engendered three to six pounds of credit in the Chesapeake.

Quite different were the activities of parish creditors such as William Burgess and the Galloways of West River; they generated their own capital for credit. In 1687, William Burgess had debts due him from 152 persons valued at £2204.48. Included were several balances in England, notably £120-3-0 from "George Cornish at London Mercht the Deceaseds Correspondent." Burgess's liabilities amounted to only £284.64, and he owed nothing to English merchants. Almost certainly, Burgess underwrote his numerous credit transactions from his own finances. Joseph Galloway, who died by 1753, did likewise. Galloway extended credit valued at £1837.90 to over 93 persons. He financed these credits from his own resources, as indicated by his debts of only £81.66. And, his account with Silvanus Grove of London indicated a hefty balance of £607-16-1. Men like Burgess and Galloway were truly independent merchants. They were not beholden to London firms as were so many of the other leading creditors in the parish.

Despite the concentration of credit value in the hands of a few parish residents, and indirectly in London firms, these leading creditors exercised little economic dominance over specific parish planters. Rarely were the leading creditors in the parish the primary or largest creditors in planter estates. Parish creditors, regardless of their volume of exchange, made small loans. Between 1660 and 1769, most of the leading creditors averaged less than £5 per debt (Table 37). The small loan typified Samuel Peele's inventory of 1733 and his first two accounts; forty-six of the credits totalled £6 or less; nineteen were between £6 and £12; and twenty-two exceeded £12. The most significant exception to the rule occurred in the 1721 inventory of Samuel Galloway, where the average credit was £213.74. Actually, Galloway did not extend credit locally; this figure represented money owed to him by four English merchants.

Within the parish, the typically small loans came from numerous credit sources. The planters borrowed from many different persons. More often than not, the planters owed their primary or largest debt to a unique creditor, i.e., his credit primacy was limited to one planter. For the 279 decedents with debt lists in their accounts, 186 separate persons appeared as primary creditors. One-hundred and forty-eight of them were unique primary creditors. Just 20.4 per cent of these persons appeared more than once as primary creditor.

With so many individuals serving as primary creditors, the structure of parish exchange was diffuse. However, the spatial structure of exchange did become more focused after the rise of London Town. Between 1710 and 1750, credit transactions increasingly centered on London Town and on London, England. Before 1710, these two places contained few primary creditors. Specifically, London Town sheltered 12 per cent of the primary creditors (mostly because of the credit activity of William Burgess who appeared on eight occasions as primary creditor) and London, England contained 5. 3 per cent. After 1710, as the London-affiliated merchants clustered in London Town, parish residents increasingly sought and found credit in the town. The new merchants, descending on London Town between 1713 and 1717, began capturing the credit trade between 1718 and 1722. They appeared frequently as primary creditors. Between 1710 and 1749, the town's merchants were the primary creditors in 24. 1 per cent of all parish accounts--a figure that doubled the pre-1710 proportion. Even more dramatically, English merchants in London placed as first creditor in over 18 per cent of all accounts. Thus, these two urban centers served as the dominant trading places for over 42 per cent of all parish decedents. These substantial revisions in the flow of parish traffic and the foci of the settlement system passed unseen by the many travellers who judged the importance of towns by their size and appearance. Tobacco towns never fared well on either score.

With the decline of London Town after 1750, trade and traffic moved elsewhere. London Town's focal position for primary parish creditors diminished to 12 per cent of all accounts; and this showing resulted almost exclusively from the activities of one merchant, James Dick. Similarly, English firms as the primary creditors fell to 13. 3 per cent. A shift in the credit foci of All Hallows was underway. Annapolis creditors appeared more frequently after 1750. One Nicholas Maccubbin, a resident of Annapolis and an extensive parish property-holder, was the primary creditor for 13. 3 per cent of the parish accounts. Yet Annapolis captured only a portion of the trade, and the town shared leadership with London Town and London. The rest of the parish's primary creditors, and probably the majority, remained scattered about the parish; the decentralized basis of trade persisted, as it always had.

CHAPTER VII

THE CADASTRE, LANDHOLDING, AND TENANCY

Fluidity characterized every element of the parish settlement system except one--cadastral boundaries. These property boundaries survived remarkably unchanged during a century and a quarter of continuous settlement. They provided an enduring stability in a settlement system otherwise in flux.

This durability of boundaries is somewhat surprising because the initial land surveys of All Hallows Parish created a cartographer's nightmare. Surveys overlapped; vacancies were tucked away in the elbows of the surveys; varied shapes and sizes were juxtaposed; and lines and areas erred by as much as 50 to 100 per cent. Several excuses for this cadastral chaos can be offered, namely, unsophisticated surveyors, crude instruments, and the practices of indiscriminate location and metes and bounds demarcation. The situation invited boundary dispute and costly litigation, but very little of either occurred. Parishioners accepted the inaccurate property lines drawn by seventeenth century surveyors so long as land was abundant and the land market was spatially concentrated.

But a growing population threatened land and boundary stability. At first, outmigration alleviated the pressure of population on the land. And the enormous increase in short-term tenancy helped perpetuate the original cadastral boundaries and the landholding structure. These tenants rented land and operated their tenements within the original cadastral framework; they did not change it. Yet inexorably, tenants increased, the man-land ratio worsened, and the shifting agricultural system approached its areal limits. By the end of the colonial years, the stability of landholdings and boundaries was put to a severe test.

Initial Survey, Consequences, and Ameliorating Procedures

The initial surveys of All Hallows Parish were essentially complete by the 1690's. By that date, the early surveyors, equipped with rudimentary skills and crude instruments, had assembled a crazy-quilt of surveys. They piled one surveying error on top of another; they mixed together a great variety of survey sizes and shapes; they left overlaps and gaps on the cadastral map. This chaos was the cumulative result of several operations in the surveying process.

Determining Location and Shape

Maryland's land system permitted the landowner to dictate the location and shape of his survey.[1] Essentially, the colony followed a policy of indiscriminate location; that policy permitted the bearer of a land warrant to locate his survey on any unsurveyed land within the county specified in the warrant. Yet, in practice, the surveyor exercised as much influence on location as did the prospective landowners. The surveyor appended later surveys onto the earlier surveys along the estuaries; indeed, almost every survey in All Hallows Parish shared a common boundary with a prior survey. With the general location established, the warrant holder took over. He gave more specific instructions on the layout of the survey. The customary tactic involved the engrossing of large stretches of water frontage, creating narrow surveys that wound around the estuaries. All Hallows planters varied this tactic slightly; they preferred small necks of land, having estuarine access on three sides. When the neck did not consume all of the acreage specified in the warrant, the surveyor simply extended the excess inland, or he returned part of the warrant acreage to the planter for his use in a later survey.

Surveys along the estuaries had simple geometric shapes of three to ten sides. The most common shape among the small necks was the rectangle; its shape conformed nicely to the configuration of the necks, that is, after the surveyors grossly generalized the estuarine wiggles. As settlement proceeded inland, geometric simplicity persisted through the 1690's (Figures 3 and 7). The surveyors' emphasis on a few simple shapes and on the geometric abstraction of drainage features was, as we shall see, a concession to their poor training and their crude instruments.

---

[1]For discussion of Maryland's land system, see Clarence P. Gould, The Land System in Maryland, 1720-1765, Johns Hopkins University Studies in Historical and Political Science 31st Series, No. 1 (1913); and John Kilty, The Land-holder's Assistant and Land Office Guide (Baltimore: n.p., 1808).

The Conduct of the Survey

Armed with location, acreage, and a crude idea of the shape of the survey, the surveyor then set about describing the limits of the parcel. The description involved a field survey, a written report of the bounds, and a great deal of error.

The ideal field survey began at an identifiable physical feature, usually a tree. After marking or notching the "beginning tree," the surveyor proceeded around the parcel, identifying and marking corner trees, determining linear distances and directions between bounding trees, all the while keeping track of the acreage specified in the warrant. But seventeenth century surveyors seldom adhered to this ideal procedure. Surveyors preferred an easier method. They measured off the desired distance along the estuary; projected the other three lines; reproduced a rectangle or a square; and quickly calculated its area. In this way, the surveyors laid out the first tier of tracts along the estuaries. The condemning evidence is found in the large number of survey corners which did not have marked trees recorded. This slipshod practice diminished by the 1670's when interior areas were surveyed. There, the surveyors ran most of the lines.

Field measurements of distance, direction, and area were usually rough-and-ready. Surveyors customarily measured distances by pacing or visually estimating from a slowly moving boat. It was a rare surveyor who measured distance with Gunter's chain, which became available in England by the 1620's.[1] Indeed, eighty years after the chain's introduction to England, one Maryland surveyor used a fishing drum line in lieu of a chain. Equally primitive were the surveyors' attempts at measuring direction. Parishioners lacked sophisticated instruments for direction measurement until the 1670's,[2] and by then most of the land had been crudely surveyed. The Assembly of 1674 recognized the imprecision of surveys, and they enacted a law that granted double the ordinary fees to surveyors who used chain, circumferentor with sights, and other surveying instruments.[3] Yet while Lord Baltimore's chief surveyors may have

---

[1]Allie W. Richeson, English Land Measuring to 1800: Instruments and Practices (Cambridge, Massachusetts: The Society for the History of Technology and the MIT Press, 1966), p. 109.

[2]The 1682 inventory of Richard Beard, a parish resident and deputy surveyor, contained "'2 old Circumferenters chaine brass seale Brass deviders'" and other instruments; Wills, 3, f. 181.

[3]Archives of Maryland, II, 393.

used the theodolite, the chain, and the circumferentor as early as 1644,[1] the typical surveyor probably did not use even a compass. Indeed, the early parish surveys recorded direction by the thirty-two points on the compass card. Degrees and minutes did not appear in the survey descriptions until 1688.[2] And sophisticated adjustments for magnetic declination came later in the eighteenth century.[3]

Area measurement was also a problem; surveyors solved it by surveying simple shapes with easily calculated areas. They did not use the ingenious English method of area measurement which compared the weights of paper cutouts, one of the survey and the other of a regular shape and a known area. Area calculation by triangles became fairly common for the elaborate land surveys made in the eighteenth century, and some plats retain the scribe marks.[4]

On completion of the field survey, the surveyor drafted a certificate containing the date of survey, surveyor, bounds, and acreage. He then returned the certificate to the Surveyor General in St. Mary's City, where it lay for six months during which time citizens could file objections to the survey. Subsequently, the landowner received a patent confirming his title.

The Consequences of Initial Survey

Parish boundaries were notoriously vague, principally because the metes and bounds reference points were transitory, and measurements of the lines

---

[1] Ibid., IV, 279. Theodolites and circumferentors are very similar. In the former, angles in a horizontal plane are found by turning the sights, while the compass needle remains in the north-south position. With the circumferentor, the sights are fixed to the instrument, and thus when positions are sited, the needle wanders back to a north-south position. Richeson, English Land Measuring, p. 93.

[2] See the survey of "Ovenwood Thickett" in 1688. Patents, 22, f. 407.

[3] One surveyor estimated that the secular variation in the needle was about six and a half degrees in ninety years at Annapolis. Deposition of Richard Shipley, Surveyor, August 1, 1749, Beard's Lessee agt. Nicholas Maccubbin, Ejectment Papers, Box No. 3. The failure of early surveyors to allow for magnetic declination is a continuing problem for Maryland surveyors. L. A. Bauer, "First Report upon Magnetic Work in Maryland including the History and Objects of Magnetic Surveys," Maryland Geological Society, I (Baltimore: Johns Hopkins Press, 1897), 405-529.

[4] Annapolis, Hall of Records MSS, Anne Arundel County Patented Certificates of Survey, No. 1564.

were woefully imprecise. The reliance on metes and bounds surveying, using trees and water courses as terminal points, created such confusion that it commanded the attention of the Assembly of 1723:

> Whereas the Bounds of Land in this Province depend chiefly upon marked Trees which are Subject to decay, or upon Bays, Rivers, Creeks or Branches, the Names whereof do frequently become obselete or change; by which Means the true Bounds of such Lands (in process of Time) become doubtful. . . .[1]

Corner trees died naturally, or were accidently or intentionally cut. And along the estuaries, shoreline erosion occasionally swept away bound trees. Names for water features were also transitory. For example, Beard's Creek was initially Jacob's Creek, and Burgess Creek, adjacent to London Town, became Shipping Creek.

Surveying errors compounded boundary confusion. The combination of crude instruments, carelessness, and the substitution of straight lines for sinuous drainage features resulted in overlapping surveys, vacancies, and gross miscalculations of area. The effects are readily apparent in the map of initial surveys (Figure 7). Acute overlapping occurred in the vicinity of Flatt Creek near South River; there, a jumble of fifty and one hundred acre surveys were enmeshed. Occasionally, an entire survey fell within the boundaries of earlier tracts. For example, the 1707 rent roll for Anne Arundel County noted that "Hester's Habitation" and "Elizabeth's Fancy" were in "elder surveys."[2] And in 1718, Philip Holeadger surrendered his patent for "Addition," "being all taken away by older surveys. . . ."[3] Other areas of the parish were a bit more tidy than Flatt Creek, partly because of the larger size of tracts; however, numerous gaps or vacancies filled the dead spaces where surveys were not contiguous.

The map of initial surveys is reconstructed from surveyors' descriptions of metes and bounds (Figure 7); the procedure involves the patching together of the surveys, by locating the earliest surveys and then appending later surveys to them. This resembles the way the surveyors proceeded, but unfortunately, our results do not agree. Note for example the jagged swath of unsurveyed land extending from south of London Town to the southern border of the parish. In reality, this gap did not exist, and the surveys on either side were contiguous.

---

[1] Archives of Maryland, XXXIX, 727.

[2] AACo Rent Roll, Liber 1.

[3] Annapolis, Hall of Records MSS, Provincial Court Judgments, VD#3, f. 235.

The gap results from surveying errors in length measurement and from the coalescense of surveys from three different estuarine "base lines." The measurement error can be estimated from the gap width; it varies from 10 to 15 per cent of an east-west transect across the entire parish. Thus, errors in length measurement probably favored the warrant holder by 10 per cent or more. The error compounded when inaccurate length measurements were used to calculate area. For example, a square-shaped survey with a 10 per cent error in side length produces an areal error of more than 20 per cent.

Consequently, survey acreages were usually inaccurate. And resurveys made in the eighteenth century embarrassingly revealed the magnitude of error. After conducting a resurvey, the surveyor noted the acreage of both the initial and corrected survey; they often specified, too, the surplus or deficiency of land in the earlier survey, and the contiguous vacant land that was added in the resurvey. Twenty-eight parish resurveys contain adequate information to determine the degree of error in initial areal calculation. Twenty contained more acres than the original survey specified, six contained less than the stated acreage, and two contained the correct acreage. As a proportion of the area specified in the original certificates of survey, the errors ranged from a surplus of 150 per cent to a deficiency of 42.1 per cent, with a mean error of 42 per cent. When the seventeenth century surveyor wrote his description for the certificate of survey, he invariably qualified the number of acres by appending "more or less." The most common error was "more"; the surveyor, by duplicity or ignorance, typically awarded more than a third again the amount intended by the Maryland proprietors.

The general uncertainty of boundary location frustrated some of the parishioners, especially those who resided along the All Hallows-St. James border. This parish boundary helped determine the number of taxables in the parish, and hence, the amount of revenue that the parish rector and vestry received from the annual county levy. Boundary problems first appeared in 1749; and about ten years later the rectors of All Hallows and St. James joined in petitioning the Assembly:

> there have been Disputes for Several Years past concerning the Limits & Bounds of the Parishes . . . which have occasioned considerable Expenses & Trouble already and will Probably be the cause of much greater, if the Parishes continue Bounded in the manner they are Supposed to be. . . . They were at first laid out by the Commissioners appointed in the year 1692 who bounded the Parishes by Plantations, which for the most part they distinguished in no other manner but by the names of those who were then in possession of them--Since that Time, some of the Plantations have been possessed by Persons of different names and Families, but some of them included with other Tracts in the same Survey, others have been sold in parts to those who held the adjoining Lands which has now rendered the bounds

> very intricate and makes it difficult to determine in which Parish some Families are, wherefore they have given in their Taxes some times in one and sometimes in the other Parish. . . .[1]

Ill-defined surveys, transitory residents, and land subdivision and consolidation all contributed to the blurring of the parish boundary. Final delimitation did not come until 1767, when the county court ordered the boundary drawn to connect the bounded trees of "Whites Plains" and "Ewen upon Ewenton."[2]

Ameliorating Procedures

The boundary dispute between All Hallows and St. James was eventually settled amicably; but in that dispute, we can see the potential for conflict and heated exchanges. Given the vague and overlapping boundaries of land, trespass, civil dispute, and litigation seemed inevitable. Yet, costly legal conflicts were unusual; the planters had simpler and less-expensive procedures for clarifying boundary lines.

Recourse to the courts was one of several remedial procedures aimed at settling boundary controversies. One party to the controversy instituted an action of trespass and ejectment in the Provincial Court.[3] The court, seeking a just decision, usually ordered a resurvey of the lands in contention. Ejectment cases, however, were not very popular. Just thirty-three such cases involving parish land came before the Provincial Court between 1684 and 1746. And several of these involved fictitious litigants, indicating that the owners sought legal clarification of their titles, and not the resolution of boundary conflicts. One "Timothy Peaceable" acted as the plaintiff in a 1737 case, in which the real purpose was to sort out title claims to "Middle Plantation."[4] Trespass and ejectment proceedings were also employed for the formal surrender of a patent that lay in "elder surveys."[5] The amount of boundary litigation coming before the Provincial Court was surprisingly small, perhaps because of the

---

[1] Annapolis, Hall of Records MSS, Black Books, X, No. 52. See also AACo Judgments, LSB#1, f. 311; Archives of Maryland, L, 9.

[2] AACo Judgments, IMB#2, f. 305; and, ibid., IMB#1, f. 871.

[3] Civil disputes involving land were not within the jurisdiction of the county courts. My understanding of ejectment proceedings was enhanced through conversations with Dr. Ashley Ellefson.

[4] Provincial Court Judgments, EI#4, ff. 156-59.

[5] Ibid., VD#3, ff. 235-36.

expense of ejectment cases.[1] The action involved lawyer's fees, surveyor's fees, and court costs for the losing party, as well as any damages awarded.[2]

A second recourse, resurveying, was far less expensive, except when the surveyor uncovered large amounts of surplus land. The resurvey procedure began with a "special warrant" from the Land Office, directing the surveyor to resurvey a specific parcel and to add in vacant land contiguous to the parcel. The procedure, by avoiding court costs and lawyer fees, entailed smaller costs than ejectment proceedings.[3] However, if the surveyor discovered surplus acreage within the original survey, then costs mounted. The provincial government reasoned that these landowners had used the surplus land without paying the annual quit-rents. And before issuing the patent on the resurvey, the Land Office demanded payment of the rent arrearages. A 1703 resurvey of "Happy Choice" disclosed eighty-eight acres of surplusage, with unpaid rents dating back to the initial survey in 1670 amounting to £12.75.[4] Honesty may have motivated a few planters to resurvey their land and pay their back rents; but most had a better reason. Resurveys gave them the opportunity of taking up vacant land adjacent to their holdings and of consolidating two or more contiguous surveys. These gains usually outweighed the costs of surplusage. In the resurveying process, boundaries were clarified; but the results were incidental to the main motive of cheaply increasing plantation size.

The spatial pattern of All Hallows resurveys appears in Figure 22. Perhaps one-half of the parish land had been resurveyed before 1776, with the highest incidence occurring in the southern, southeastern, and northwestern portions of the parish. Resurveying diminished on the Patuxent side of the parish and, surprisingly, in the cluttered zone around Flatt Creek; about the only com-

---

[1] Archives of Maryland, XXXIX, 727.

[2] Surveyor's fees could be costly. In an ejectment case of 1768 to 1771, surveyor's fees amounted to 1,926 pounds of tobacco, or the equivalent of two laborers' annual tobacco production. Itemized charges included resurvey, plats, running lines, journey fees, and certificates. In addition, 96 pounds of tobacco was paid to a chain carrier for four days work. Anderson agt. Iiams, 1768-1771, Ejectment Papers, Box No. 1.

[3] There were, however, occasional court-ordered surveys from the county court. They were conducted by the sheriff, the deputy surveyor, and a jury of twelve men, usually local citizens. These jury resurveys seem to have been limited to the determination of boundaries and areas of orphan's estates. See AACo Deeds, WT#2, ff. 354-55, 358-60.

[4] Patents, EI#1, ff. 453-54.

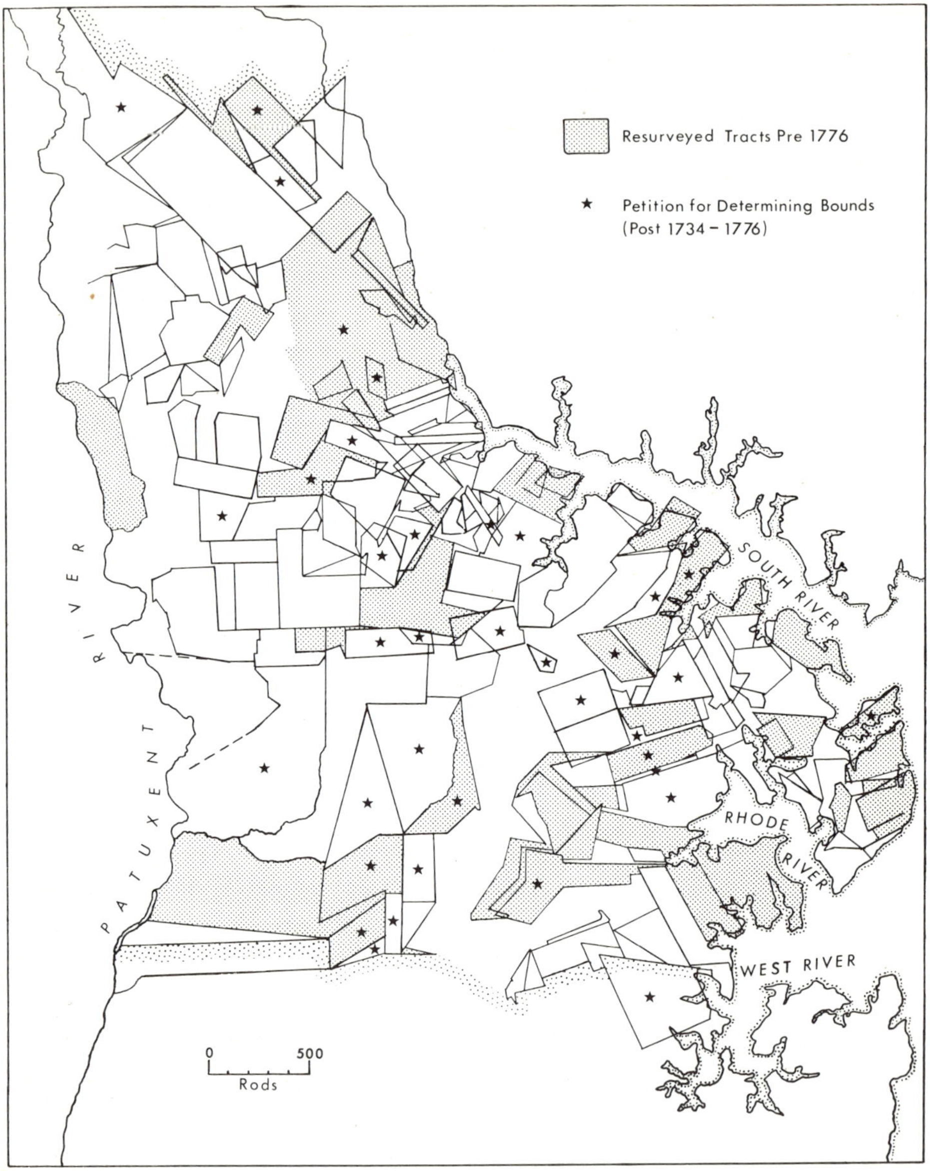

Fig. 22.--Location of Resurveys and Petitions to Examine Bounds

monality shared by these two areas was their late settlement, generally after 1665 (Figure 3). Perhaps they benefited from more skillful surveying.

Resurveys may have been cheaper than court litigation, but both procedures were out of reach for the small planter, earning five fo fifteen pounds annually. In determining their land bounds, they required even less costly procedures, such as relying on the word of an "Antient Liver." Parishioner Richard Iiams did precisely that when he sought to clarify the bounds of "Burgess Choice" before he purchased part of it:

> and wanting to know the bounds Certainly Applyed himselfe to Walter Phelps who was an Antient Liver in those partes to shew him the bounds And the said Walter went wth him round the Land and Shewd him the trees. . . .[1]

The word of men like Walter Phelps did not carry the force of law, but their word carried more than ordinary weight. When boundary litigation arose, these judicious, long-livers were frequently the first persons called to give depositions on boundary trees and lines.

Besides litigation, resurveys, and the word of "antient livers," boundary disputants also resorted to third party arbitration, with the disputants entering into a bond to accept the ruling.[2] Arbitration, however, does not seem to have been widely used to solve boundary problems.

A fifth procedure, the processioning of cadastral bounds, made little headway in Maryland, though this periodic renewal of boundary lines and markers was legally required in neighboring Virginia.[3] The Maryland Assembly of 1748 did pass a bill "for Processioning of Lands . . . ," but the Upper House quashed it. While recognizing the usefulness of renewing cadastral bounds, that body rationalized that "very few would in all Probability desire their Bounds to be Processioned. . . ."[4]

By far the most effective procedure for boundary delimitation was contained in a 1723 act "for the Ease of the Inhabitants in Examining evidences re-

---

[1]Deposition of Richard Iiams, February 20, 1722, Godiah Spray, Lessee of Richard Snowden agt. Anne Lee, Ejectment Papers, Box S.

[2]AACo Deeds, SY#1, ff. 100-102; ibid., WT#1, ff. 286-88.

[3]By a Virginia act of 1662, freeholders were to meet every four years to examine and renew the boundary marks of land within parts of their parishes; this was processioning. William H. Seiler, "Land Processioning in Colonial Virginia," William and Mary Quarterly, 3rd Series, VI (July, 1949), 416-36.

[4]Archives of Maryland, XLVI, 30-31.

lating to the Bounds of Land. . . ."[1] The act dealt explicitly and exclusively with boundaries, thus minimizing fears that surplus land would be discovered and arrearages charged. The procedure began with the landowner; he submitted a petition to the appropriate county court. In turn, the court commissioned four disinterested and "capable freeholders" to examine evidences regarding boundaries. The act empowered two or more of the commissioners with the authority to issue summons to individuals nominated by the petitioner. Public notice of the examination was affixed to the parish church at least three Sundays in advance; other notices were required at public places at least twenty days in advance. The results of the boundary examination were recorded in the county court records. The boundary disputants found the procedure inexpensive, and their only costs were the fees paid to the commissioners and to the evidences. Neither surveyors nor lawyers were required. By this act, the Assembly tacitly acknowledged that cadastral boundaries were based on customary bounds as proven by reliable local residents and not on the inaccurate descriptions given by incompetent seventeenth century surveyors.

The determination of boundaries by petition and examination was much more frequent than litigation, resurvey, or arbitration. Unfortunately, court judgments in Anne Arundel County lapsed immediately after the act. But they resumed in 1733, and from that date until 1771 parish residents submitted 37 petitions which involved 51 initial surveys or an average of almost one petition per year, or nearly twice the average for ejectment cases. Petitions tended to cluster, with 6 occurring between 1738 and 1740; 16 between 1743 and 1753; and 12 between 1756 and 1763. There was no apparent relationship with booms or busts.

The spatial pattern was very similar to that of resurveys (Figure 22); however, the distribution was more widespread, especially on the "Ridge" and in the Flatt Creek area, where overlapping was prevalent.

In sum, a variety of remedial procedures minimized the havoc wrought by seventeenth century surveyors. Given the magnitude of their errors, the parishioners' demands for litigation, resurvey, petition, and processioning were surprisingly modest. The boundaries of many original surveys were never redefined. Some planters had their boundaries redetermined once, but rarely twice. Specifically, petition and resurvey on the same parcel occurred in just 13 per cent of all the original surveys. This paucity of boundary litigation and

---

[1] Ibid., XXXIX, 727-30.

conflict was the direct result of several stabilizing aspects of the settlement system, to which we now turn.

Stabilizing Aspects of the Land System

In an economy based on tobacco, corn, livestock, and wheat, and in which 80 to 90 per cent of the household heads were planters, the meaning of land was patently obvious. Freemen sought to become freeholders exercising fee simple ownership over land; and the brisk land market attested to these desires. But despite the dynamism of the land market, landownership proved a stabilizing element in the settlement system. The initial surveys persisted as the basic cadastral framework.

The Market for Land

Until 1683, land was usually acquired from the proprietor in return for the transportation of white immigrants into the colony. Thus, the rapid growth of population in the parish corresponded with equally rapid land acquisition. By the 1690's most of the land had been surveyed; prospective freeholders had to buy in the private market. Even before 1683,[1] some persons purchased parts of the initial surveys. The buyers consisted mainly of second-generation sons of the first settlers. They were logical participants in the land market, especially when they could not afford to pay an immigrant's passage for land rights. The main sellers in this frontier land market were English heirs of Marylanders who died without relations in the colony. These English heirs were usually anxious to sell, and at very reasonable prices. Large speculators played both the buying and the selling ends of the land market. Thus, the private land market was brisk during the early years, but it became even more so after the 1690's.

Parish land transactions, including deeds of sale, gift, and mortgage, varied considerably in volume. These transactions between 1658 and 1771 appear in Figure 23;[2] on the graph, transactions are grouped by three-year periods.

---

[1]The head-rights system in Maryland was abandoned after 1683, and the proprietor substituted a cash payment for land that was surveyed and patented. Edward I. McCormac, White Servitude in Maryland, 1634-1820, Johns Hopkins University Studies in Historical and Political Science, 22nd Series, Nos. 3-4 (1904), p. 27.

[2]The data are extracted from various libers of AACo Deeds between 1658 and 1774.

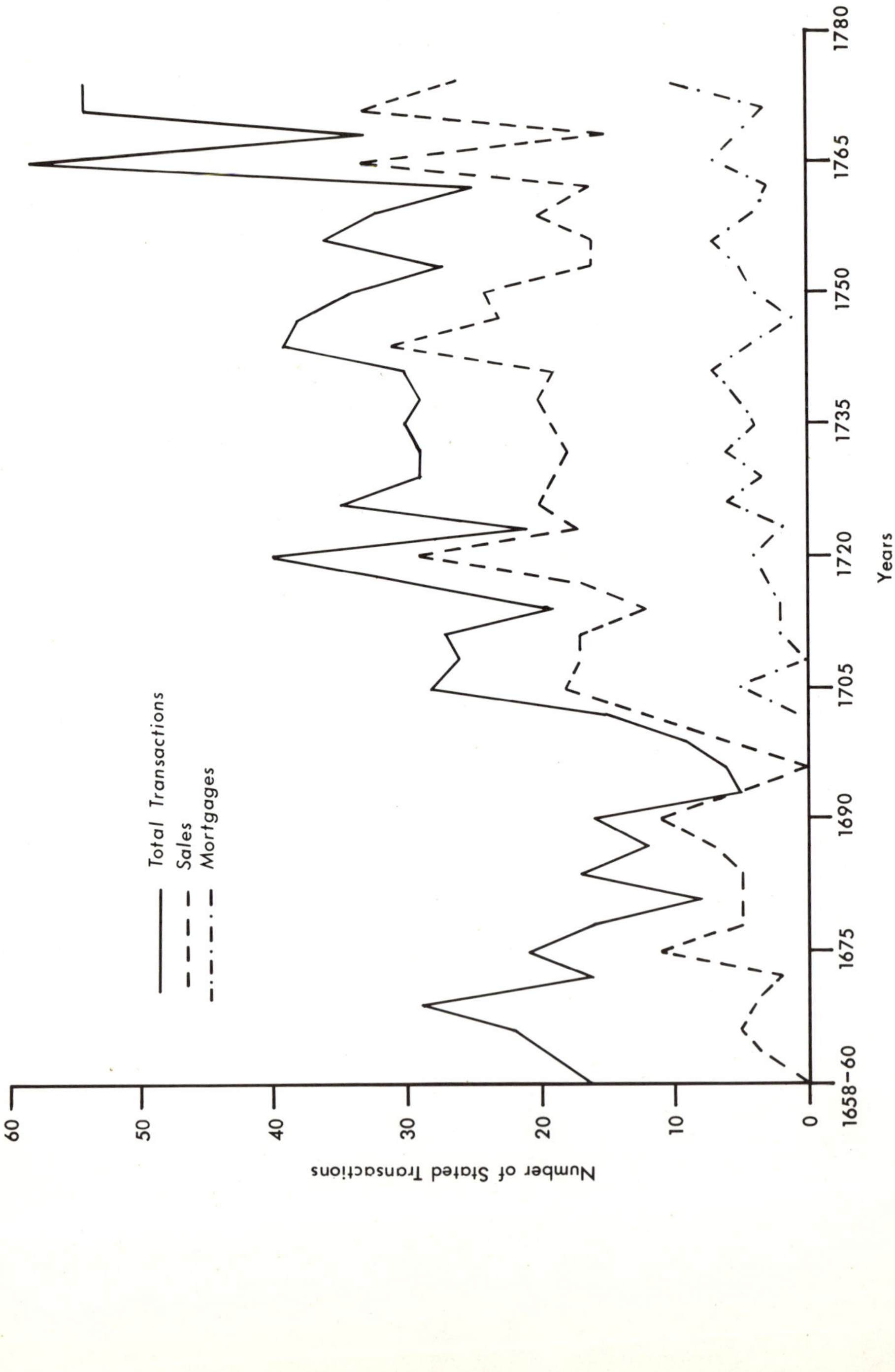

Fig. 23.--Land Transactions, 1659-1774

The figures before 1703 must be used with especial caution because they are derived from re-recorded land deeds. Parish land transactions ranged from a low of eight in 1679-1681 to a high of fifty-eight in 1763-1765. Sales constituted the majority of land transactions. A recurrent pattern of peaks and troughs characterized land sales, but they did not fluctuate with respect to economic conditions. Sales peaks occurred in 1673-1675, a boom; 1688-1690, a bust; 1703-1705, a transitional phase; 1718-1720, a transitional phase; 1742-1744, a transitional phase; and 1763-1765, a bust. The regular spacing between sales peaks suggests that demographic factors may have been more influential than economic ones. The year-intervals between sales peaks were 15, 15, 24, 21, and 24; stated differently, land sales peaked at about half a human generation of 32 years. Sales of land tended to rise when large population cohorts came of age and entered into the land market. Indeed, replacement rate peaks tended to coincide with peaks in land sales between the 1680's and 1740. The first sales peak in the 1670's probably resulted from freed servants acquiring land; but after that, the demographic correlation became stronger. The replacement rates for the successive land sale peaks were 2.14 in 1691-1695; 1.31 in 1703-1705; 1.46 in 1716-1718; and over 3.00 in 1742-1744. The naturally increasing parish population may have had the effect of lengthening the sales peak interval. Because of rising replacement rates and falling death rates, parish children had more cohort competitors for scarce resources. Land prices were pushed up; sons may have deferred marriage, household formation, and land purchases for five to ten years until they acquired the capital to buy land and start their own plantation. The upshot was that land sales peaks came at intervals of twenty years or so instead of the usual fifteen years.[1]

Mortgages on land for the purposes of capital acquisition were infrequent. That is if we assume that all mortgages were recorded in the county land records. Mortgages tended to increase during depressions, especially after 1730; mortgage peaks came in 1730-1732, 1739-1741, 1754-1756, 1763-1765, and

---

[1]There does appear to be some cyclicity in the number of land sales, and the spacing accords fairly well with the twenty-two and one-half year cycles in the demographic model of P. M. G. Harris. However, the interval spacing here seems to divide into fifteen year intervals prior to 1704, and longer intervals thereafter. In other words, there is probably a secular trend reducing opportunity to acquire land. P. M. G. Harris, "The Social Origins of American Leaders: The Demographic Foundations," Perspectives in American History, III (1969), 159-344. One further qualification is that the peaks of land sales in the mid-1670's and again in 1703-1705 are weakly related to replacement rates, and probably reflect the entry into the land market of freed servants, imported during recent boom years.

1772-1774. Land mortgages thus provided collateral for some of the credit extension during depressions. Another source of collateral was from mortgages of personal property, which also became more common after 1730. By contrast to the middle years of the eighteenth century, the years before 1730 saw mortgages peaking in the boom years of 1703-1705, 1718-1720, and 1724-1726. Unfortunately, no mortgage data survive for the pre-1700 period.

In All Hallows Parish, then, land was a commodity to be bought, sold, and mortgaged. Consequently, the volume of land business was considerable. Every three years, forty to eighty parishioners conducted twenty to forty land sales--a substantial showing for a parish containing 312 households before 1776.

The Cadastre: Turnover, Subdivision, and the Persistence of Names

This dynamic land market had little effect on the cadastral framework, which retained its seventeenth century identity. Two factors explain the remarkable persistence of the initial surveys: the spatial concentration both of land sales and of land subdivision within the initial surveys.

The majority of land sales between 1730 and 1774 were concentrated among a small number of surveys (Table 39). Of 149 survey parcels, 30.2 per cent contained no sales; 25.5 per cent contained one sale; 14.1 per cent contained two sales. Thus, 69.8 per cent of all surveys were marginally involved in the parish land market. The typical survey averaged 2.29 sales, but this figure was inflated considerably by two surveys containing fifteen and nineteen sales. Respectively, these two surveys were "Scorton & Burgh," which encompassed London Town, and "Snowden's Reputation Supported," located near the head of South River in the vicinity of numerous mills and the Anne Arundel County School. Land sales were most frequent in the area around the head of South River; along the road leading from London Town south to Anne Arundel Manor; and by the Patuxent near Kilkenny and Queen Anne's Town (Figure 24). The remainder of the parish area had low sales turnover; and in these areas, marginally involved in the land market, boundary clarification was non-essential.

Boundary confusion increased wherever land subdivision proceeded rapidly. Yet this practice of carving out smaller properties from the initial surveys was very confined. Undivided surveys accounted for 75.6 per cent of all the surveys as of 1707; by 1783, the proportion had fallen a trifle to 66.8 per cent (Table 40).[1] For these same dates, surveys containing one division or less con-

---

[1]The source for 1707 is Anne Arundel County Rent Rolls, Liber 1; minor

TABLE 39

SALES TURNOVER PER SURVEY, 1730-1774

No. of Sales	Surveys with Stated No. of Sales
0	45
1	38
2	21
3	12
4	9
5	7
6	3
7	3
8	3
9	3
10	5

TABLE 40

FREQUENCY OF SUBDIVISION IN INITIAL SURVEYS,
1707 AND 1783

No. of Parcels in Initial Survey	1707	1783 Total	Upper Rhode 1783	Lower Rhode 1783	South River 1783
1	127	127	67	35	25
2	22	33	18	9	6
3	8	14	9	0	5
4	5	9	5	2	2
5	4	2	2	0	0
6	1	3	1	0	2
7	1	1	1	0	0
8	0	1	0	0	1
n	168	190	103	46	41

stituted 88.7 per cent and 84.2 per cent, respectively; and with two divisions or less (three parcels or less), 93.5 per cent and 91.6 per cent. The overwhelming majority of initial parish surveys were subdivided less than twice, and contained three or fewer parcels.

Subdivision's uneven spatial pattern mirrored the pattern for land sales (Figures 25 and 26). As of 1707, subdivision occurred mainly on the "Ridge" in

---

corrections are made by collating with deeds. For 1783, the source is the Federal Assessment of 1783.

Fig. 24.--Sales Turnover: Number of Sales per Survey, 1730-1774

the central part of the parish. By 1783, subdivision had become more widespread; however, areal concentrations persisted. The zone of maximum subdivision shifted from the Ridge toward the head of South River; near the numerous bridges over Patuxent; and along the major transport routes leading south and west from London Town.

The spatial concentration of sales turnover and survey subdivision reinforced one another; both were highest in areas with access to main or public roads, especially along the inter-colonial routeways through the parish. Boundary ambiguity, indicated by resurveys and petitions, was most acute in the very areas where land was actively transferred and subdivided.[1] Yet these accessible corridors made up a very small share of parish land. Lying beyond these corridors was the majority of parish surveys. They were marginally involved in the parish land market; and the scarcity of sales and subdivision insured their territorial integrity through time.

Thus, in many parts of the parish, the initial surveys provided the basic cadastral outline up until the American Revolution. This durability was especially evident in the century-long survival of the names given to initial surveys. Survey names bestowed in the seventeenth century appeared over and over in the federal assessment of 1783. The assessors sometimes corrupted spellings, but the original names are usually recognizable. For example, "Foldland," named after George Nettlefold who surveyed the parcel in 1661, became "Foreland"; and "Hester's Habitation" became "Ester's."[2] On the 1783 assessment list for Upper Rhode River Hundred, there appeared 172 parcel names, some of which were repeated several times; 136, or 79 per cent, of these names had been bestowed on pre-1707 surveys. Of the 36 new names, many were attached to resurveys. In about 5 per cent of the cases, new names resulted from subdivisions of an initial survey. When Benjamin Burgess sold all of his inherited land at the beginning of the eighteenth century, the parcels took on the names of the purchasers. Thus the initial survey of "Burges Choice" was sundered into "Charles Frolick," after its new owner Charles Cheney, and "Ijams Purchase," for Richard Ijams.[3] Names created in this fashion are here considered as new names; however, even they endured for over eighty years.

---

[1]This is perhaps more true of the petitions to examine evidences, which are collected for 1734-1774, a period of route elaboration and realignment.

[2]See, Patents, 5, ff. 290-91; ibid., 20, ff. 187-88.

[3]AACo Deeds, WT#1, ff. 84-88; ibid., WT#2, ff. 237-40.

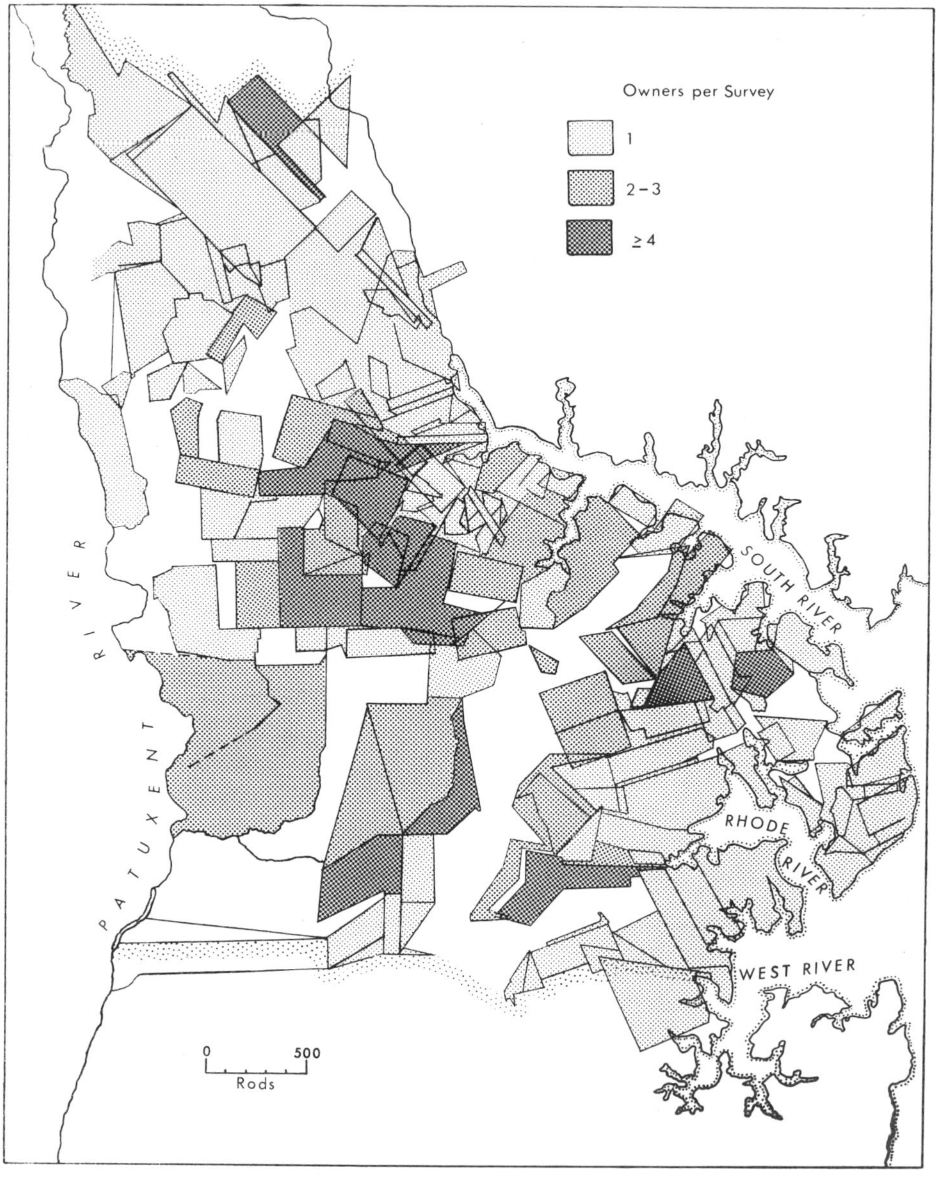

Fig. 25.--Survey Subdivision, 1707

Fig. 26.--Survey Subdivision, 1783

To summarize briefly, the majority of parish boundaries changed little during the colonial period. These bounds, as imprecise and vague as they were, helped maintain territorial stability. In just a few areas of high accessibility, a vigorous land market prevailed. There, boundary confusion was more severe; and buyers and sellers resorted frequently to the several remedial procedures designed to clarify the boundaries of plantations.

Landholding and Tenancy

Because many parish landholdings were marginally involved in the land market and in subdivision, these properties remained basically unchanged during the colonial years. Consequently, the parish landholding structure of 1675 was nearly identical to the structures of 1707 and 1783.[1] These three cross-sections, though largely determined by the availability of data, represent such distinctively different times and economic conditions as to constitute a fair test of the stability of landholding. The year 1675 fell in the midst of a boom in tobacco prices; 1707 came during a severe depression; and 1783 marked the last year of the American Revolution. If parish landholdings experienced major revisions, these should be readily apparent in these three divergent time periods.

In order to discuss landholding patterns, it is necessary to carefully define terms. Consistency of definition is attained by using the definition stated in the tax law of 1782. This law specified which tenures were assessible as real property and hence, were owned or held by the taxpayer. They were:

> all lands held or enjoyed immediately by Tenants in fee simple, or fee simple conditional, or executory or Fee tail, or by Tenants for Life without any Contingency and impeachment of waste and who pays no rent, or by Tenant by the Courtesy shall be wholly valued to such tenants; And land assigned to and held by Tenant in Dower shall be assessed to such tenant, and where divers persons have Particular estates or interests carved out of the same inheritance, as for years, with a reversion or remainder for life or in fee, a just computation should be made in proportion to the value of their particular interest therein. . . .[2]

This definition is followed with two slight exceptions. On a holding with a reversion or a remainder, I count the part-owner in possession of the land as the landowner. Additionally, I list the guardians of orphans as owners because guardians conducted the affairs on orphans' plantations.

---

[1]For 1675, the landholding pattern is reconstructed from initial surveys and deeds; for 1707, from the Anne Arundel County Rent Roll, supplemented by deeds; and for 1783, from the Federal Assessment of 1783.

[2]Annapolis, Hall of Records MSS, Laws, Liber TBH#A, f. 226.

Landholding in All Hallows was remarkably stable (Figure 27). The rank-size distribution of landholdings, which ranks the amount of land held by individual owners or possessors, was similar in all three cross-sectional years. The curve gradually ascended to holdings of about 400 acres, and then it turned abruptly upward. The median size of holdings ranged moderately from 300 acres in 1675 to 176 acres in 1707, and 204 acres in 1783. The largest holdings were similarly stable; in chronological order, they were 3,800 acres, 3,799 acres, and 2,887 acres. Further evidence of landholding stability is found in Table 41. For example, landholdings exceeding 300 acres numbered 42 in 1675; 46 in 1707; and 50 in 1783. However, some selective shifting did occur in size categories of less than 300 acres. Between 1675 and 1707, holdings of less than 199 acres increased by 166.7 per cent. Further shifts occurred between 1707 and 1783, with the largest increase (138.5 per cent) occurring among 200- to 299-acre holdings. Aside from these shifts, acreage categories exhibited only minor changes. Thus, the sizes of landholdings in 1783 retained marked similarity to those more than one hundred years earlier. The one notable change involved the growing number of small and intermediate holdings of less than 299 acres.

Tenancy and Population Growth

One reason for the static land structure was that the body of landowners grew very slowly; by contrast, the parish population grew rapidly. More and more parish households did not own land; most of them functioned as agricultural tenants. The figures dramatize the disparity in the growth of population and landownership. From 1675 to 1707, parish households increased by 82.2 per cent while landowners increased by only 30 per cent. Between 1707 and 1783, the comparable proportions were 73 per cent for households and 12.7 per cent for landowners. These low entry rates into parish landownership buttressed stability on the land. But such stability was of dubious value for the increasing population of non-landowners. They faced one of two alternatives: tenancy or outmigration.[1]

---

[1]The stability of landholdings in All Hallows seems strikingly different from Lockridge's conclusions for New England towns. There, land became scarce in the late eighteenth century; in numerous towns, the average amount of land available for white males over 21 fell to 30-70 acres, a dramatic decline from seventeenth century levels. Applying Lockridge's methodology to All Hallows, we find that the average acreage per white adult male decreased slightly from 136 acres in 1707 to 121 acres in 1776. Following Lockridge's logic we

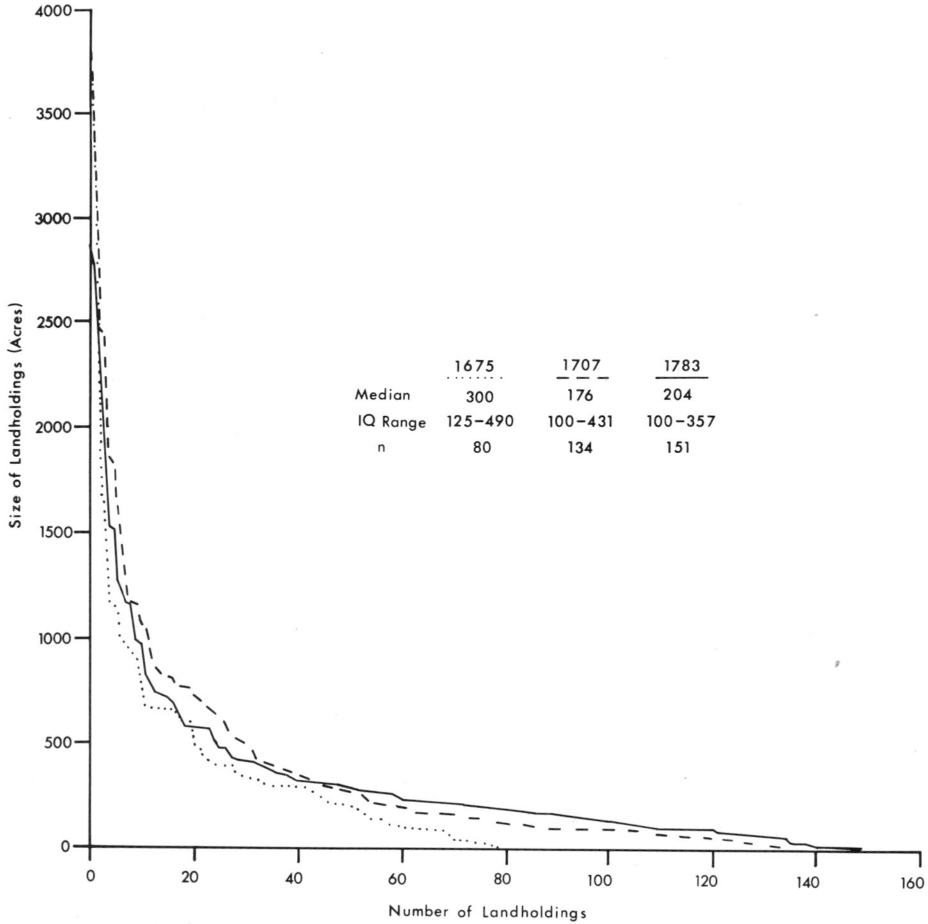

Fig. 27.--Number and Size of Landholdings, 1675, 1707, and 1783

TABLE 41

FREQUENCY DISTRIBUTIONS OF LANDHOLDING IN ALL HALLOWS PARISH, 1675-1783

Acres	1675 (n=80) Frequencies		Percentages	1707 (n=134) Frequencies		Percentages	1783 (n=151) Frequencies		Percentages
0-49	5}	10	12.5	8}	27	20.2	15}	29	19.2
50-99	5}			19}			14}		
100-149	12}	17	21.3	29}	45	33.6	24}	41	27.2
150-199	5}			16}			17}		
200-249	7}	11	13.8	8}	13	9.7	21}	31	20.5
250-299	4}			5}			10}		
300-349	11}	14	17.5	7}	12	8.9	11}	17	11.3
350-399	3}			5}			6}		
400-449	6}	8	10.0	3}	4	2.9	6}	8	5.3
450-499	2}			1}			2}		
500-999	13		16.3	20		14.9	15		9.9
≥1,000	7		8.8	10		7.4	10		6.6

Leasing land was an alternative chosen by many parishioners during the eighteenth century; yet tenancy was not uncommon in earlier years. Indeed, John Hammond recommended the practice for seventeenth century immigrants:

> my advice is that they neither sojourn, for that will be chargeable; nor on the sudden purchase, for that may prove unfortunate; but that they for the first year hire a house (for seats are always to be hired) and by that means, they will not onely finde content and live at a cheap rate, but be acquainted in the Country, and learn the worth and goodness of the Plantation they mean to purchase; and so not intangle themselves in an ill-bargain. . . .[1]

Hammond perceived tenancy as a temporary status along the way toward land-ownership; however, by the 1670's, perhaps 20 per cent of the parish heads of household carried this status to their graves.

Tenancy figures for the seventeenth century are, at best, rough estimates; however, the two different methods and sources used here produce virtually identical results. The first method uses inventories and deeds in order to estimate the non-landowners. For each inventoried decedent, three questions had to be answered: (1) was the decedent a landowner? (2) was he a head of household? (3) was he engaged in agriculture (Table 42)? Land ownership is determined from the land records, wills, inventories, and accounts. In the special case of men holding rights to land through marriage to widows, I always include them as landowners. Household heads are defined as decedent inventories possessing two or more of the following goods: furniture, beds, and cooking utensils (what the colonials called "household stuffe"). Inventories are also used to determine agricultural activity, which is indicated by possession of any one of the following: (1) livestock (except one horse, which probably indicates use for transport); (2) agricultural implements; (3) steelyards; (4) crop listings.

Based on these procedures, seventeenth century tenants comprised 29.8 per cent of all households between 1663 and 1699; but the proportion of tenants was on the rise from 23.3 per cent for the pre-1680 period; to 31.4 per cent for 1680-1689; and 33.3 per cent for 1690-1699. Agriculture was the main livelihood for almost 65 per cent of the non-landowning households during the seventeenth century. In addition to these plantation tenants, the parish contained a body of persons who had neither land nor households; they worked as laborers

---

would conclude that little change had occurred in parish landholding. When in fact, changes of enormous import had taken place, namely, the growth of a substantial non-landowning population with uncertain tenure. Kenneth A. Lockridge, "Land, Population and the Evolution of New England Society, 1630-1790," Past and Present, No. 39 (April, 1968), pp. 62-80.

[1] Hammond, "Leah and Rachel," p. 294.

TABLE 42

DISTRIBUTION OF LAND, HOUSEHOLDS, AND AGRICULTURAL ACTIVITY, ALL HALLOWS PARISH INVENTORIES, 1663-1699

	1663-79	1680-89	1690-99	Totals, 1663-1699
1. No. of inventories	35	55	39	129
2. No. of households	30	51	33	114
3. Households, no land	7	16	11	34
4. Households, no land, agric.	5	11	6	22

and "lived in" with parish families. In a colony where land purportedly was cheap and easily acquired, one of ten parishioners were landless laborers, as indicated by the seventeenth century inventories; and two to three out of ten were tenants.

The majority of tenants and inmates were poor (Table 43). Of the tenants, 61.8 per cent had estates smaller than £50 sterling; however, more than a fifth of them enjoyed a fair prosperity with estates valued in excess of £100.[1] By contrast, just 17.3 per cent of the landowners left estates of less than £50, and 59.3 per cent were worth more than £100 at their deaths. Inmates had very meager fortunes; over three-quarters of their inventories fell below £25.

The number of non-landowning households can be estimated a second way, and the results compare favorably to the inventory method. This second approach compares the number of households to the number of resident landowners.[2] In 1675, there were 80 landowners in the parish, almost all of whom were residents; households numbered an estimated 101. By subtraction, the parish of 1675 contained 21 non-landowning households, or 20.8 per cent of all households. This proportion estimated by the second method is very similar to

[1]These more prosperous non-landowners included a young man engaged in mercantile activity, who died before his wealthy father had settled land upon him; several inmates who probably lived in London Town and engaged in commerce; and a small group of householders who specialized in non-agricultural occupations, such as blacksmithing, milling, and boat construction.

[2]The method was devised and presented by Lois Green Carr, "County Government in Maryland, 1689-1709" (unpublished Ph.D. dissertation, Harvard University, 1968), Chapter VII.

TABLE 43

TOTAL ESTATE VALUE RELATED TO LANDOWNERSHIP AND HOUSEHOLDS, ALL HALLOWS PARISH INVENTORIES, 1663-1699

	Estate Value (personalty, credits only) in pounds Sterling									
	0-25	25-50	50-75	75-100	100-200	200-300	300-400	400-500	500-1000	1000+
No land nor household	10	1	1	0	1	1	0	0	0	0
No land, household	12	9	1	2	6	0	1	0	1	0
Land and household	8	6	10	9	20	10	4	4	6	4
Totals	30	16	12	11	27	11	5	4	7	4

the inventory-deeds estimate of 23.3 per cent for 1663-1679. The second method also provides an estimate of tenancy in 1707. But first it is essential to remove the number of landowners residing outside parish bounds. Twelve of the 134 owners are excluded as non-residents.[1] After this adjustment, the proportion of non-landowners comes to 33.7 per cent in 1707; and again the estimate is very close to the inventory estimate (method one) of 33.3 per cent for 1690-1699.

At the end of the colonial period, tenancy is estimated more easily. The tax list of 1783, after minor adjustments, indicates that 49.1 per cent of all households did not own land.[2]

Tenancy in the parish increased from about 20 per cent in the 1670's to over 30 per cent in the first decade of the eighteenth century, and reached nearly 50 per cent by the Revolution. Between 1675 and 1707, tenant households grew at an annual rate of .4 per cent (arithmetic mean); had that rate continued after 1707, tenancy would have reached 40 per cent by 1723 and 50 per cent by 1748. Undoubtedly, the rate slowed in the eighteenth century because the 50 per cent mark still prevailed in 1776. Probably by the 1720's, non-landowners found it difficult to acquire land either in fee simple or by lease. The land shortage worsened as population grew by natural increase. Under such conditions, outmigration became imperative.

Economic factors also contributed to the inexorable growth of tenancy. Population pressure drove up prices of land. A few patrician planters may have helped raise land prices through social hoarding of land for their progeny or for social status, but in general, planters regarded land as a commodity. Prices rose with increased demand. Tenants seeking to become landowners were caught in an economic squeeze. They faced ascending land prices and declining incomes.

---

[1]Non-residents are usually identified in the rent roll, though a few are determined from deeds. Of the non-residents, five were from Prince George's County; one was from St. James' Parish; two were from Baltimore County; one was from Calvert County; and three resided in London, England. AACo, Rent Rolls, Liber 1.

[2]The minor adjustments involve using genealogical materials to determine which of the taxables were not heads of households, and then to allocate them to the correct household. Fathers and sons are placed within the same household, except when it is clear from the tax list that the son had his own residence; separate residence is inferred if the son had more than one category of taxable property and one or more white inhabitants listed with his name. This grouping reduces the number of taxables from 359 to 301. Non-landowning figures are higher if this procedure is not performed. This task was done in conjunction with Dr. Ronald Hoffman of the University of Maryland.

This economic squeeze made it very difficult for tenants to progress up the agricultural ladder. The majority of tenants had small annual incomes from tobacco. With good weather and prices, the typical tenant working alone earned perhaps £8 to £10 for his 2,000 pounds of tobacco. To purchase a 25-acre plantation, or preferably a 50- to 100-acre holding, was a heavy drain on his income. When land was cheap before 1690, an average acre of land purchased in the private market cost less than seven shillings (Table 44 and Figure 28). Thus, 25 acres required an outlay of £8.75 sterling, or the equivalent of one laborer's annual output of tobacco. But, after 1690, land prices rose markedly to about ten shillings per acre, hovering there until the 1750's. At ten shillings per acre, 25 acres cost £12.5. But the successful planter needed even more land. About 1775, an anonymous author claimed that a tobacco planter required at least 50 acres of land;[1] if correct, this doubled the land purchase cost to £25, or two and a half times his annual income in boom years.

TABLE 44

LAND PRICES PER ACRE IN ALL HALLOWS PARISH GROUPED TO APPROXIMATE BOOMS AND BUSTS, 1660-1769

Years	n	Mean Land Price in shillings sterling per acre
1660-78	10	6.32
1679-96	26	5.88
1697-1705	31	13.03
1706-17	55	9.45
1718-26	36	10.25
1727-32	36	8.58
1733-41	46	9.77
1742-50	67	10.35
1751-53} 1757-62} 1766-69}	75	14.81
1754-56} 1763-65}	45	14.63

Fluctuations of land prices compounded the tenant's dilemma. When his income rose during boom years, he found that land prices increased even more rapidly (Table 44). For example, when tobacco prices peaked between 1698 and

[1] American Husbandry, p. 165.

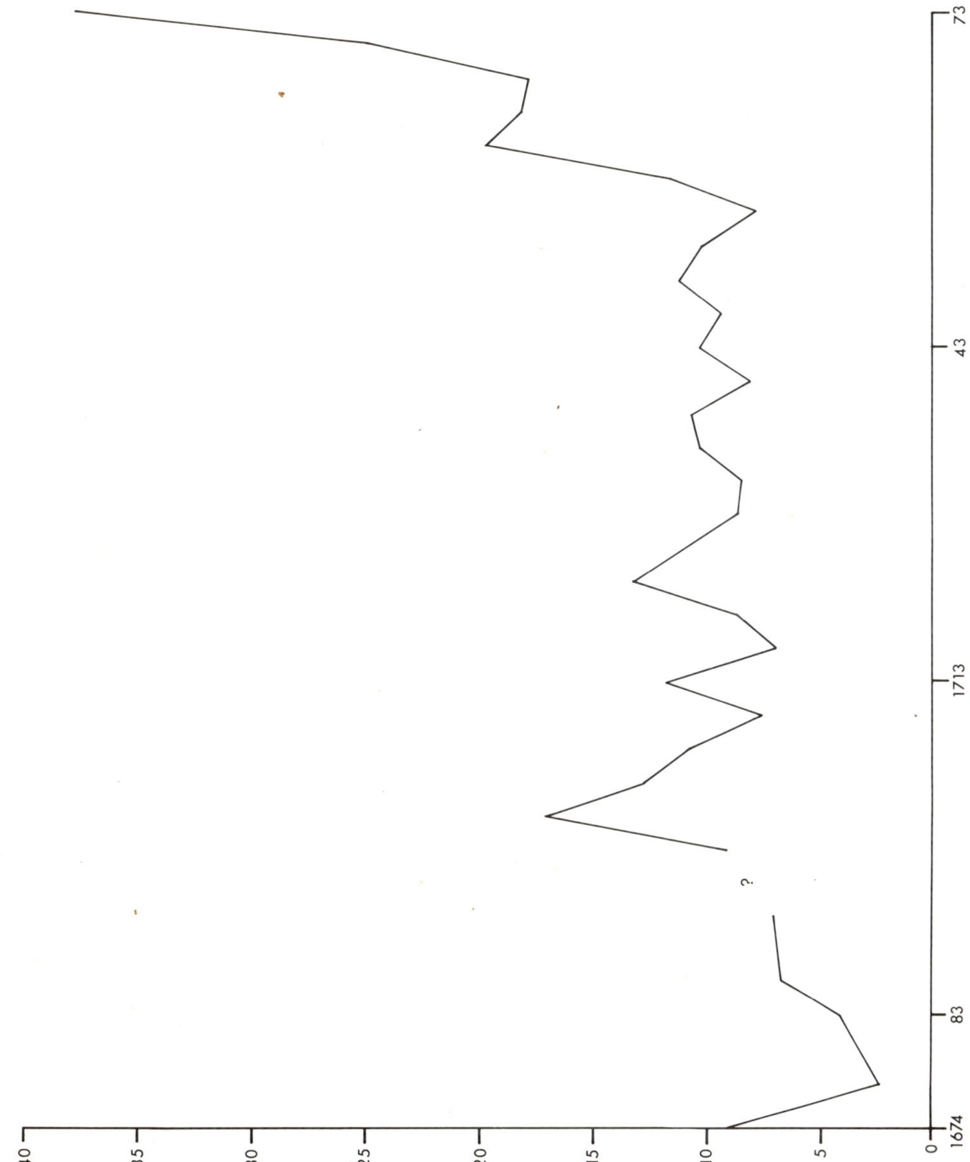

Fig. 28. --Mean Land Prices, 1673-1774

1704, rising by 19.5 per cent over the mean of the previous bust period, mean land prices rose by 121.6 per cent. During depressions, when small planters could least afford land purhcases, the market offered the best bargains. For example, land prices fell by 27.5 per cent between the boom of 1698-1704 and the bust of 1705-1718; meanwhile, tobacco prices fell by only 10 per cent.

As tenancy expanded in the eighteenth century, landlords exacted concessions from their tenants. This is the main conclusion that emerges from an examination of scattered lease agreements that survive from the eighteenth century. Yet the conclusions must remain very tentative because so many tenants made verbal agreements to lease land for a short term. The length of leases in recorded agreements varied from one year to ninety-nine years. Leases for natural lives or for ninety-nine years were probably considered as freeholds.[1] The acreage leased to tenants ranged widely, but one hundred acres was the most common figure. Landlords collected the rents in late Autumn, Winter or early Spring; in other words, at the end of the harvest year. The tenants usually made their payments in tobacco, although some landlords requested currency or kind. Per annum payments varied from 450 pounds of tobacco per hundred acres to around 800 pounds. The sporadic data do not expose a clear trend in lease rates, but the higher figure seems to have been very common by the 1740's.[2] In 1767, a parcel at the head of South River contained five tenements yielding £50 annually, or £10 per tenement. In sterling, this amounted to about £6.67, or roughly 800 pounds of tobacco valued at two pence per pound. In neighboring St. James' Parish, the viewers of an orphan's estate estimated a rental of 1,600 pounds of tobacco for 240 acres containing two old dwelling houses, one log house, and four tobacco houses.[3] This rental came to 666.7 pounds per hundred acres. Tenant agreements frequently required capital improvements, such as the planting of apple trees,[4] the construction and mainte-

---

[1] See again the tax law of 1782; Laws, TBH#A, f. 226.

[2] Landlord-tenant agreements appear in AACo Judgments, G, ff. 24-25; ibid., ff. 253-54; ibid., TB#1, ff. 7-11; AACo Deeds, WT#1, f. 234; ibid., WT#2, ff. 241-43, 426-29; ibid., SY#1, ff. 73-74; ibid., RB#3, ff. 346-47; ibid., BB#2, ff. 229-30; ibid., BB#3, ff. 501-2; Wills 3, f. 412; Inventories & Accounts 6, f. 330; ibid., 7, f. 58. In 1748, land in Prince George's County was advertised for rent; the first two years were rent free, and afterwards 800 pounds of tobacco per annum; Maryland Gazette, March 24, 1748.

[3] Maryland Gazette, October 1, 1767. AACo Judgments, G, ff. 253-54.

[4] For example, AACo Deeds, RB#3, ff. 346-47.

nance of dwelling houses,[1] and the fencing of orchards or pastures.[2] As timber became scarce, leases sometimes stipulated how much land could be cleared annually,[3] and in one case the tenant's lease restricted his labor force to his family and one servant, or two servants if his children could not work.[4]

It is, I think, a reasonable conclusion that tenant rentals increased toward a ceiling of around 800 pounds of tobacco per hundred acres by the late 1740's; and furthermore, that only top or good tobacco was accepted.[5] It is logical to assume that the growth of landowning households increased demands for leaseholds and drove up rentals. But the tenant-planter with only household labor could pay no more; he already was pressed to the limit. Rentals of 800 pounds of tobacco consumed between 50 and 80 per cent of his annual crop and income. Perhaps some tenants bolstered their incomes by hiring wage laborers or by leasing slaves, but labor costs were usually prohibitive.[6] Lease rates approached a ceiling when they neared 800 pounds of tobacco per hundred acres. The small tenant, producing about 1,000 pounds of tobacco (after the 1747 inspection act), could not bear a higher rental. After paying the annual rent, the tenant retained about 200 pounds of tobacco for purchases and savings. His prospects for climbing the agricultural ladder were decidedly poor.

The dual growth of population and tenancy exerted pressures on the limited supply of parish land and on the cadastral framework. Surprisingly, these pressures did not boil over into vast amounts of boundary litigation, resurvey, or examination by petition. Boundary confusion and dispute were held in abey-

---

[1]Ibid., WT#2, ff. 426-29.

[2]AACo Deeds, RB#3, ff. 346-47; AACo Judgments, TB#1, ff. 7-11.

[3]AACo Deeds, BB#3, ff. 501-2. [4]Ibid., RB#3, ff. 346-47.

[5]Maryland Gazette, April 28, 1747. This commentator stated specifically that landlords customarily took the best tobacco. In 1706, Amos Garrett wished 600 pounds of tobacco "'free from trash'" for about 100 acres. AACo Deeds, WT#2, ff. 426-29. Payment of rents by currency, coin, or bills of exchange never made much headway, which is surprising given the fluctuation in tobacco prices. This would have stabilized landlord revenues, but perhaps would have discouraged tenants, especially in depressions.

[6]The extent of these practices is uncertain. In 1774, Father Mosley, on the Eastern Shore, noted that: "'Negroes hire from £16 to £20 per annum, according to their age, health and strength . . .'"; Devitt, "Letters of Father Joseph Mosley," p. 300. This is probably in current money, which reduces to £12 to £15 sterling. Renting slaves for tobacco culture at these rates would have been irrational.

ance because man-land pressures did not become acute until the end of the study period. The critical subsistence ratio of fifty acres per laborer was not surpassed until 1767 when All Hallows contained 1, 017 taxables. By 1776, they numbered 1, 156. They needed 57, 800 acres, but the finite parish provided only 50, 850 acres. The man-land ratio of forty-four acres per laborer on the eve of the American Revolution signalled the beginning of a new and critical phase in the settlement history of All Hallows Parish. Even the massive outmigration of parishioners since the 1720's had failed to halt the steady march of a naturally increasing population.

CHAPTER VIII

ENSEMBLE

> The Road today has been very hilly & sandy; the Sand deep, & had it not been for the Rain the Traveling would have been very tedious. Passed through thirty two Gates today. Saw in my way a small red Bird, such as I do not remember to have met with to the Northward. Houses for curing Tobacco in (called here Tobacco Houses) begin to be more plenty than in the Parts of Maryland I have travelled hitherto. They are generally large & consist of only the outside Shell; in Appearance they resemble our Barns. The Business of Farming is carried on by Negroes, who have an Overseer appointed them; his Business is to see that they do the Work which he directs to be done. . . . There are sometimes several hundred Negroes belonging to one Man, who is as absolute as the grand Turk.[1]

These were the observations of Philadelphian Ebenezer Hazard in 1777 after passing through All Hallows Parish. Other commentators remarked of dispersed plantations, diminutive towns, and retreating woodlands. All Hallows heralded entrance into a regional core quite different from northern Maryland and Pennsylvania. Travellers like Ebenezer Hazard were keenly sensitive to regional differences in landscapes, economy, and society; but of necessity their vignettes on the tobacco coast captured only one scene in a lengthy scenario. Eluding them were the incessant changes in economy, resources, population, and settlement systems. A recapitulation of these changes serves the dual purpose of summarizing the more important conclusions of this study and sketching the outline of an evolutionary model of settlement systems in the Chesapeake and, more generally, in staple economies.

Tobacco economy, resources, and population provided the changing context for the settlement system of All Hallows Parish. Four generations of parish planters retained their commitment to tobacco as the staple commercial crop, which was a noteworthy achievement considering the obstacles of trans-Atlantic marketing, war-time interruptions, changing continental demands, and erratic prices. Tobacco prices rose and fell in cycles of boom and bust. Before 1750, the boom-bust cycle was fairly long and averaged slightly over twenty-two years. The typical boom of high prices lasted about ten and one-half

[1] Shelley, "Ebenezer Hazard's Travels through Maryland in 1777," p. 50.

years, while low prices lasted for about twelve years. The secular trend of prices, however, was downward. But abrupt changes occurred in the third quarter of the eighteenth century. The full cycle collapsed from more than twenty-two years to eight and one-half years. The quick succession of boom and bust played havoc with planter investment, which was attuned to lengthier cycles. The trend of prices also changed dramatically as a direct result of legislation. Before 1747, Maryland planters complained about tobacco prices, and occasionally designed statutory remedies to improve quality and price. In that year, a most significant law passed the Assembly; the tobacco inspection act attempted to improve tobacco prices by eliminating inferior tobacco from the market. The act was successfully enforced and prices rose sharply; however, rising prices were a bit of an illusion. The improved prices rarely compensated for the excluded tobacco which amounted to almost half a laborer's crop.

The staple economy placed extremely heavy demands upon resources. Parish planters were especially profligate in their use of wood for hogsheads, buildings, fences, casks, coffins, carts, boats, and furniture. In light of the abundant and seemingly inexhaustible seventeenth century hardwood forest and the lack of alternative materials in the stoneless coastal plain, the environmental irresponsibility of planters is understandable. But by the end of that century, the more open landscape was a harbinger of changing times. After the 1730's boom, timber became scarce. By 1765, timber was scarce or lacking on half or more of the land.

Parish planters were far more judicious in their exploitation of the soil. All Hallows contained some of the finest bright tobacco soils in southern Maryland, and despite cultivation for more than a century, they remained productive. Yields of tobacco declined very little between 1660 and 1769. A combination of factors helped maintain soil productivity. Tobacco was an intensive crop and one laborer tended about three acres per year. Thus, tobacco did not take up much land, and parish tobacco fields never occupied more than 5 per cent of the total area in any one year. On the other hand, tobacco lands were exhausted after three or four years of cultivation. The planter's solution was to shift to a new parcel every three or four years; meanwhile, the exhausted old fields were allowed to recuperate. Grass, shrubs, and eventually trees invaded the old fields. The re-appearance of the forest, which took about twenty years, signaled that fertility had been restored and the field could be recultivated. Thus the availability of abundant land in combination with an exhaustive, intensive crop were joined in an agrarian system of intensive shifting cultivation. This mobile system of agriculture was effective so long as the ratio of land to labor exceeded twenty to one--this land-man ratio was not approached in All Hallows during the colonial period. In addition, yields of tobacco were maintained by gentle relief, sandy soils, and a legacy of Indian planting practices which impeded runoff. The traditional view of tobacco culture irreparably destroying the soil is in need of refinement. That view assumes that ragged old fields were permanently exhausted, and it exaggerates the amount of land in tobacco production. Even more egregious is the inference of economic decline from the landscape of old, unpainted buildings and unkempt old fields. In fact, landscape atrophy was a necessary and normal part of this transient agricultural system.

The increased pressures upon timber and, to a lesser extent, soils came from an increasing population which experienced three phases of growth. The most dramatic phase occurred before 1675; it was followed by moderate growth until 1705, after which growth slowed to about one per cent per annum. Immigration accounted for the more rapid growth in the seventeenth century. These immigrants were mainly English whites, both free and servant, until the 1680's and 1690's when Negro slave importations became especially heavy. After 1705, the low rate of growth resulted from a complex of demographic changes. Between 1710 and 1730, these critical changes became apparent. Immigration waned, while outmigration picked up velocity and reached levels of 40 to 50 per cent of the total taxables after the 1720's. But the parish continued to add people because the high replacement rates and the decline in the death rate more than offset migrational losses. The parish population advanced slowly but steadily, all the while encroaching on timber land and the essential land required for subsistence. For the support of himself and his dependents, a laborer required about fifty acres for tobacco, subsistence crops, timber, and pasture. By 1766, each laborer had exactly that amount. A decade later, the average laborer could count on only forty-four acres.

Negro slaves made up an increasing proportion of the population. In 1776, they comprised nearly 68 per cent of the laborers (taxables) and about 50 per cent of the total population. The growth of Negro population outpaced white because of higher birth rates and differential outmigration, in which white tenants without slaves left more frequently, thereby increasing the proportion of slaves who were not free to move.

By the American Revolution, the parish was on the brink of a second critical period. The parish contained too many people and too little land for the practice of the traditional economy. The situation surely warranted new economic or demographic strategies; fortunately, Revolutionary planters were heirs of a long history of adjustment which had modified plantations and activities to the uncertain pulsations of the tobacco economy.

The plantation was the predominant settlement type in All Hallows Parish. Planters comprised 80 per cent or more of all heads of households throughout the colonial period. However, the term "plantation" masked a great variety of settlements, and this variety expanded as planters altered their settlements to more effectively cope with an erratic economy. Buffeted by recurrent depressions, some planters ameliorated hard times by rearranging their plantation investments and by increasing their potential self-sufficiency. A regular sequence of plantation changes were set in motion as the planter girded for the depression. Midway through the boom portion of the cycle, some planters anticipated the inevitable decline in tobacco prices. Accordingly, they began to reallocate their relative investments. First, they reduced tertiary goods, and as the depression broke over them more drastic measures were taken. Consumption expenditures were cut back while primary investment, mostly in agriculture, rose. In addition, numerous new items appeared on the plantation. These items of potential self-sufficiency enabled the planter to produce at home what he normally would have imported. The process of import replacement was never total, but it did permit the flexible planter a temporary respite when tobacco prices were low. As the depression waned, some assumed a boom stance. Tertiary investment increased, followed by growth in consumption and decline in primary investment. Imports were being resumed. Potential self-sufficiency levelled off, but at higher levels than in the preceding boom. This sequence of changes recurred in every boom and bust until 1750. Thereafter, economic cycles changed. The typical cycle telescoped from twenty-two years down to eight. The change eluded planters, who continued to adjust their investments as they always had. Their adjustments always lagged one phase behind the accelerated cycles.

Charles Carroll once remarked that planter prosperity depended upon the gentle rise or fall of tobacco prices. Carroll perceptively identified the engine of change in the colonial Chesapeake, but he left ambiguous the relationship between prices and prosperity. The statement may be clarified by noting that low prices brought prosperity to the large plantations; high prices meant prosperity for the small. Stated somewhat cryptically, one man's wine was another man's poison.

In each succeeding depression, large plantations grew in value, at least until 1740 to 1748. In that depression, larger planters saw their plantation values fall by over 20 per cent; whereas in previous depressions these values had risen a minimum of 70 per cent. The inequality of plantation scales was also less pronounced than in the typical depression, and, in fact, resembled the boom years. For the larger planters, depression wine had suddenly and inexplicably turned to poison. Quite naturally they attributed their crisis to sinking tobacco prices, and to relieve their woes the large planters in the Maryland Assembly passed the tobacco inspection act in 1747 when tobacco price hit an all-time low. Unfortunately, these men misperceived the cause of their immediate crisis and the source of past depression growth. In every depression up to 1740, the large planters extended liberal credit. They did not do so in the 1740's depression. The failure to extend credit was the result of paper currency emitted by Maryland in 1733. This was the first paper currency issued by Maryland. Demands for paper were not great during the boom of the 1730's. But by 1738 as the depression approached, paper currency became scarce, and the exchange rate soared to 100 per cent. Instead of extending credit as they had in the past, large planters in the parish apparently demanded paper. But little paper was available, and then only at exorbitant rates. As a consequence, the parish economy wrenched to a standstill, and large planters suffered along with the small.

During the colonial era, the plantations of All Hallows increased in scale (or total estate value). Thus, I find myself in general agreement with Aubrey C. Land's conclusions based upon a more comprehensive study of the Chesapeake. One refinement is added. Growth was not linear, but was characterized by fits and starts. Dramatic gains occurred in depressions, but they were confined to the larger plantations. Middling and smaller planters prospered during the booms. Finally, the conclusions for All Hallows confirm what I believe is Land's most perceptive insight, i.e., the source of growth among large and rising planters was not agriculture, but more diversified investments. In All Hallows, these investments were in credit.[1]

Throughout this century and a quarter of change, parish plantations were scattered or dispersed, despite the increase in population densities. The traditional interpretation of the rural settlement pattern is correct, as far as it goes. Plantation dispersal resulted from the abundance of land, which was easily ac-

---

[1]Aubrey C. Land, "Economic Base and Social Structure," pp. 639-54; and his "Economic Behavior in a Planting Society: The Eighteenth-Century Chesapeake," Journal of Southern History, XXXIII (November, 1967), 469-85.

quired through the headright system before 1683, and from the intricate estuarine configuration, which encouraged the engrossment of riparian holdings. There is little evidence, however, to support the cultural interpretation which states that initial settlers came from the dispersed pasture farming areas of highland England and the West Country. In fact, there is the contrary evidence of efforts to create towns and villages, such as Jamestown, St. Mary's, and Providence in Anne Arundel County.[1] In these places, clustered settlement with agrarian components provided the initial design. The traditional interpretation which stresses cheap estuarine sites is inadequate because it does not explain the persistence of plantation dispersal. By 1776, parish densities exceeded four persons per square mile and woodlands were in retreat, yet travellers made no mention of settlement clustering either along the estuaries or highways. Dispersed settlement persisted for two reasons. First, as the plantation became relatively more autarchic through diversification and potential self-sufficiency, planters depended less upon external exchange. Hence, location with regard to other plantations was less important, and the siting of plantations could be decided by internal constraints. Second, the chief internal constraint was the shifting agricultural system which encouraged central location within the cadastre or leasehold. This location minimized the movement of labor, materials, and crops between the dwelling house and mobile fields, but it maximized the distances to near neighbors.

Although plantations were numerically dominant in the parish settlement system, the small number of non-agrarian activity sites were especially important. Occupational specialists such as merchants, doctors, coopers, carpenters, boatwrights, innholders, tailors, ministers, and school teachers provided services which went beyond the capabilities of most plantations. These occupations were potentially urban. In All Hallows Parish, the potential urban population never exceeded 20 per cent of the household heads; nevertheless, they provided the base for revolutionary, but shortlived, urban growth.

Potential urban occupations exhibited three phases of spatial distribution. The first phase extended from initial settlement to about 1713. Occupational specialists were scattered or decentralized. The only hint of urban concentration came at London Town which was laid out in the 1680's; but hopes for urban growth were dashed when the town's founder and leading merchant died and An-

---

[1]H. Roy Merrens, "Settlement of the Colonial Atlantic Seaboard," Paper presented at Conference on the National Archives and Research in Historical Geography (Washington, D. C., 1971). AACo Deeds, IT#5, ff. 68-71; Patents, 5, ff. 57-58.

napolis won out as the site for the provincial capital. Phase two brought a rekindling of hope for London Town. Between 1710 and 1719, the town became a haven for merchants with English connections. They arrived on the heels of the Treaty of Utrecht which ended European hostilities. Speculating that the peace would be durable and the tobacco trade prosperous, about ten new merchants clustered in London Town. They super-imposed a unique and viable urban place on the dispersed and decentralized system. Urban flourescence lasted for nearly forty years, during which time between 40 and 50 per cent of the potential urban population were concentrated in London Town. This was a revolutionary change in settlement structure, even though the town had only thirty-five to forty houses and perhaps 200 people. The waning of London Town was evident by the 1750's. The merchants who sponsored town growth succumbed to death or migrated to other parts. They were not replaced by recruits from the parish, although there existed a pool of men with sufficient wealth to enter into specialized merchant activity. In this third phase the spatial pattern of All Hallows became once again decentralized.

The decline of London Town and its merchants was attributable to changes on the plantation, in tobacco marketing, and in the relative location of the parish. The merchant specialists of London Town were out of harmony with changes in the plantations. Planters adapted to the cyclical economy by diversifying agriculture and increasing potential self-sufficiency. During bad years, more and more planters substituted home production for imports; during booms they resumed importation. Merchants were more specialized, and hence less flexible; as they rode out the depression, they watched their flexible customers cut back purchases. Merchant rigidity boded ill in an economy where at least half the years were depressed. Although the evidence is slim, merchant indebtedness seemed to be on the rise between 1710 and the 1760's.

Another harsh blow to the town's future came from the tobacco inspection act of 1747. The act shifted the focus of the tobacco trade to the inspection house located upstream from London Town in the freshes of South River. In addition, the act set in motion intense competition among the parish merchants. Tobacco production was nearly halved by the provisions of the act, and merchants had to vie for the reduced crop. As a consequence, merchant numbers fell, customers were reallocated, and hinterlands were expanded. With the growth in hinterlands, the location of London Town became even more eccentric, and the unsettled situation was conducive to merchant re-location.

Finally, London Town fell victim to developments elsewhere in Maryland.

Colonial highways were realigned to accommodate settlement in the Piedmont and the back country. The development of Baltimore, Frederick, and Georgetown caused the transportation axis of the colony to rotate clockwise; consequently, London Town forfeited its position as one of the most accessible sites in the Maryland colony.

Perhaps this exposé of London Town's rise and fall will lead to a much-needed reevaluation of urbanization in the Chesapeake. It is necessary to look beyond the small size and the transitory nature of tobacco ports and examine the role they played. In addition, we should include all persons who were potentially urban, whether they were centralized or not. London Town drastically revised both the locational pattern and the flow of traffic during the forty year reign. Occupational centralization may have been greater in All Hallows than it was in the more heavily urbanized area of southeastern Pennsylvania. In all likelihood, similar developments took place in other tobacco ports like Port Tobacco, Oxford, Elkridge, and Joppa.

The settlements of All Hallows Parish were meshed in a commercial economy which involved long-distance trade, European markets, and fluctuating prices. The smooth flow of goods, persons, and messages was imperative, and numerous improvements were made which expedited these movements. The long-distance exchange of tobacco for European goods, slaves, and other imports was facilitated by the intricate interpenetration of land and water in the Chesapeake estuaries. No point in the parish exceeded five miles from a navigable landing. A variety of vessels probed these estuaries. Ships and brigs entered the open sea, the Chesapeake Bay, and the larger estuaries. But their draft precluded them from the smaller estuaries and, at an early date, smaller schooners and sloops were employed to collect tobacco and distribute imports. Even smaller were the flats which hauled several hogsheads of tobacco from shallow creeks or lightered from landings to ships.

Perhaps the most important transport improvement was the dispatch with which vessels were loaded and sent for England. Delays of weeks and even months were common in the seventeenth century; but later, turnaround time was reduced to about two weeks. One cause of this efficiency was the change in the mechanisms and agents of exchange. For much of the seventeenth century, barter trade between planter and ship captain or supercargo was not uncommon. But by the 1690's, planters increasingly consigned their tobacco to English merchants who acted as middlemen. The consignment method of trade was important because it heightened planter cognizance of the market and of events in

England and Europe; in short, he was less provincial. But more importantly, the planter consignor, by retaining ownership of his tobacco, was compelled to pay freight rates. And if he had to pay these rates, it was in his interest to get the tobacco to market early in order to receive the best prices. Too many sales opportunities were lost when the ship lay over the winter in Maryland waters. After 1713, another marketing method became significant through efforts of native merchants and English factors. These merchants purchased tobacco directly or outright. It is safe to say that the direct purchase and consignment trades vied in the eighteenth century, and that consignment probably gained ground during the 1720's and 1740's. In any case, both methods decreased turnaround time. Tobacco transactions were completed in advance by a resident merchant or factor or by letter from planter to English merchant. The ship captain by-passed negotiations with shrewd planters and proceeded to pick up his tobacco. In some cases, the tobacco was even collected in advance, further speeding departure. No longer did the ship captain have to seek a full load and send his sailors hither and yon to roll the tobacco from the plantations. In addition, turnaround speed was gained by the chartering of vessels. Sea-going vessels were increasingly chartered by a single party; and if a planter wished to consign to that merchant it was necessary to do so early to ensure a place for his tobacco. Single charters were also more efficient in England for all of the tobacco went directly to one merchant.

Local travel among the dispersed population also demanded adjustments. Estuaries were obstacles to travel since few parishioners had water craft. By the 1680's, parish planters had switched to the horse, road, and ferry for both local trips and for longer ones to the county or provincial courts. The change was very rational as horses were cheaper and more flexible than water vessels. Chesapeake horses were cheap to maintain, and they had more stamina than their English counterparts, perhaps because of the stoneless, well-drained, sandy soils. The planter preferred to ride around the heads of estuaries rather than to cross them, at least until public ferries and bridges became common. The ease of road construction also contributed to the horse's triumph. Parish roads were inexpensive, narrow swaths, crudely grubbed by private parties or taxables summoned by the overseer of the highways. Roads proliferated, and they frequently proved annoying because of redundance or by the multitude of gates which were erected to protect roadside crops. The belief that Chesapeake residents were amphibians is grossly inaccurate, and an equestrian image seems more appropriate.

The horse and road made local travel easy, and they encouraged interdependence among the dispersed sites in the parish. Meanwhile, overseas exchange was expedited by shipping and marketing improvements. Of course, we would expect considerable traffic and exchange in a developing staple economy; the exceptional feature is the marked variation of exchange in time and space. Plantation exchange "rolled with the punches" of the economy. A plantation's exchange depended on its flexibility (potential self-sufficiency) and the state of the economy. During depressions, flexible plantations initiated what I have called import replacement and thereby decreased exchange and relative indebtedness. In the boom they resumed imports and indebtedness generally rose. Rigid plantations did not possess these options; and during depressions their imports and indebtedness remained high, unless they chose austerity. Two points need underlining. First, flexibility was a trait of many parish plantations. During the eighteenth century, flexible and intermediate plantations, which increasingly behaved alike, usually comprised over 80 per cent of all plantations. Second, plantation flexibility was not limited to slave plantations. True, many of them had slaves, but some did not. Flexibility was foremost a response to economic depression, and it did not depend on slave labor for success.

Many persons participated in the economy of All Hallows Parish, and accordingly exchange was diffuse; but paradoxically, when credit transactions were valued in money, exchange was highly concentrated. The paradox arose because the largest parish creditors, usually a handful of persons, made many small loans; meanwhile, others made few loans, but they often turned up as the primary creditor to a parish resident. Hence, the typical planter was usually beholden to a person who was not the primary creditor for any other parishioner. In this sense, exchange was diffuse. It was also spatially diffuse until dramatically revised by the growth of London Town. Between 1710 and 1750, merchants in London Town and London, England became the foci for credit. After 1750, both places diminished as centers of exchange, which again became spatially diffuse, although Annapolis made some headway as a new focal point for credit.

The confused boundaries of land were remarkably stable in an otherwise fluid parish settlement system. The chaotic cadastral pattern, bequeathed by poorly-trained and poorly-equipped surveyors, survived with only slight changes until the American Revolution. Civil disputes over land were few since the expense of court fees dissuaded many from pursuing litigation. Other less costly procedures, such as resurveying and boundary examination by petition, were used more often; but these too were infrequent. Vague boundaries were tolerable so long as there was abundant land, concentrated land turnover, and little growth in the ranks of landowners. Although the market for land was generally brisk, most of the sales and subdivision were spatially concentrated on parcels near public highways. Landholdings in the rest of the parish were marginal participants in the land market. Also, the number of landowners increased slowly. Most of the increment occurred in the plantations between one hundred and three hundred acres, which were the average size of holdings. Given these conditions, there was little need for precise boundary delimitation.

Of course, hazily-defined boundaries exerted few effects upon the settlement system. Neither the alignment of routes nor the spatial pattern of exchange were guided by boundaries. Their greatest impact was felt in the location of activity sites such as the parish church, the county free school, and plantation sites.

Stability on the land was endangered by the increase of tenancy. The proportion of tenant households rose from about one-fifth in 1675 to one-third in 1707 to one-half by the Revolution. Tenancy was inevitable with the growth of population and the relatively few new entrants into landownership. In tandem, they forced up land prices to over ten shillings per acre during the eighteenth century. Rentals also began to creep upward. Rents may have doubled from 400 pounds of tobacco per hundred acres in the early 1700's to about 800 pounds by the 1740's. When half or more of the tenant's annual crop went for rent, the prospects for climbing the agricultural ladder were not good. And so, by the end of the colonial period, tenants left the parish in far greater numbers than their landed neighbors. But outmigration was no panacea. Population and tenancy continued to grow after the 1720's, and by the 1760's the man-land ratio turned unfavorable. This portentous change threatened the stability on the land which parish planters had long enjoyed.

The settlement system of All Hallows Parish was the evolutionary product of 125 years and four generations of parish planters. The results were not pleasing to the eye (some continue to infer southern laziness from the disheveled landscape), but beyond esthetics, the settlement system was eminently functional and adaptable to changes in the economy, society, and polity. While my conclusions frequently depart from the conventional wisdom regarding the Chesapeake, many of these differences will be resolved as other detailed local studies become available. Until that time, the findings for All Hallows Parish should be cautiously accepted as hypotheses which will apply in varying degrees to other parts of the tobacco coast.

At the moment, extrapolation to other staple economies is premature, but eventually comparative generalization may be possible. Of course, some would object that Negro slavery created such peculiarity in the Chesapeake and the American South that generalization is impossible. While conceding that Negro slavery has provided the traditional explanation of Southern life, I submit that economics was far more important in shaping the settlement system. Slaves did not cause tenancy and the decline of the yeomen. Nor was Negro labor the principal cause of plantation self-sufficiency. Nor did the alleged careless cultivation by Negroes destroy the soil. Nor was plantation growth (scale) attributable to slavery. The "grand Turk" with "several hundred Negroes" was exceedingly rare in the Chesapeake. In summary, the quest for generalizations about settlement systems need not be obstructed by Negro slavery in the Chesapeake.

APPENDIX

TOBACCO PRICES AND EXCHANGE RATES: CHESAPEAKE PRICES OF MARYLAND TOBACCO AND STERLING EXCHANGE RATES, 1711-1775

The table below contains Chesapeake prices of Maryland tobacco valued in current money and in sterling along with an exchange rate between these two currencies. Prices and exchange rates all derive from the probate records, inventories and accounts, for Anne Arundel and Prince George's counties between 1711 and 1775. At least eight tobacco prices survive for each year, which extends from January 1 to December 31.

The need for these three series (tobacco prices in current money, in sterling, and exchange rates) requires brief comment. All entries in the probate records are valued in Maryland currencies, which, in turn, are overvalued in relation to sterling. To convert the former to sterling values, we need an exchange rate; and the rates of exchange between Maryland current money and sterling appear regularly in the inventories and accounts. These administered exchange rates provide the data for the series below. Usually, the exchange rates within a given year show the same value, and therefore, I use the modal exchange rate for that year. Exceptions occur in the years 1757, 1772, and 1773. In 1757, no single exchange rate prevails, and hence the mean is used instead of the mode. For 1772 and 1773, exchange rates of $33\frac{1}{3}$ and $66\frac{2}{3}$ appear with nearly equal frequency; accordingly, two exchange rates and two sets of tobacco prices are listed for these years.

As scholarly understanding of the Chesapeake deepens, we may find better ways of converting current money values in the probate records to sterling. There is a growing suspicion that the administered exchange rates in the inventories and accounts may be governed as much by custom as by market changes. Two alternative ways of converting inventory values to comparative money units are now under study by John McCusker, Russell Menard, Allan Kulikoff, and myself. One alternative is the use of commercial rates of sterling exchange, as appear in the records of merchants. These rates would permit the conversion of inventory values to their current value in sterling, and the prices would reflect greater sensitivity to market fluctuations. The second alternative aims at a constant value series based on a weighted price index of Chesapeake commodities.

Continuing research may arrive at more appropriate exchange rates or indices for converting values from current money to sterling; in any case, we can continue to apply these refined procedures to the current money tobacco prices that appear below.

CHESAPEAKE PRICES OF MARYLAND TOBACCO IN PENCE PER POUND AND STERLING EXCHANGE RATES FOR MARYLAND CURRENT MONEY, 1711-1775

Year	n	Current Money Mean	Sterling			Exchange Rates
			Mean	High	Low	
1711	12	.97	.97	1.00	.60	Par
1712	16	1.00	1.00	1.00	1.00	Par
1713	17	1.00	1.00	1.00	.95	Par
1714	19	.94	.71	.75	.29	33⅓
1715	10	.96	.72	.75	.45	33⅓
1716	18	1.07	.80	1.44	.63	33⅓
1717	12	1.05	.79	1.13	.75	33⅓
1718	16	1.19	.89	1.35	.75	33⅓
1719	20	1.39	1.04	1.50	.75	33⅓
1720	12	1.58	1.19	1.50	.75	33⅓
1721	11	1.29	.97	1.50	.45	33⅓
1722	14	1.15	.86	1.13	.75	33⅓
1723	12	1.42	1.07	1.13	.75	33⅓
1724	10	1.20	.90	1.08	.72	33⅓
1725	11	1.39	1.05	1.80	.54	33⅓
1726	11	1.22	.91	1.13	.26	33⅓
1727	14	1.09	.82	1.13	.75	33⅓
1728	14	.89	.67	.75	.26	33⅓
1729	9	.94	.70	.99	.38	33⅓
1730	15	.90	.67	1.13	.27	33⅓
1731	10	.87	.65	.90	.23	33⅓
1732	9	.99	.74	.90	.36	33⅓
1733	13	1.12	.84	1.13	.54	33⅓
1734	28	1.29	.97	1.26	.54	33⅓
1735	16	1.24	.93	1.50	.45	33⅓
1736	14	1.36	1.02	2.25	.36	33⅓
1737	10	1.24	.93	1.50	.45	33⅓
1738	18	1.36	1.02	1.80	.45	33⅓
1739	8	1.34	1.01	1.50	.45	33⅓
1740	29	1.61	.80	1.20	.30	100
1741	23	1.23	.62	1.05	.24	100
1742	50	1.33	.67	1.00	.30	100
1743	36	1.35	.67	1.20	.19	100

Year	n	Current Money Mean	Sterling			Exchange Rates
			Mean	High	Low	
1744	41	1.25	.63	1.00	.15	100
1745	26	1.12	.56	1.20	.15	100
1746	11	1.21	.61	1.00	.30	100
1747	30	.90	.45	1.00	.00	100
1748	16	1.33	.67	1.00	.24	100
1749	26	1.53	.76	1.50	.00	100
1750	16	2.32	1.16	1.89	.60	100
1751	15	2.03	1.16	1.54	.31	75
1752	11	2.21	1.48	1.60	.80	50
1753	24	1.74	1.16	1.60	.60	50
1754	16	1.56	1.04	1.33	.60	50
1755	16	1.28	.85	1.60	.40	50
1756	11	1.76	1.07	1.21	.91	65
1757	17	1.83	1.16	1.90	.63	57.78
1758	14	2.12	1.29	2.73	.73	65
1759	13	3.07	2.05	3.00	1.28	50
1760	15	2.40	1.60	2.72	.80	50
1761	12	2.30	1.54	2.00	1.00	50
1762	30	2.08	1.39	3.00	.80	50
1763	20	1.65	1.10	1.44	.88	50
1764	10	1.68	1.26	1.50	1.04	$33\frac{1}{3}$
1765	12	1.77	1.33	1.62	.90	$33\frac{1}{3}$
1766	10	1.93	1.45	1.80	1.17	$33\frac{1}{3}$
1767	22	2.18	1.63	2.16	.72	$33\frac{1}{3}$
1768	14	2.41	1.81	3.00	1.13	$33\frac{1}{3}$
1769	14	2.98	2.23	3.00	1.35	$33\frac{1}{3}$
1770	26	2.75	2.06	2.52	1.13	$33\frac{1}{3}$
1771	18	2.53	1.90	2.70	.90	$33\frac{1}{3}$
1772	19	2.18	1.64	2.40	1.08	$33\frac{1}{3}$
1772	19	2.40	1.44	1.92	.86	$66\frac{2}{3}$
1773	10	2.19	1.64	2.93	1.13	$33\frac{1}{3}$
1773	10	2.22	1.33	2.34	.86	$66\frac{2}{3}$
1774	12	1.88	1.41	2.52	.90	$33\frac{1}{3}$
1775	14	2.23	1.67	2.43	1.20	$33\frac{1}{3}$

CITED BIBLIOGRAPHY

Manuscripts and Manuscript Collections

Library of Congress, Washington, D. C.

Galloway-Maxcy-Markoe Collection.

Maryland Hall of Records, Annapolis, Maryland.

Accounts.

Anne Arundel County Deeds.

Anne Arundel County Judgments.

Anne Arundel County Patented Certificates of Survey.

Anne Arundel County Unpatented Certificates of Survey.

Black Books.

Charles County Land Records.

Ejectment Papers.

Galloway-Maxcy-Markoe Collection, Gift Collection, Gift Collection D634.

Inventories.

Inventories and Accounts.

Laws.

Original Wills.

Patents.

Prince George's County Accounts.

Prince George's County Inventories.

Proceedings of the Visitors of the Free School of Anne Arundel County, 1724. Gift Collection, G610.

Protestant Episcopal Church Records.

Provincial Court Judgments.

Provincial Court Land Records.

Quaker Records.

Rent Rolls.

Testamentary Papers.

Testamentary Proceedings.

Wills.

Maryland Historical Society, Baltimore, Maryland.

Scharf Collection, Federal Assessments of 1782 and 1783.

Public Record Office, London, England.

Audit Office, 12/79, Maryland Loyalist Claims, 1786-1787, ff. 134-35.

Audit Office, 13/30, folder GII.

Primary Materials: Public Documents and Books

American Husbandry. Edited by Harry J. Carman. New York: Columbia University Press, 1939, reprinted by Kennikat Press, Inc., Port Washington, New York, 1964.

Archives of Maryland. 70 vols. Baltimore: Maryland Historical Society, 1883-date.

Beverley, Robert. The History and Present State of Virginia. Edited by Louis B. Wright. Chapel Hill: University of North Carolina Press for the Institute of Early American History and Culture at Williamsburg, Virginia, 1947.

Bordley, John Beale. A Summary View of the Courses of Crops in the Husbandry of England and Maryland; with a Comparison of their Products; and a System of Improved Courses Proposed for Farms in America. Philadelphia: n.p., 1784.

Brumbaugh, Gaius Marcus. Maryland Records: Colonial, Revolutionary, County and Church, from Original Sources. 2 vols. Baltimore: Genealogical Publishing Company, 1967.

Burnaby, Reverend Andrew. Travels through the Middle Settlements in North America, 1759 and 1760. 3d ed. London: T. Payne, 1798.

Calendar of State Papers, Colonial Series, America and West Indies. 44 vols. London: His Majesty's Stationery Office, 1860-date.

Danckaerts, Jasper. Journal of Jasper Danckaerts, 1679-1680. Edited by Bartlett Burleigh James and J. Franklin Jameson. Original Narratives of Early American History. New York: Charles Scribner's Sons, 1913, and reprinted by Barnes & Noble, Inc., New York, 1959.

des Cognets, Louis, Jr. English Duplicates of Lost Virginia Records. Princeton, New Jersey: n.p., 1958.

Eddis, William. Letters from America. Edited by Aubrey C. Land. Cambridge, Massachusetts: The Belknap Press of Harvard University Press, 1969.

Farish, Hunter Dickinson, ed. Journal & Letters of Philip Vickers Fithian 1773-1774; A Plantation Tutor of the Old Dominion. Williamsburg, Virginia: Colonial Williamsburg, Incorporated, 1965.

Greene, Jack P., ed. The Diary of Colonel Landon Carter of Sabine Hall. 2 vols. Charlottesville: The University Press of Virginia for the Virginia Historical Society, 1965.

Herndon, G. Melvin. William Tatham and the Culture of Tobacco Including a facsimile reprint of An Historical and Practical Essay on the Culture and Commerce of Tobacco. Coral Gables, Florida: University of Miami Press, 1969.

Narratives of Early Maryland, 1633-1684. Edited by Clayton Colman Hall. Original Narratives of Early American History. New York: Charles Scribner's Sons, 1910, reprinted by Barnes & Noble, Inc., 1959.

Papers Relating to the Church in Maryland, A.D. 1694-1775. Edited by William Stevens Perry. N.p.: privately printed, 1878.

Rochefoucault-Liancourt, Duke de la. Travels through the United States of North America . . . in the Years 1795, 1796, and 1797. Translated by H. Newman. 4 vols. London: R. Phillips, 1799.

The Secret Diary of William Byrd of Westover, 1709-1712. Edited by Louis B. Wright and Marion Tinling. Richmond: The Dietz Press, 1941.

Smyth, J. F. D. A Tour in the United States of America. 2 vols. London: J. Robson and J. Sewell for G. Robinson, 1784.

Travels and Works of Captain John Smith, President of Virginia and Admiral of New England. Edited by Edward Arber and A. G. Bradley. 2 vols. Edinburgh: n.p., 1910, and reprinted by Burt Franklin, New York, n.d.

Thomas, Sir Dalby. "An Historical Account of the Rise and Growth of the West-India Colonies, London, 1690." Harleian Miscellany, IX (1810), 403-45.

Primary Materials: Articles

"An Account of the Number of Souls in the Province of Maryland, in the Year 1755." Gentlemen's Magazine, XXXIV (June, 1764), 261.

Devitt, Reverend Edward I., S.J., ed. "Letters of Father Joseph Mosley, S.J. and Some Extracts from his Diary (1757-1786)." American Catholic Historical Society of Philadelphia, Records, XVII (1906), 180-210, 289-311.

Gordon, Lord Adam. "Journal of an Officer Who Travelled in America and the West Indies in 1764 and 1765." Travels in the American Colonies. Edited by Newton D. Mereness. New York: Macmillan Company, 1916. Pp. 267-413.

G., R. "Virginia's Cure: or an Advisive Narrative Concerning Virginia." Tracts and Other Papers Relating Principally to the Origin, Settlement, and Progress of the Colonies in North America. Vol. III. Edited by Peter Force. N.p.: n.p., 1844, reprinted for Peter Smith, Gloucester, Massachusetts by the Murray Printing Company, Forge Village, Massachusetts, 1963. Pp. 1-19.

"Itinerant Observations in America, 1745-1746." Collections of the Georgia Historical Society, IV (1878), 29-47.

"Journal of a French Traveller in the Colonies, 1765, II." American Historical Review, XXVII (October, 1921), 70-89.

Kammen, Michael G., ed. "Maryland in 1699: A Letter from the Reverend Hugh Jones." Journal of Southern History, XXIX (August, 1963), 362-72.

"Narrative of a Voyage to Maryland, 1705-1706." American Historical Review, XII (January, 1912), 327-40.

Quincy, Josiah. "Journal of Josiah Quincy, Junior, 1773." Edited by M. A. DeWolfe Howe. Massachusetts Historical Society Proceedings, XLIX (1915-1916), 424-81.

Shelley, Fred, ed. "Ebenezer Hazard's Travels through Maryland in 1777." Maryland Historical Magazine, XLVI (March, 1951), 44-54.

Other Primary Materials

Herrman, Augustin. Virginia and Maryland . . . Surveyed and Exactly Drawne by Augustin Herrman. London: W. Faithorne, Sculpt., 1673.

Maryland Gazette. 1729-1792.

Secondary Materials: Books and Monographs

Behrens, Kathryn L. Paper Money in Maryland, 1727-1789. Johns Hopkins University Studies in Historical and Political Science, 41st Series, No. 1. Baltimore: Johns Hopkins University (1923).

Craven, Avery Odelle. Soil Exhaustion as a Factor in the Agricultural History of Virginia and Maryland, 1606-1860. University of Illinois Studies in the Social Sciences, Vol. XIII, No. 1. Urbana, Illinois: University of Illinois, 1926, and reprinted by Peter Smith, Gloucester, Massachusetts, 1965.

Craven, Wesley Frank. The Southern Colonies in the Seventeenth Century, 1607-1689. Edited by Wendell Holmes Stephenson and E. Merton Coulter. A History of the South, I. N.p.: Louisiana State University Press and the Littlefield Fund for Southern History, The University of Texas, 1949.

Craven, Wesley Frank. White, Red, and Black: The Seventeenth-Century Virginian. Charlottesville: The University Press of Virginia, 1971.

Gould, Clarence P. The Land System in Maryland, 1720-1765. Johns Hopkins University Studies in Historical and Political Science, 31st Series, No. 1 (1913).

________. Money and Transportation in Maryland, 1720-1765. Johns Hopkins University Studies in Historical and Political Science, 33rd Series, No. 1 (1915).

Gray, Lewis C., assisted by Thompson, Esther Katherine. History of Agriculture in the Southern United States to 1860. 2 vols. Carnegie Institution of Washington Publication No. 430. U. S. A.: Carnegie Institution of Washington, n. d., reprinted by Peter Smith, Gloucester, Massachusetts, 1958.

Hall, Clayton C. The Lord's Baltimore and the Maryland Palatinate. Baltimore: John Murphy Company, 1902.

Hartsook, Elisabeth and Skordas, Gust. Land Office and Prerogative Court Records of Colonial Maryland. Publications of the Hall of Records Commission No. 4. Baltimore: Genealogical Publishing Company, 1968.

Kelly, J. Reaney. Quakers in the Founding of Anne Arundel County, Maryland. Baltimore: J. H. Furst Company for the Maryland Historical Society, 1963.

Kilty, John. The Land-holder's Assistant and Land Office Guide. Baltimore: n.p., 1808.

Lemon, James T. The Best Poor Man's Country: A Geographical Study of Early Southeastern Pennsylvania. Baltimore: The Johns Hopkins Press, 1972.

McCormac, Eugene I. White Servitude in Maryland, 1634-1820. Johns Hopkins University Studies in Historical and Political Science, 22nd Series, Nos. 3-4 (1904).

Maryland. Board of Natural Resources. Department of Geology, Mines and Water Resources. Shore Erosion in Tidewater Maryland. Bulletin 6. Baltimore, 1949.

Maryland. Maryland Geological Survey. Harold E. Vokes. Geography and Geology of Maryland. Revised by Jonathan Edwards, Jr. Bulletin 19. Baltimore: Maryland Geological Survey, 1957, revised and reprinted, 1968.

Merrens, Harry Roy. Colonial North Carolina: A Study in Historical Geography. Chapel Hill: University of North Carolina Press, 1964.

Middleton, Arthur Pierce. Tobacco Coast: A Maritime History of Chesapeake Bay in the Colonial Era. Newport News, Virginia: The Mariner's Museum, 1953.

Morriss, Margaret Shove. Colonial Trade of Maryland, 1689-1715. Johns

Hopkins University Studies in Historical and Political Science, 32nd Series, No. 3 (1914).

Plantation Systems of the New World. Edited by Vera Rubin. Social Sciences Monographs, VII. Washington, D. C.: Pan American Union, 1959.

Richeson, Allie W. English Land Measuring to 1800: Instruments and Practices. Cambridge, Massachusetts: The Society for the History of Technology and the MIT Press, 1966.

Shepherd, James F. and Walton, Gary M. Shipping, Maritime Trade, and the Economic Development of Colonial North America. London: Cambridge University Press, 1972.

Smith, Abbot E. Colonists in Bondage: White Servitude and Convict Labor in America 1607-1776. Chapel Hill: University of North Carolina Press, 1947, reprinted by Peter Smith, Gloucester, Massachusetts, 1965.

Soltow, James H. The Economic Role of Williamsburg. Williamsburg Research Studies. Williamsburg, Virginia: Colonial Williamsburg, Inc., 1965.

Tilghman, Oswald. History of Talbot County Maryland, 1661-1861. 2 vols. Baltimore: Williams & Wilkins Company, 1915.

Thirsk, Joan, ed. The Agrarian History of England and Wales, 1500-1640. Vol. IV. Cambridge, England: University Printing House, 1967.

U.S. Bureau of the Census. Historical Statistics of the United States, Colonial Times to 1957; a Statistical Abstract Supplement. Washington, D. C.: Government Printing Office, 1960.

U.S. Department of Agriculture. Soil Conservation Service. Soil Survey Maps of Anne Arundel County, Maryland. 2 vols. College Park, Maryland: n.p., 1968.

U.S. Department of Agriculture. Soil Conservation Service in Cooperation with the Maryland Agricultural Experiment Station. Soil Survey, Prince Georges County, Maryland. Washington, D. C.: Government Printing Office, 1967.

U.S. Department of Commerce and Labor. Bureau of the Census. A Century of Population Growth: From the First Census of the United States to the Twelfth 1790-1900, by W. S. Rossiter. Washington, D. C.: Government Printing Office, 1909.

Wrigley, E. A. Population and History. World University Library. New York: McGraw-Hill Book Company, 1969.

Wyckoff, Vertrees J. Tobacco Regulation in Colonial Maryland. Johns Hopkins University Studies in Historical and Political Science, New Series, No. 22 (1936).

Secondary Materials: Articles

Barker, Howard F. "National Stocks in the Population of the United States as indicated by Surnames in the Census of 1790." Annual Report of the American Historical Association, XXXI (1931), 126-359.

Bauer, L. A. "First Report upon Magnetic Work in Maryland including the History and Objects of Magnetic Surveys." Maryland Geological Society, I. Baltimore: Johns Hopkins Press, 1897. Pp. 405-529.

Carroll, Kenneth L. "The Anatomy of a Separation: The Lynam Controversy." Quaker History, LV (Autumn, 1966), 67-78.

Ducatel, J. T. "Outlines of the Physical Geography of Maryland, embracing its prominent Geological Features." Transactions of the Maryland Academy of Sciences and Literature, I (1837), 24-54.

Gould, Clarence P. "The Economic Causes of the Rise of Baltimore." Essays in Colonial History Presented to Charles McLean Andrews by his Students. New Haven: Yale University Press, 1931. Pp. 225-51.

Harris, P. M. G. "The Social Origins of American Leaders: The Demographic Foundations." Perspectives in American History, III (1969), 159-344.

Hemphill, John M., II. "Annapolis: Colonial Metropolis and State Capital." The Old Line State. Edited by Morris L. Radoff. Maryland Hall of Records Commission Publication No. 16. Baltimore: Twentieth Century Printing Company, Inc., 1971. Pp. 177-91.

________. "Freight Rates in the Maryland Tobacco Trade, 1705-1762." Maryland Historical Magazine, LIV (March, 1959), 36-60.

________. "Freight Rates in the Maryland Tobacco Trade, 1705-1762: Appendix." Maryland Historical Magazine, LIV (June, 1959), 153-87.

Jones, Alice Hanson. "Wealth Estimates for the American Middle Colonies, 1774." Economic Development and Cultural Change, XVIII (July, 1970), 1-172.

Karinen, Arthur E. "Maryland Population: 1631-1730: Numerical and Distributional Aspects." Maryland Historical Magazine, LIV (December, 1959), 365-407.

________. "Numerical and Distributional Aspects of Maryland Population 1631-1840: Part II, Distributional Characteristics 1631-1730." Maryland Historical Magazine, LX (June, 1965), 139-59.

Klingaman, David C. "The Significance of Grain in the Development of the Tobacco Colonies." Journal of Economic History, XXIX (June, 1969), 268-78.

Land, Aubrey C. "Economic Base and Social Structure: The Northern Chesapeake in the Eighteenth Century." Journal of Economic History, XXV (December, 1965), 639-54.

________. "Economic Behavior in a Planting Society: The Eighteenth Century

Chesapeake." Journal of Southern History, XXXIII (November, 1967), 469-85.

Lockridge, Kenneth A. "Land, Population and the Evolution of New England Society, 1630-1790." Past and Present, No. 39 (April, 1968), pp. 62-80.

Marye, William B. "The Great Maryland Barrens." Maryland Historical Magazine, L (March, June, and September, 1955), 11-23, 120-42, 234-53.

McCusker, John J. "The Current Value of English Exports, 1697-1800." William and Mary Quarterly, 3rd Series, XXVIII (October, 1971), 608-28.

Menard, Russell R. "Farm Prices of Maryland Tobacco, 1659-1710." Maryland Historical Magazine, LXVIII (Spring, 1973), 80-85.

Merrens, H. Roy. "Historical Geography and Early American History." William and Mary Quarterly, 3rd Series, XXII (October, 1965), 529-48.

Pattison, William D. "Geography and the Discovery of Education." Social Science in the Schools: A Search for Rationale. Edited by Irving Morrissett and W. William Stevens, Jr. New York: Holt, Rinehart and Winston, Inc., 1971. Pp. 35-44.

Price, Jacob M. "The Economic Growth of the Chesapeake and the European Market, 1697-1775." Journal of Economic History, XXIV (December, 1964), 496-511.

Seiler, William H. "Land Processioning in Colonial Virginia." William and Mary Quarterly, 3rd Series, VI (July, 1949), 416-36.

Trewartha, Glenn T. "Types of Rural Settlement in Colonial America." Geographical Review, XXXVI (October, 1946), 568-96.

Webb, John M. "Basic Concepts in the Analysis of Small Urban Centers in Minnesota." Annals of the Association of American Geographers, XLIX (March, 1959), 55-72.

Wyckoff, V. J. "Seventeenth Century Maryland Prices." Agricultural History, XII (July, 1938), 299-310.

Other Secondary Materials

Carr, Lois Green. "County Government in Maryland, 1689-1709." Unpublished Ph. D. dissertation, Harvard University, 1968.

Hemphill, John M. "Virginia and the English Commercial System, 1689-1733." Unpublished Ph. D. dissertation, Princeton University, 1964.

Jones, Alice Hanson. "Wealth Estimates for the Southern Colonies about 1770." Paper presented at the Annual Meeting of the Organization of American Historians, Chicago, 1973.

Karinen, Arthur. "Numerical and Distributional Aspects of Maryland Population, 1631-1840." Unpublished Ph. D. dissertation, University of Maryland, 1958.

Maryland. Maryland Geological Survey and Maryland Agricultural Experiment Station. Soil Map Anne Arundel County, Maryland. N.p., n.p., 1928.

Menard, Russell. "The Growth of Population in Early Colonial Maryland, 1631-1712." Annapolis, 1972. (Typewritten.)

Merrens, H. Roy. "Settlement of the Colonial Atlantic Seaboard." Paper presented at Conference on the National Archives and Research in Historical Geography, Washington, D.C., 1971.

THE UNIVERSITY OF CHICAGO

DEPARTMENT OF GEOGRAPHY

RESEARCH PAPERS (Lithographed, 6×9 Inches)

(*Available from Department of Geography, The University of Chicago, 5828 S. University Ave., Chicago, Illinois 60637. Price: $5.00 each; by series subscription, $4.00 each.*)

84. KANSKY, K. J. *Structure of Transportation Networks: Relationships between Network Geometry and Regional Characteristics* 1963. 155 pp.
91. HILL, A. DAVID. *The Changing Landscape of a Mexican Municipio, Villa Las Rosas, Chiapas* NAS-NRC Foreign Field Research Program Report No. 26. 1964. 121 pp.
94. MC MANIS, DOUGLAS R. *The Initial Evaluation and Utilization of the Illinois Prairies, 1815–1840* 1964. 109 pp.
97. BOWDEN, LEONARD W. *Diffusion of the Decision to Irrigate: Simulation of the Spread of a New Resource Management Practice in the Colorado Northern High Plains* 1965. 146 pp.
98. KATES, ROBERT W. *Industrial Flood Losses: Damage Estimation in the Lehigh Valley* 1965. 76 pp.
102. AHMAD, QAZI. *Indian Cities: Characteristics and Correlates* 1965. 184 pp.
103. BARNUM, H. GARDINER. *Market Centers and Hinterlands in Baden-Württemberg* 1966. 172 pp.
105. SEWELL, W. R. DERRICK, et al. *Human Dimensions of Weather Modification* 1966. 423 pp.
106. SAARINEN, THOMAS F. *Perception of the Drought Hazard on the Great Plains* 1966. 183 pp.
107. SOLZMAN, DAVID M. *Waterway Industrial Sites: A Chicago Case Study* 1967. 138 pp.
108. KASPERSON, ROGER E. *The Dodecanese: Diversity and Unity in Island Politics* 1967. 184 pp.
109. LOWENTHAL, DAVID, et al. *Environmental Perception and Behavior.* 1967. 88 pp.
110. REED, WALLACE E. *Areal Interaction in India: Commodity Flows of the Bengal-Bihar Industrial Area* 1967. 210 pp.
112. BOURNE, LARRY S. *Private Redevelopment of the Central City: Spatial Processes of Structural Change in the City of Toronto* 1967. 199 pp.
113. BRUSH, JOHN E., and GAUTHIER, HOWARD L., JR. *Service Centers and Consumer Trips: Studies on the Philadelphia Metropolitan Fringe* 1968. 182 pp.
114. CLARKSON, JAMES D. *The Cultural Ecology of a Chinese Village: Cameron Highlands, Malaysia* 1968. 174 pp.
115. BURTON, IAN; KATES, ROBERT W.; and SNEAD, RODMAN E. *The Human Ecology of Coastal Flood Hazard in Megalopolis* 1968. 196 pp.
117. WONG, SHUE TUCK. *Perception of Choice and Factors Affecting Industrial Water Supply Decisions in Northeastern Illinois* 1968. 96 pp.
118. JOHNSON, DOUGLAS L. *The Nature of Nomadism* 1969. 200 pp.
119. DIENES, LESLIE. *Locational Factors and Locational Developments in the Soviet Chemical Industry* 1969. 285 pp.
120. MIHELIC, DUSAN. *The Political Element in the Port Geography of Trieste* 1969. 104 pp.
121. BAUMANN, DUANE. *The Recreational Use of Domestic Water Supply Reservoirs: Perception and Choice* 1969. 125 pp.
122. LIND, AULIS O. *Coastal Landforms of Cat Island, Bahamas: A Study of Holocene Accretionary Topography and Sea-Level Change* 1969. 156 pp.
123. WHITNEY, JOSEPH. *China: Area, Administration and Nation Building* 1970. 198 pp.
124. EARICKSON, ROBERT. *The Spatial Behavior of Hospital Patients: A Behavioral Approach to Spatial Interaction in Metropolitan Chicago* 1970. 198 pp.
125. DAY, JOHN C. *Managing the Lower Rio Grande: An Experience in International River Development* 1970. 277 pp.
126. MAC IVER, IAN. *Urban Water Supply Alternatives: Perception and Choice in the Grand Basin, Ontario* 1970. 178 pp.
127. GOHEEN, PETER G. *Victorian Toronto, 1850 to 1900: Pattern and Process of Growth* 1970. 278 pp.
128. GOOD, CHARLES M. *Rural Markets and Trade in East Africa* 1970. 252 pp.
129. MEYER, DAVID R. *Spatial Variation of Black Urban Households* 1970. 127 pp.
130. GLADFELTER, BRUCE. *Meseta and Campiña Landforms in Central Spain: A Geomorphology of the Alto Henares Basin* 1971. 204 pp.
131. NEILS, ELAINE M. *Reservation to City: Indian Urbanization and Federal Relocation* 1971. 200 pp.
132. MOLINE, NORMAN T. *Mobility and the Small Town, 1900–1930* 1971. 169 pp.
133. SCHWIND, PAUL J. *Migration and Regional Development in the United States, 1950–1960* 1971. 170 pp.

134. PYLE, GERALD F. *Heart Disease, Cancer and Stroke in Chicago: A Geographical Analysis with Facilities Plans for 1980* 1971. 292 pp.

135. JOHNSON, JAMES F. *Renovated Waste Water: An Alternative Source of Municipal Water Supply in the U.S.* 1971. 155 pp.

136. BUTZER, KARL W. *Recent History of an Ethiopian Delta: The Omo River and the Level of Lake Rudolf* 1971. 184 pp.

137. HARRIS, CHAUNCY D. *Annotated World List of Selected Current Geographical Serials in English, French, and German* 3rd edition 1971. 77 pp.

138. HARRIS, CHAUNCY D., and FELLMANN, JEROME D. *International List of Geographical Serials* 2nd edition 1971. 267 pp.

139. MC MANIS, DOUGLAS R. *European Impressions of the New England Coast, 1497–1620* 1972. 147 pp.

140. COHEN, YEHOSHUA S. *Diffusion of an Innovation in an Urban System: The Spread of Planned Regional Shopping Centers in the United States, 1949–1968* 1972. 136 pp.

141. MITCHELL, NORA. *The Indian Hill-Station: Kodaikanal* 1972. 199 pp.

142. PLATT, RUTHERFORD H. *The Open Space Decision Process: Spatial Allocation of Costs and Benefits* 1972. 189 pp.

143. GOLANT, STEPHEN M. *The Residential Location and Spatial Behavior of the Elderly: A Canadian Example* 1972. 226 pp.

144. PANNELL, CLIFTON W. *T'ai-chung, T'ai-wan: Structure and Function* 1973. 200 pp.

145. LANKFORD, PHILIP M. *Regional Incomes in the United States, 1929–1967: Level, Distribution, Stability, and Growth* 1972. 137 pp.

146. FREEMAN, DONALD B. *International Trade, Migration, and Capital Flows: A Quantitative Analysis of Spatial Economic Interaction* 1973. 202 pp.

147. MYERS, SARAH K. *Language Shift Among Migrants to Lima, Peru* 1973. 204 pp.

148. JOHNSON, DOUGLAS L. *Jabal al-Akhdar, Cyrenaica: An Historical Geography of Settlement and Livelihood* 1973. 240 pp.

149. YEUNG, YUE-MAN. *National Development Policy and Urban Transformation in Singapore: A Study of Public Housing and the Marketing System* 1973. 204 pp.

150. HALL, FRED L. *Location Criteria for High Schools: Student Transportation and Racial Integration* 1973. 156 pp.

151. ROSENBERG, TERRY J. *Residence, Employment, and Mobility of Puerto Ricans in New York City* 1974. 230 pp.

152. MIKESELL, MARVIN W., editor. *Geographers Abroad: Essays on the Problems and Prospects of Research in Foreign Areas* 1973. 296 pp.

153. OSBORN, JAMES. *Area, Development Policy, and the Middle City in Malaysia* 1974. 273 pp.

154. WACHT, WALTER F. *The Domestic Air Transportation Network of the United States* 1974. 98 pp.

155. BERRY, BRIAN J. L., et al. *Land Use, Urban Form and Environmental Quality* 1974. 464 pp.

156. MITCHELL, JAMES K. *Community Response to Coastal Erosion: Individual and Collective Adjustments to Hazard on the Atlantic Shore* 1974. 209 pp.

157. COOK, GILLIAN P. *Spatial Dynamics of Business Growth in the Witwatersrand* 1975. 143 pp.

158. STARR, JOHN T., JR. *The Evolution of Unit Train Operations in the United States: 1960–1969—A Decade of Experience* 1975.

159. PYLE, GERALD F. *The Spatial Dynamics of Crime* 1974. 220 pp.

160. MEYER, JUDITH W. *Diffusion of an American Montessori Education* 1975. 109 pp.

161. SCHMID, JAMES A. *Urban Vegetation: A Review and Chicago Case Study* 1975.

162. LAMB, RICHARD. *Metropolitan Impacts on Rural America* 1975.

163. FEDOR, THOMAS. *Patterns of Urban Growth in the Russian Empire during the Nineteenth Century* 1975.

164. HARRIS, CHAUNCY D. *Guide to Geographical Bibliographies and Reference Works in Russian or on the Soviet Union* 1975. 496 pp.

165. JONES, DONALD W. *Migration and Urban Unemployment in Dualistic Economic Development* 1975.

166. BEDNARZ, ROBERT S. *The Effect of Air Pollution on Property Value* 1975. 118 pp.

167. HANNEMANN, MANFRED. *The Diffusion of the Reformation in Southwestern Germany, 1518-1534* 1975.

168. SUBLETT, MICHAEL D. *Farmers on the Road. Interfarm Migration and the Farming of Noncontiguous Lands in Three Midwestern Townships, 1939-1969* 1975. 228 pp.

169. STETZER, DONALD FOSTER. *Special Districts in Cook County: Toward a Geography of Local Government* 1975. 189 pp.

170. EARLE, CARVILLE V. *The Evolution of a Tidewater Settlement System: All Hallow's Parish, Maryland, 1650–1783* 1975. 249 pp.